Representations

ESSAYS ON LITERATURE AND SOCIETY

Steven Marcus

COLUMBIA UNIVERSITY PRESS

NEW YORK

Representations

Essays on Literature and Society

Columbia University Press Morningside Edition
Columbia University Press
New York   Oxford
Copyright © 1975, 1990 by Steven Marcus

Library of Congress Cataloging-in-Publication Data

Marcus, Steven.
Representations :
essays on literature and society /
Steven Marcus.
p. cm.
Reprint. Originally published:
New York : Random House, 1975.
ISBN 0-231-07400-X (cl.)
ISBN 0-231-07401-8 (pbk.)
1. English literature—History and criticism.
2. American literature—History and criticism.
3. Literature and society.
I. Title.
PR99.M3247   1990
820.9′3—dc20
90-39364
CIP

Morningside Edition 1990

Casebound editions of Columbia University Press books are Smyth-
sewn and printed on permanent and durable acid-free paper

∞

Printed in the U.S.A.

c 10 9 8 7 6 5 4 3 2 1
p 10 9 8 7 6 5 4 3 2 1

To Gertrud

AUTHOR'S NOTE

All of the pieces in this volume have been printed in some form before. Some of them are reprinted here without change. Others have been moderately revised. And two of them, "Awakening from the Nightmare?" and "Freud and Dora," which were abridged for reasons of space when they first appeared, are now printed in the form I originally intended.

I should like to thank Berenice Hoffman for her editorial efforts on my behalf.

Preface to the Morningside Edition

Although the reprinting of a volume of essays is naturally an occasion of pleasure for its author, such a juncture equally provokes reflections about things that have occurred in the interval between the volume's first appearance and the present. In the world of literary criticism, which has now become almost completely an institution of academic literary pursuits, extraordinary changes have taken place. This is not the moment to discuss them; they are constantly being discussed in numberless quarters, and taking some account of them here would not be appropriate, in my view, or even useful.

There is, however, one assertion which is made in the original Introduction to this volume, and that is carried out by different means in the essays that follow it, that I should like to direct attention to as carrying a continuing salience of pressure. That statement has to do with the cognitive function and value of both literature and the disciplined study and discussion of it. Today, I believe, such an emphasis is even more timely and cautionary—not to say admonitory—than it was almost fifteen years ago. I will not vex this question further than to say that the relation of literature, and its languages, as well as the relation of the various discourses in which literature is discussed, to the referential world remains for me a matter of central importance. Its pertinence has not been diminished despite the circumstance that such relations have been in various contexts denied, trivialized, displaced and even kidnapped. To address attention to the place of literature and the critical study of it in an actual historical world, and in a culture in which we are all intractably situated, seems to me still a worthwhile thing to do.

Contents

Contents □ xii

Introduction

If there is a common theme or tendency in the essays and other pieces in this volume it is their preoccupation with the imagination of society. That preoccupation has intensified and become more deliberate and conscious in the most recently written of these pieces, but it is to be found, I believe, in all of them. The imagination of society is a phrase whose inflationary impetus is checked by its circularity and duplicity. What I mean by this subject, on the one hand, is the way that certain writers—in particular, novelists—represent or imagine the world in which we live. They imagine through the language of writing a social world or worlds; in another sense, however, they also act as the imaginations of the actual societies in which they live and for whom they write. On the other hand, I am also pointing to the way certain other kinds of writers, who are not primarily literary figures in the conventional sense—for example, historians or social scientists or theorists or psychologists—also represent or imagine society in their written work. Their writing too, when it is closely examined, reveals what should be obvious—that it is powerfully informed and influenced by preconceptions of what it is they are writing about, and that their representations or imaginations of society often differ from their conscious and explicit awareness of what it is that they are doing or describing. (Similar disparities, to be sure, are to be found among the first group of writers or novelists.) In another sense, again, these so-called non-literary writers also act in their writings as the imaginations of the real societies in which they live and whose nature they in their own ways express. Between these two groups or kinds of writers, then, we may hope to discover something about how society imagines itself, which is to say, how societies represent their realities—their own existence—to themselves. It should go without saying that these imaginations amount to only a small fraction of the myriad forms in which society and societies represent or imagine themselves; small as it may be, this fraction amounts nonetheless to a significant group of figures and of forms and means, and I believe that there is something to be learned from attending to the imagination of society in the several senses that these remarks suggest and that the pieces in this volume variously touch upon.

To put the matter in another way, both kinds of activities are interpretations or, if you like, fictions. They are fictions in the original and etymological sense that they are made or constructed. Such constructions are in fact acts of the imagination, whether they are made by an anthropologist in the field in Bali or in his study at Princeton, or whether they are made by an English novelist writing in

1862 about Savonarola in Florence in 1492 or by a Swiss Professor of History writing about the same subject in 1860. These fictions tend to be the ordinary and indispensable means by which we go about understanding the world or society about us, although we also ordinarily tend to be largely unaware that this is what we are doing. And if in the title of this book I have used the word "Representations" instead of "Fictions" or "Imaginations," it is largely because I wanted to communicate in it first the comparatively normal, neutral or uncharged sense that the term representation customarily carries. Nevertheless, representations remain inescapably fictions or imaginations, and there is no easy way out of this epistemological puzzle, whatever our perspective or whatever linguistic means or conceptual devices we use in our constructions or imaginations of the social world.[1]

The foregoing assertions entail, I believe, a number of further considerations. In the first place, they entail the view that literature represents a world. The structures of literature are in the first instance formal; they tend to create an internally coherent literary world and refer with some degree of self-sustaining autonomy to themselves, to the linguistic universe that any work of literature constitutes. But this same literary world is also connected to the real world—whatever that is and however we may wish, according to the occasion, to describe or define it. The structures of literature refer to this real world, comment upon it, represent it by means of a written language that is part of it, and are hence themselves parts of the same real world that they refract and reconstitute imaginatively. If this is so, then it seems to me that literature has a cognitive value and function, that it is or can be a valid way of knowing or apprehending the world. And a similar inference is to be

---

[1] See Clifford Geertz, *The Interpretation of Cultures* (New York, 1973), pp. 15f.

drawn about the secondary discourse that is appropriate to the analysis, interpretation and discussion of literature, the discourse of literary criticism.

If these inferences hold, then it is possible to put forward at least two further related statements. If literature and the study of literature are valid forms of knowledge, then it seems likely that our understanding of both can only benefit from the introduction into the context of literary study certain kinds of knowledge and instruments of analysis that have been developed in other, related cognitive disciplines—I am thinking in particular of history, the social sciences, and psychology. But it also seems to me that the instruments of literary criticism and analysis can and should be applied to the reading of supposedly non-literary texts, texts of historical interest, of social theory, of psychological and anthropological inquiry and speculation. And if my view is correct, then such an application should generate new and perhaps surprising and perhaps sometimes even convincing meanings in works of these reputed "non-literary" orders. In a number of the essays that follow, sometimes one procedure is in general pursued and sometimes the other. On a few rare occasions I have tried to do both at once.[2]

I do not by such statements mean that these pieces are, or were ever, systematic in either intention or anticipated results, or that some ideal project of literary studies is foreshadowed in them or that provisions for implementing such a project ought to be—or can be—envisaged. Nothing could be further from my mind. Nevertheless, it seems to me that the two kinds of procedures that I have referred to should be brought together more often than they ordinarily are in literary criticism. This is to say that the part of literary

---

[2] And then there are other occasions in which the goings-on seem to me too loose and non-specific to be dignified by calling them procedures, but in which something else of interest may be happening.

criticism that is formal in the sense that it attends to the internal and quasi-autonomous structures—linguistic, thematic, generic and so on—of works of literature should be brought together with the part of literary criticism that is referential. It then becomes referential in the sense that it refers and pays regard to the real world that literature itself refers to, refracts and is part of, and yet remains deeply committed to the enterprise of literature and to the due measure of autonomy that the imagination of society both exercises and requires. This is one way—though not the only way—in which the claims to intellectual seriousness on the part of literary studies can be reasserted and perhaps sustained.

New York
June 1975

Representations

ESSAYS ON LITERATURE AND SOCIETY

Hunger and Ideology

Famine seems to be the last, the most dreadful resource of nature.... The vices of mankind are active and able ministers of depopulation. They are the precursors in the great army of destruction; and often finish the dreadful work themselves. But should they fail in this war of extermination, sickly seasons, epidemics, pestilence, and plague, advance in terrific array, and sweep off their thousands and ten thousands. Should success be still incomplete, gigantic inevitable famine stalks in the rear, and with one mighty blow, levels the population with the food of the world.
—Thomas Malthus

As every schoolboy knows, the Irish famine is one of the capital disasters of history. It broke upon a people who had been dominated by a foreign power for seven hundred years, and who lived in almost bestial servitude, poverty, misery, ignorance, and helplessness. The accounts of contemporary travelers uniformly attest to the extremity of Ireland's condition: one witness asserted that "no mode of life in Europe could seem pitiable after one had seen Ireland . . . the poorest among the Letts, the Esthonians and the Finlanders, lead a life of comparative comfort"; another wrote that "the

Negro in his chains" suffered less misery. Subsisting under conditions of systematic exploitation and classic peonage, the Irish peasants had been reduced to living off a single crop, the potato. Indeed, in certain back areas of Ireland "cooking any food other than the potato had become a lost art." And yet, as if to demonstrate the ghastly truth of Malthus' theory, the population of Ireland had been steadily increasing. The calamity began with the blight of the potato crops in 1845 and 1846. A variety of public and private schemes for relief were undertaken, but such measures soon proved inadequate as the famine extended through the following years and began to take cumulative effect. Hunger was succeeded by disease, primarily by an epidemic of typhus, but bacillary dysentery, hunger edema, scurvy, and cholera were also general. The vegetable blight was thus followed by human blight; the lightning-like reproduction, spread, and infestation of the spores of the potato fungus were equaled only by the rapidity with which typhus propagated itself. "A brush in passing was enough to transfer the fever-transmitting louse or its dustlike excrement to a new victim, and one fever-stricken person could pass on infection to a hundred others in the course of a day."

Hunger and disease were followed by emigration, the third great agent in the depopulation of Ireland, and "historically the most important event of the famine." More than a million emigrants from Ireland left the unspeakable conditions of their homeland, journeyed under unspeakable conditions across the Atlantic, and were treated unspeakably when they arrived in North America. An even larger number crossed the Irish channel to take up existence in Liverpool, Glasgow, and the ports of South Wales. Ireland was more than decimated by the famine; according to the best estimates—which are very rough—between twenty-five and twenty-seven per cent of its population was in one way or another lost.

These are some of the gross facts of the famine, as they

are retold in Cecil Woodham-Smith's *The Great Hunger*,[1] a week-by-week account of the long disaster and a work of unrelieved grimness and horror. Mrs. Woodham-Smith goes in neither for picturesque detail nor comic-pathetic diversions and almost never generalizes. Fact after relentless fact falls on the mind, but they do not deaden perception. In Mrs. Woodham-Smith's hands, abstract statistics come alive as human beings, as she paradoxically undoes the usual effect of statistics, which is to impersonalize, average out, and distance our response to concrete experience. *The Great Hunger* is a work of unusual distinction, informed at every point by the knowledge that facts alone do not amount to history unless we include among them the fact of consciousness.

As the historian G. M. Young once remarked, "the real, central theme of History is not what happened, but what people felt about it when it was happening." The Irish famine itself occurred at a time in which consciousness was in the course of dramatically shifting. If we compare it, for example, with the Black Plague of 1348–1349, the differences are instructive. The earlier event is the worst catastrophe of this millennium of European history; modern authorities estimate that about one-third of the population of the Continent perished. But how was the plague interpreted at the time of its occurrence? According to one scholar, Norman Cohn, it was regarded "in normal medieval fashion, as a divine chastisement for the transgressions of a sinful world." And the religious excesses, such as the flagellant processions, which then sprang up were "in part an attempt to divert the chastisement." After reading such accounts, the reader must conclude that these attitudes and practices were, to adapt a sociological term, "legitimate" responses to the situation—that is to say, they corresponded both to

---

[1] Cecil Woodham-Smith, *The Great Hunger: Ireland 1845–1849* (New York, 1962).

the means or resources then available for dealing with that situatiori, and to the furthest spiritual and intellectual stage of development to which society had then attained. At the time of the Irish famine, however, a similar attitude no longer elicits our assent. When Charles Edward Trevelyan, the Treasury official in charge of all the programs for Irish relief, gives voice to such sentiments, the reader detects in his pieties not only indifference and hard-heartedness but flummery as well. Mrs. Woodham-Smith dryly observes that "The 'thought that famine was the will of God was a consolation to him, and he hoped that the Catholic priests were making this clear." And Trevelyan himself wrote: "It is hard upon the poor people that they should be deprived of knowing that they are suffering from an affliction of God's providence." A number of considerations converge to make this reference to Providence morally unacceptable. In the first place, means had been developed and were at hand to deal with and alleviate both famine and plague, but they were not fully employed. In the second, the religious argument or explanation is at this moment serving a classic ideological function—it is being used to screen other interests and motives, and as a partial extenuation of the British government's failure to provide adequate relief to the starving Irish. And third, at the time Trevelyan was writing, a humane consciousness had already come into existence which challenged the validity of his assumptions and the necessity of his conclusions.

The discrepancy between Trevelyan's attitude and what had become an authentic moral possibility at that moment in history leads us to note that death itself is relative and historical. Death as a fact is absolute, of course, but as civilization's control over nature advances, the number of morally legitimate or acceptable forms of death or dying steadily decreases. (In our culture today, for instance, death in a nuclear war seems on the verge of ceasing to exist as a moral possibility.) One of the things that makes the Irish famine an episode of large historical significance is that we can detect in it just such a shift in consciousness—it is in all likelihood the first disaster of its kind in history which was widely responded to, and continues to be thought of, as a moral outrage.

Still another kind of consciousness can be felt to exist in Mrs. Woodham-Smith's book. And this is the consciousness of our own time, of World War II, concentration camps, and race-murder. The charge has been brought against the British government that its treatment of the Irish people during the famine amounted to genocide, and it "has been accused, and not only by the Irish, of wishing to exterminate the Irish people . . . as Hitler wished to exterminate the Jews." As a historian, Mrs. Woodham-Smith is properly wary of such tempting analogies, and remarks that the 1840's must not be judged by today's standards; moreover, she adds, "whatever parsimony and callousness the British Government displayed towards Ireland, was paralleled seven years later by the treatment of their own soldiers which brought about the destruction of the British Army in the Crimea." Such disclaimers to the contrary notwithstanding, Mrs. Woodham-Smith's book was written in our time and could not have been written before it; the very form of the narrative, the choice of significant details, the emphases and shadings are all in some measure dictated by that fact. Just as in literature a classic work renews itself by impersonating a modern one, so also, as Philip Rahv once remarked, "the past retains its vitality in so far as it impersonates the present, either in its aversions or ideals." Indeed, on a strict definition, history can only be a study of the present, the past itself being in fact one mode which the present takes. *The Great Hunger* would not be so interesting and important a work did it not offer this peculiar historical relevance, or if one were unable to feel that the past was being revealed in it as a genuine mode of the present.

It is in the scenes of mass horror and death that the

impersonation of modernity can be felt most strongly. If the natural calamities of blight and plague were bad enough by themselves, the treatment of the Irish by their landlords and by the British government, that is to say, by other human beings, was terrible in the extreme. The terror, of course, has to do with the fact that they weren't being regarded or treated as human beings, that their humanity was being denied. One of the first results of the blight, for example, was the mass eviction of Irish tenants from off the land. Troops and police would move in and demolish the tenants' houses on the spot. "The scene was frightful; women running wailing with pieces of their property, and clinging to door-posts from which they had to be forcibly torn; men cursing, children screaming with fright. That night the people slept in the ruins; next day they were driven out, the foundations of the houses were torn up and razed, and no neighbour was allowed to take them in." Homeless in their own homeland, alienated by official decree from their brothers, the evicted sought refuge "in what was called a 'scalp.' A hole was dug in the earth, two to three feet deep, roofed over with sticks and pieces of turf, and in this burrow a family existed." It is almost as if they were preparing graves for themselves beforehand; yet when these living dead were discovered in their holes in the ground, they were "remorselessly hunted out."

The scenes of mass starvation and death endlessly follow: of human beings dying alone, deserted, forgotten, abandoned by their very families; of bodies lying unburied and unknown along the roads and in ditches; of corpses of persons who died of starvation being eaten by cats and rats who were themselves skeletons. The island had become a vast death-camp, an emerald Golgotha, a green and pleasant pit of despair. Out of a multitude of such reports, one will have to serve as representative of the rest. Here are the Irish children:

The worst sufferers were the children; starving children were skeletons, many too far gone to be able to walk. The skin over the chest-bones and upper part of the stomach was stretched so tight that every curve of the breast-bone and ribs stood out in relief. . . . Starvation had affected the children's bones; the jaw-bone was so fragile and thin that a very slight pressure would force the tongue into the roof of the mouth. In Skibbereen, Elihu Burritt met children with jaws so distended that they could not speak; in Mayo the starving children had lost their voices. Many were in the stupor characteristic of death by starvation. Sidney Godolphin Osborne visited workhouses, infirmaries and hospitals and never heard a single child utter a cry or moan of pain—"in the very act of death still not a tear nor a cry. I have scarcely ever seen one try to change his or her position . . . two, three or four in a bed, there they lie and die, if suffering still ever silent, unmoved." By April, 1847, children were looking like little old men and women of eighty years of age, wrinkled and bent . . . even the babies were "aged."

A curious phenomenon was the growth of hair on starving children's faces. The hair on the head fell out and hair grew on the face. . . .

The descriptions of the Irish sufferings during the plague, of what they endured at the hands of the shipping agents and aboard the emigrant vessels, and of what further degradation awaited them on their arrival in Canada and the United States are more of the protracted same. Upon all of which, direct comment is almost bound to prove inadequate. In *Past and Present*, an extraodinary book written in 1843, Thomas Carlyle addressed himself to the "condition of England"—which was bad enough. At one point he introduces the anecdote of a poor Irish widow in Edinburgh, who "went forth with her three children, bare of all resource, to solicit help from the Charitable Establishments of that City." She was refused by all, helped by none, until, exhausted, she sank down with typhus, died, and infected her lane with fever so that "seventeen other persons died of fever there in consequence." It is a very curious matter, Carlyle observes. "The forlorn Irish Widow applies to her fellow-creatures, as if saying, 'Behold I am sinking, bare of help: ye must help me!' They answer, 'No; impossible; thou art no sister of ours.' But she proves her sisterhood; her typhus-fever kills *them*: they actually were her brothers, though denying it! Had human creature ever to go lower for a proof?" It is a very impressive piece of writing, and yet one wants to ask if even this is adequate to the reality of the experience, or if anything could be.

One of the more striking implications of Mrs. Woodham-Smith's account has precisely to do with the consciousness of the witnesses of the famine, with the disparity that existed between what was happening and their understanding of what was happening, or between experience and their ability to respond to, much less master, it. The constant refrain of those who observed the famine is, "It cannot be described." "The scenes which presented themselves were such as no tongue or pen can convey the slightest idea of. . . ." "It is impossible to go through the detail. . . ." "Believe me, my dear Sir, the reality in most cases far exceeded description. Indeed none can conceive what it was but those who were in it." The modern reference seems apposite again; the refrain recalls the statements made by witnesses when the concentration camps were opened at the end of the Second World War. Reality itself had grown so monstrous that human consciousness could scarcely conceive or apprehend it; reality overwhelmed the human capacity to respond coherently to it. The relations between reality and consciousness are, it goes without saying, inexhaustibly complex, but it may be said that sometime during the middle of the nineteenth century the disparity I have been outlining began to be sensed or felt. One of the chief causes which brought about this development was the growth among the British middle classes of an awareness of what the life of the poor, of the urban and industrial working classes, was like.

If we turn to literature, that part of an age in which we expect consciousness to exist in its fullest and most precise reach, the disparity is even sharper. Dickens was the one novelist of the period who was anywhere near remotely strong enough to grasp directly and imaginatively this order of experience. Indeed, he was regularly accused from various sides of "exaggerating" the facts of social distress. Yet if anything emerges clearly from a work like *The Great Hunger* (as it does from other similar documents of the age), it is, as Dickens himself often protested, that his art was a mild representation of what was actually happening. It was mild not by intention but because reality wholly outstripped the capacities of art, the capacities of consciousness, to encompass it. And it is during the Victorian period that an important modern truth begins to emerge—that however mad, wild, or grotesque art may seem to be, it can never touch or approach the madness of reality.

But the statements of the observers that Mrs. Woodham-Smith cites, or of men like Dickens and Carlyle, represented only one segment of British opinion. Had more men been capable of such sentiments, the Irish distress would not have been so enormous. But in fact the dominant British consciousness at the time remained fixed at an opposite pole. This attitude was compounded of several elements. To begin with, there was a strain of sheer Podsnappery among the English; there were large and frequent denials that any such thing as a famine was actually occurring, or that the potato blight was anything but a false alarm and "the invention of agitators." To profess a belief that the blight existed, wrote one reliable contemporary, "was as sure a method of being branded as a radical as to propose to destroy the Church." And if at last it ceased to be possible to deny the blight and the famine, then the suffering of the Irish was their own fault. Ireland was a disturbing thought to the English, Mrs. Woodham-Smith writes, and "it was therefore a comfort to be able to believe that the Irish were not starving or, if some of them were, the depravity of the Irish was such that they deserved to starve; and to treat Ireland's desperate appeals . . . as merely another whine from a professional beggar."

The belief in the economic theory of *laissez faire* was undoubtedly the controlling influence in England's treatment of Ireland during the famine. The ideas which combine to make this theory—such as the sacred rights of property, complete liberty of enterprise, the laws of the market and of supply and demand, and of government non-intervention in the economic sphere—were held with fanatical, religious intensity by the largest majority of British politicians and authorities. Any plan for the relief of the Irish was preconditioned by the requirement that private enterprise was in no way to be interfered with. Most of the time this naturally led to no relief. For example, during the first year of the famine, the British government bought certain small amounts of Indian corn with which it both hoped to keep market prices on grain down and to feed a few of the Irish. Since no trade in Indian corn existed in the United Kingdom, this was not construed as an interference with private enterprise. But the scheme, of course, failed: you cannot keep prices down in a market where food does not exist because prices themselves cease to exist. Moreover, the British might as well have purchased stones or rock salt, for all the relief the Indian corn provided. Corn was unknown as a food in Ireland; the special facilities needed for milling it did not exist, and so the corn went unground. Inspired with divine ignorance, the authorities then suggested that the Irish eat it unground—in which state Indian corn is not merely indigestible but downright dangerous. Luckily, however—if such an expression in this context has any meaning—most of the corn remained in warehouses, since the British had, in addition, neglected to supply a way of distributing it to the people. The vaguely lunatic atmosphere of this episode recurs throughout the other operations of relief: from the recipes for soup, composed by Alexis Soyer "the famous French chef of the Reform Club," which "created a sensation in London," to the projects for public works which succeeded in ruining the roads of Ireland, it is all nightmare, impotence, and disaster.

The point is that the English did not really want to relieve the Irish; they did not believe it was morally right, and from the standpoint of economic theory it was unsound and "unnatural." One of the diagnostic attributes of any culture is its attitude toward poverty, and one can read the economic, social, and moral history of England in the history of its Poor Law. Confronted with eight million starving Irish, Charles Edward Trevelyan could write: "dependence on charity is not to be made an agreeable mode of life." Trevelyan was not simply unaware of the almost demented irony of this statement; in it he was expressing doctrines altogether typical of the British governing classes. On the one hand, poverty was an inevitable part of the economic system; the workings of this system were identified with laws of nature and so were not to be tampered with; on the other, poverty was the result of improvidence on the part of the poor for which they were not to be rewarded but punished. One of the results of such thinking is that by the nineteenth century in England poverty had come to be regarded as a kind of crime, and the poor were treated as criminals—if relief were made as "unattractive and difficult to obtain as possible," then the poor would presumably not be so willing to seek it. This more or less insane solution was applied wholesale to Ireland, but it, too, did not work.

When it was proposed to allow destitute able-bodied men to receive relief by entering the workhouse, it was discovered that the workhouses had to be emptied first "of the aged and the infirm, of widows and children." Apart from producing still more suffering, this measure came to nothing, since it proved difficult or impossible to carry out: in the immense workhouse at Tralee the inmates could not be turned out because they had "no clothes to put on and no shelter to which to return, for landlords customarily took advantage of destitute persons being forced to enter the workhouse to pull their cabins down." In the end nothing worked.

In the end nothing worked, and Ireland was left, according to Trevelyan's suggestion, to the "operation of natural causes"—which is to say that it was abandoned. These causes were not only the workings of supply and demand and Providence but the causes enumerated in Malthus' theory as well, mass death from starvation and disease. Nassau Senior, the political economist and adviser on economic affairs to the British government, remarked that he "feared the famine of 1848 in Ireland would not kill more than a million people, and that would scarcely be enough to do much good." The Irish sickened, suffered, fled, and died in their millions; whether enough of them died to do much good is difficult to determine.

What becomes evident, then, is that the Irish people were as much the victim of ideas as they were of nature's indifference to humanity. They were the victims of intellectual error, and the Irish famine is an unsurpassable instance of the effects of ideology in its purest sense. For the doctrines of political economy and of Malthus were unadulterated ideology; they were laws of society pretending to be laws of nature—or as Marx was to phrase it, they represented the "bourgeois relations of production as eternal categories." And even though this ideological thinking worked to the material advantage of the British ruling classes, they too, we now can see, may be counted among its victims. For they were condemned to live in falsehood, and falsehood is always corrupting. Out of the intellectual falsehood in which the British ruling classes were steeped and the spiritual corruption which was its consequence sprang the enduring horror of the Irish famine—the unforgivable selfishness, indifference, and brutality with which the English permitted themselves to treat the Irish. That this treatment was sanctioned by what was then thought of as "scientific" and enlightened principles, and that the English administrators of this inhumanity were sincere in their beliefs and convinced of the advanced and even the benign nature of their views serves only to compound the desperate pathos of the event. But it serves as well to emphasize in that event what is exemplary in a modern way.

For these horrors were perpetrated by the most enlightened and civilized nation in the world during one of the greatest periods of its history. The Victorian period is universally and correctly thought of as the "age of reform"; during that time an unparalleled series of intellectual, scientific, social, and political advances took place in England. The spirit of humanity was abroad then as it has rarely been in human history; the literature of that period, the great novelists and the great Victorian critics, is in sum an incomparable contribution to our humanity and provides an incomparable humane heritage. To be sure, it was also a time of enormous social injustice; but what one usually feels in this regard is that during the Victorian period men had for the first time come into full possession of the consciousness of what social injustice is and means, that they were trying to do something about it, and that the reforming spirit, given enough time, would work successfully toward amelioration. And yet it is also a fact that Victorian England was directly and irretrievably responsible for the incomparable monstrousness of the Irish famine. The lessons for modernity to read in this are self-evident.

Whether these lessons will be read is something else again. For we, too, are by both temperament and tradition a reforming society confronted by problems whose solutions reform alone probably cannot bring about. And we, too, are an enlightened civilization bound in by ideology of which we are largely unaware and by contradictions with which we can scarcely cope. Whether we consider domestic problems—civil rights, unemployment, the farm problem—or international ones—the Cold War, aid to underdeveloped areas—the difference between what might possibly be done and what will actually be done, is actually being done, is staggering. This difference, this gap between resources and performance, is in considerable measure a result of ideology, of thought which is socially determined yet unconscious of its determination. Since all political and historical knowledge, as Karl Mannheim has demonstrated, is ideological in the sense that it is inseparable from the particular values and position of a thinking subject and a social context, we cannot in such matters hope to attain some kind of absolute or transcendent truth. We can, however, enlarge our awareness of the truth that the ideas of all groups, including our own, are socially determined, that we as well as our adversaries think in ways or styles which are limited by our concrete social and historical situations. Only in this way can we reduce to a minimum the tendency toward self-apotheosis which is so characteristic of political and social ideas and so fatal in its consequences. The British in 1845–1849 were unable to do this, and the black record of the Irish famine was the result. If we today prove equally unable, the outcome is likely to be even worse.

(1963)

Authority and Obedience

Beginning in 1960, Stanley Milgram, who was then a member of the psychology department at Yale, conducted a series of experiments on human beings which quickly became famous if not notorious and provided a variety of grounds for heated professional debate. *Obedience to Authority*[1] is his considered account of that research. It is also a work that represents, in many important ways, current conditions in certain of the social sciences.

The experiments themselves, as Milgram describes them, are worthy of Kafka; and in their sinister combina-

[1] Stanley Milgram, *Obedience to Authority: An Experimental View* (New York, 1974).

tion of melodrama and visual excitement call to mind such early films of Fritz Lang as *M* and *Dr. Mabuse*. Participants were recruited by placing advertisements in the local newspaper calling "for people of all occupations" to help complete "a scientific study of memory and learning . . . at Yale University." A cross section of the occupational community did in due time voluntarily show up, and in the long run more than a thousand people took part in the experiments.

These volunteers were the actual "subjects" of the experimental research project, although they did not know it. The "scientific study of memory and learning" was in fact an elaborate set of hoaxes. Their staging ran typically as follows: the volunteer, or naïve subject, is ushered into a laboratory fitted out with appropriate-looking apparatus or props. Here he meets two other persons. One of them is introduced as another volunteer in the same experiment. This is a falsehood; he is an outside member of the experimental team (although not a psychologist) who has been "trained for the role" he is about to play.

The third member of the triad is dressed in a gray technician's coat and is also part of the act. His role is to play the experimenter. The "experimenter" then "explains" to the other two that the study they are working on is concerned with "the effects of punishment on learning." By a series of manipulations the real volunteer is chosen to be the "teacher," and the fake volunteer to be the "learner." The "learner" is then taken to an adjacent room, strapped into a chair, and an electrode is attached to his wrist.

The "teacher" is in turn seated in front of "an impressive shock generator," on which there are thirty switches ranging from fifteen to 450 volts and accompanying written designations ranging from "SLIGHT SHOCK" to "DANGER —SEVERE SHOCK." He is told to administer a verbal learning test to the man in the next room. Whenever an incorrect answer is given, the "teacher" is to give the other an electric shock in return, starting at fifteen volts and going up in fifteen-volt intervals to the end.

The "teacher" or subject—who thinks all this is for real —begins. (No one has ever simply refused and walked out of the laboratory.) "At 75 volts, the 'learner' grunts. At 120 volts he complains verbally; at 150 he demands to be released from the experiment. His protests continue as the shocks escalate, growing increasingly vehement and emotional. At 285 volts his response can only be described as an agonized scream." There are still 165 volts left to go. The "teacher" or subject usually becomes troubled somewhere in around here (or earlier) and turns to the "experimenter" for advice; the "experimenter" enjoins him to continue, and he commonly does, right up to the maximum.

These procedures, arrangements, and settings were modified in a variety of ways as the experiments continued. But the results were always comparable and compatible with the findings in the basic experiment. In that experiment nearly two-thirds of the "teachers" or subjects kept pressing away to 450 volts—and when in one modified form of the experiment the further hoax that the "learner" had a bad heart was introduced, and when he began to shout and scream about pains in the chest, it made no difference at all. Sixty-five per cent kept pressing the switches.

If the shocks administered in the experiment were only simulated, the shock produced by its results was perfectly real. Dismay and consternation were given voice to on all sides—by the experimenters themselves, by numbers of the subjects who had to confront what they had done and how they had behaved, and by those in the outside world who became aware of the "Eichmann experiment," as it came inevitably to be called. Debate among scientists spread to academic humanists and spilled over into the pages of newspapers and magazines, which carried stories about the controversy.

Part of the disturbance arose from surprise. No one had predicted anything remotely resembling the results that were reached; everyone, including those who had designed the experiments, had anticipated the reverse. And when, in a further effort of checking, different groups—such as psychiatrists, college students, and middle-class adults—were systematically questioned on this score, their predictions were as wide of the mark as those made before the experiments began.

Everyone predicted that he would himself at some point disobey the experimenter's orders to proceed with the punishment. And when the same respondents were asked about others, they predicted "that virtually all subjects will refuse to obey the experimenter; only a pathological fringe, not exceeding one or two per cent, was expected to proceed to the end of the shockboard." The psychiatrists predicted just as poorly as everyone else. Among many other things, science acts to upset our settled assumptions (the earth is flat) and disconfirm our inherited, collective certitudes (man is a rational creature in conscious control of his existence). On this account, the Milgram experiments certainly looked like science.

In addition to this, however, the experiments themselves were a cause of distress and debate among professional psychologists, and Milgram came in for harsh criticism for having both devised and gone through with them. He was accused of unethical practices in manipulating his subjects and in not protecting them beforehand from what might be the consequences upon them of their behavior in an extremely stress-filled experimental situation. The high levels of deceit, fraud, misrepresentation, and chicanery necessary to perform such research were also attacked as being incompatible with the conduct of science. At times it became difficult in the furor to know which was to be more condemned —the results of the experiments or the experimental activity itself.

In *Obedience to Authority* Milgram defends himself against all such charges and concludes, without warrant, that there is nothing problematical about his undertaking. I find it impossible to take an unqualified or absolute position on this matter. On the one side, there can be no doubt that these experiments were designed—whether consciously or not—to bring out the worst in us. They are brutal and ingenious dramatic inventions, little masterpieces of scientific bad faith. And the cruelty they inflict upon their unwitting subjects is surpassed only by the cruelty that they elicit from them. Moreover, the consequences of such an experience for the volunteer subjects are simply incalculable—one participant later reported that his wife remarked: "You can call yourself Eichmann." On the other side, it may be argued in retrospect that the information gathered by such research was valuable enough to justify it—if not its continuance; that it remains important that we know, or that we do not forget, these things about ourselves.

At the same time, there is something slightly academic about the debate in this form. These experiments were performed in the early 1960's, in those palmy days of research in the behavioral sciences when pretty much anything went. It is a real question whether this particular research project would be funded or supported today. Precisely because of incidents such as the Milgram experiments, standards of permissibility for experimental research upon human beings have generally tended to become rigorous—which doesn't mean that barbarities are not committed regularly. On balance, then, it may be reasonable to propose that although it is a useful thing that we have the knowledge that came out of these experiments, it is at least as desirable that research conducted according to such methods be interdicted.

The second question of interest that arises from this work has to do with how Milgram handles his data, what he does with it, what meanings he discovers, what theoretical schemes and explanations he enlists and arrives at, what conclusions he is led to draw. At this point, it has to be said, general disaster sets in. It is hard to know where, in this woeful and lamentable performance, to begin, and I shall have to limit myself to discussing only a few of the intellectual calamities that make up so much of this book.

Let us begin with something relatively simple. At the outset, Milgram says that he has studied his subject—the dilemmas of obedience to authority—with "the aim of understanding rather than judging it from a moral standpoint." This remark is, one supposes, his version of scientific impartiality or value-free research. Yet I have rarely read a book that is so moralistic, so obtrusively preachy, as *Obedience to Authority*. Here, for example, is a typical description, by Milgram, of one of the people who volunteered to help him with his experiments:

> Mr. Batta is a thirty-seven-year-old welder. . . . He has a rough-hewn face that conveys a conspicuous lack of alertness. His over-all appearance is somewhat brutish. An observer described him as a "crude mesomorph of obviously limited intelligence" . . . [yet] he relates to the experimenter with a submissive and deferential sweetness. . . .

> When the learner first complains, Mr. Batta pays no attention to him. . . . All the while he maintains the same rigid mask. The learner, seated alongside him, begs him to stop, but with robotic impassivity, he continues the procedure. What is extraordinary is his apparent total indifference to the learner; he hardly takes cognizance of him as a human being. . . .

Far from being non-judgmental in a moral sense, this passage simply reeks with moral attitudes, and is in fact a continuous activity of moralizing. Milgram is apparently unaware that this is so; worse still, he is unaware that these characterizations are being written from a very high horse, and that they communicate to the reader a distinct impression that Milgram regards their objects with outright contempt. For a researcher whose chief discoveries have to do with how weak and fragile the civilized constraints in most human beings can be, this is hardly the recommended attitude.

When Milgram pauses to generalize outward, his conceptual discourse is equally revealing. His experiments demonstrate, he writes, "the capacity for man to abandon his humanity, indeed, the inevitability that he does so, as he merges his unique personality into larger institutional structures." When an individual human being "merges his person into an organizational structure, a new creature replaces autonomous man . . . freed of humane inhibition, mindful only of the sanction of authority." And these experiments "raise the possibility that human nature, or—more specifically—the kind of character produced in American democratic society, cannot be counted on to insulate its citizens from brutality and inhumane treatment at the direction of malevolent authority."

The mutilated syntax of that last sentence expresses precisely the quality of thought in it. These are simply empty pious sentiments; and phrases like "autonomous man" and "malevolent authority" are just as simply reified entities that walk around in this book—and in Milgram's mind and language—as if for all the world they were concrete objects or creatures that could be picked up and handled and probed with one's finger.

Milgram's theoretical account of his material is worse yet. The explanatory model he has chosen comes from general systems theory and cybernetics and runs in outline as follows: Human beings are conceived of as "automata . . . each designed to function in isolation." They "dwell apart as self-regulating omnivores," in a word, as autonomous automata, a pretty bad joke in itself.[2] At some unspecified point they are brought together to form a social organization, at which moment regulations, constraints, and inhibitions to prevent them from acting against one another (otherwise known as "omnivoring") have to be built into them. These latter are known as conscience or superego. (Milgram characteristically fails to distinguish between the two.) As the levels of organizational structure or hierarchy become more complex, however, "higher-level components" of coordination and control take over, and the automata begin to behave in an "organizational mode" or a "systemic mode." As parts of a "system," the built-in regulations and inhibitions are "diminished" at the point of entry into hierarchical relations and at the behest of their successful functioning. Hence Eichmann.

It should be perfectly plain that this mishmash explains virtually nothing. The incongruences between the general systems model and what goes on in human beings are overwhelming. According even to Milgram himself, a "person entering an authority system no longer *views himself* as acting out of his own purpose but rather comes to *see* himself as an agent for executing the wishes of another person. Once an individual *conceives* his action in this light, profound alterations occur in his behavior." (Italics mine.)

---

[2] The bad joke is to be found in the circumstance that the notion of autonomous automata accurately describes electronic computers that have crossed a certain threshold of complexity. Such computers respond not merely to stimuli that enter them from the outside world; they respond as well to the demands of the internalized model or representation of some aspect of the real world that has been built into them. The bad joke is compounded by the circumstance that Milgram never overtly acknowledges that one element of the theoretical model he is using to describe and analyze the behavior of human beings is in fact based upon the idea of a computer.

I am grateful to Professor Joseph Weizenbaum of the Massachusetts Institute of Technology for bringing this point to my attention.

In other words, what is being described is a subjective state, the state of an active, knowing subject, and neither of these can be analyzed apart from the assumptions carried by such terms. In the model, however, the same state is represented thus: "a self-regulating entity is internally modified so as to allow its functioning within a system of hierarchical control." The unannounced shift from active to passive is essential. In the systems model the emphasis falls heavily on "inputs" from the external object world.

Milgram himself at one point allows as how there may be some slight discrepancies between the two conceptual schemes, such as "an element of free choice [which] determines whether the person defines himself in this way or not," but he asserts that this difference is of no substantial importance. In short, nothing has been explained. And a considerable part of that nothing has to do with the thirty-five per cent or more who disobeyed in the experiments. About these, Milgram has nothing to say.

But there is really no point in belaboring a dead behavioral horse. All the theoretical and explanatory parts of the book exist at this abysmal pitch of discourse. They stand in extreme contrast to the experiments themselves, which were devilishly ingenious, cleverly thought out, and—whatever one thinks of them—extremely provocative and probably important. This contrast—and the failures it implies—suggests something about the state of certain of the social and behavioral sciences today.

In one sense at least that state may be described as the opposite of the one which obtained for the great social theorists of the past. In Hegel or Marx (especially the younger Marx), in Freud or Durkheim—to list only a few outstanding instances—the disproportions were all the other way. Their great explanatory systems were formulated with the help of relatively little data or information—or what is considered such today. The transhistorical power of those systems of explanation may indeed be connected with the exceptional rigor and relevance with which the data that were to be applied within them were pre-selected. The situation today, on the contrary, is characterized by an overwhelming production of new information and apparently vital data, accompanied by explanatory schemes and theoretical proposals whose intellectual poverty has become increasingly evident.

This circumstance forms one part of what is coming to be widely recognized as the crisis which the social and behavioral sciences in our society are currently suffering. The causes and meanings of this state of affairs cannot be discussed here; but part of the general difficulty is represented in symptomatic perfection by Milgram's book, in which certain theoretical constructions and systematic contrivances taken from the contexts of the natural sciences and their dependent technologies are applied mechanically —without reflection and without understanding—to the qualitatively different contexts of human and social behavior.

Even so, Milgram's book is by no means to be ignored or overlooked. Perhaps something in the way of explanation may yet be intimated. It is Freud who supplies us with some needful hints—especially the later Freud. In his later years Freud ruminated at length over questions that concern the superego, in particular the question of its historical fate. The superego, he realized, was the hero-villain of our civilization. And the great disasters and crimes of history, he suggested, do not occur through outbreaks of repressed, anarchic sexuality. They occur when the superego, with all its organized powers of punishment and aggressivity, is enlisted in the active service of the very highest causes.

It is when the superego sanctions us to act freely and punitively in the name of some of humanity's highest ideals —whether it be the Deity, or the Nation, or Democracy, or the Revolution, or Science itself—that the great horrors of human aggressivity, violence, and destruction are unleashed. Milgram's book is an excellent exemplification of this notion, since it is really about the authority of Science rather than about authority in general. This explanation does not, of course, explain very much, but may at least begin to put matters in such a way that real understanding can become possible.

(1974)

Snopes Revisited

The Town,[1] sequel to *The Hamlet* and the second part of a long-projected trilogy about the Snopes family, is the most interesting book William Faulkner has published in fifteen years. Though it falls short of being a success, it manages to transcend many of the moral and rhetorical ineptitudes into which Faulkner's more recent work has fallen. It is not, like *Intruder in the Dust*, a novel with a broken back, half narrative, half Dixiecrat sociology. Its technical adventuresomeness does not, as it did in *Requiem for a Nun*, obscure the novel's main line of interest. Nor is its preoccupation with the largest moral issues so ponderous, so ab-

[1] William Faulkner, *The Town* (New York, 1957).

stract, or so personal that *The Town* is continually being surrendered, as *A Fable* was, to that monologue of musing and ranting about universals which turns up whenever Faulkner's dramatizing impulse wears thin. *The Town* revives the direct, dramatic mode of *As I Lay Dying*—the story is presented through the consciousness of several characters. It is remarkable for the extraordinary and intelligent self-awareness it contains, and for the definitive moral and social criticism it represents.

Beginning where *The Hamlet* leaves off, *The Town* covers approximately the next twenty years of the Snopes history, ending sometime in 1927. Its scene is Jefferson, its subject the impact of Flem and his family on Jefferson, and the reciprocal impact of Jefferson upon them. In Jefferson, Flem, the closest thing in American literature to a perpetual-motion machine of connivance and chicanery, parlays his interests with the same secret and preternatural genius for making money that enabled him to outman the "old pirate" of Frenchman's Bend, Will Varner. He eliminates his partner in the ownership of a restaurant; he invests in real estate; he becomes manager of the town power plant; he continues to lend money usuriously to the tenant farmers on whom "the entire cotton economy of the country was founded and supported," and becomes a power among them. Using his father-in-law's influence with impenetrable deviousness, he gets himself elected vice-president of one of Jefferson's two banks, finally becomes its president, a deacon in the Baptist church, an unshakably respectable "solitary widower," and owner and master of "the old de Spain house which he had remodeled into an ante-bellum Southern mansion." It is a great American story of success, and a typical one. Inside of forty years, Flem, son of an outlawed, bushwhacking tenant farmer from the back hills— "Scratch?" says Gavin Stevens; "Scratch was euphemism indeed for where he started from"—has transformed himself into a rich and responsible citizen in a respectable old community, a defender of "civic jealousy and pride," a pillar of society.

But the rise of Flem Snopes, which Irving Howe has called "an inverted and sinister picaresque adventure," is only one of several stories which make up the novel's elaborate organization. Another and more continuous narrative concerns Eula, Flem's wife, and her affair with Manfred de Spain, saber-scarred veteran of the Spanish-American War, romantic, rakehell, former mayor of Jefferson, and after the death of Colonel Sartoris, president of the bank. It is revealed in this book that Flem Snopes is impotent, and Eula, as we recall from *The Hamlet*, is a kind of bucolic Venus and Brünnehilde, a glimpse of whom is enough to send most men into nympholepsy. The affair of Eula and de Spain goes on for eighteen years within "a kind of outrageous morality of adultery . . . based on an unimpugnable fidelity"; they come together in a "simple unadulterated uninhibited immortal lust," one of those characteristically fateful and annihilating grand passions through which Faulkner has frequently expressed his sense of the limits of feeling, of emotions whose splendor of commitment and selflessness is inevitably accompanied by barrenness and isolation: de Spain is driven out of town and Eula shoots herself. Flem knows about the affair all along and effortlessly contrives to make it serve his monomaniacal ambition —the adultery of Eula and de Spain is in fact the wave on which Flem rides into respectable society. Faulkner's sense of the social immorality that allows Flem's schemes to succeed is particularly acute, and out of it emerges the extremely critical judgment on Jefferson life which the novel pronounces.

The only way Flem can hurt Eula is through her daughter Linda, who is ignorant of her mother's adultery and of the fact that Flem is not her father. It is her innocence (inexplicably, she loves Flem) that is to be protected at all costs from the truth and from the scandal and violence that a public exposure would create. For this reason Eula and de Spain are from the very beginning enlisted in Flem's intrigues, which would destroy them in any case. Eula in turn engages Gavin Stevens in the defense of her daughter and herself, and in effect of Flem too. Thus, Stevens, who has always thought of himself as the champion of the tradition opposing what Snopes stands for, becomes Flem's principal if unwilling ally. "Just say I represent Jefferson and so Flem Snopes is my burden too," he intones.

The third main subdivision of the narrative is composed of tales about the double dealings of Flem and other Snopeses who have drifted in his wake to Jefferson. In this respect *The Town* most closely resembles *The Hamlet*, which contains such consummately humorous stories as "Spotted Horses" and the horse-trading of Pat Stamper and Ab Snopes. *The Town* contains four such stories. Like "Spotted Horses," two of them—"Mule in the Yard" and "Centaur in Brass"—are reworkings of previously published material and are considerably improved by revision. They are longer, their style is more dense and their action more complete. "Mule in the Yard," I think, can now be read with "Spotted Horses" as one of the minor masterpieces of American literature. It tells about a certain enterprise of I. O. Snopes, who some ten years before the story's action begins bought mules for fifty dollars each, took them at night to a blind curve on the railroad, where they were run down, and collected indemnity of sixty dollars a mule from the railroad company. His assistant in this business, a man named Hait, had managed to get himself killed one night along with a string of the mules. Hait's widow collected $8500 from the railroad's insurance company, and I. O. has been stewing for years because he never received what he calculated was his share of the money. One foggy day a mule of I. O.'s breaks into the Widow Hait's tiny yard. Old Het, the peripatetic Negress from the poorhouse, is there; so are Mrs. Hait's cow and chickens, and so, soon, is I. O.

A fantastic chase begins to flow around the house, and Faulkner's prose breaks forth with that unique, brilliant energy of perception which transforms the most chaotic and violent activity into fluid, comic grace.

> "In the cellar, fore God!" old Het hollored. She didn't wait either. "Go round the other way and head him!" she said. And she said that when she and Mrs Hait turned that corner, there was the mule with the flying halter once more seeming to float lightly onward on a cloud of chickens with which, since the chickens had been able to go under the house and so along the chord while the mule had to go around on the arc, it had once more coincided. When they turned the next corner, they were in the back yard again.
>
> "Fore God!" Het hollored. "He fixing to misuse the cow!" She said it was like a tableau. The cow had come out of the shed into the middle of the back yard; it and the mule were now facing each other about a yard apart, motionless, with lowered heads and braced legs like two mismatched book-ends, and Snopes was half in and half out of the now-open cellar door on the coping of which the scuttle of ashes still sat. . . .

Passages like this remind us of one of Faulkner's essential sources of strength: the legacy of Mark Twain. Like Twain, Faulkner has learned to assimilate the folk culture of a part of the country to the literary tradition. He has been able to do so partly because of the nature of that culture, because it possessed in its actual life the complication of social and moral assumptions that a true folk culture always has and that makes it so accessible to traditional literary modes. But he could not have done it in the way he has without the precedent of Twain; it is difficult to conceive of Faulkner at his characteristic best without being reminded that Twain stands in the immediate background.

The other three stories, though not so memorable as "Mule in the Yard," are sustained with impressive intelligence and humor. In the last of them, for example, the extraordinary vignette with which the novel ends, Byron Snopes, who has embezzled a couple of thousand dollars from the bank and fled to Texas, ships four of his children by "a Jicarilla Apache squaw" to Flem. "They looked like snakes. Or maybe that's too strong too. Anyway, they didn't look like children; if there was one thing in the world they didn't look like it was children." Like Faulkner's idiots, these children are natural objects forced to inhabit a civilized world; the laws of their being are irrelevant to the conventions by which man lives, even such conventions as the Snopeses find it necessary to observe. Since their Snopesian inheritance has been enriched with Apache blood, they exist by a kind of essential destructiveness, a natural, inarticulate, unblinking, aggressive appetite: they eat and they destroy. A five-hundred-dollar pedigreed Pekingese disappears inside of them; they almost perform an *auto-da-fé*, Apache style, with their cousin Clarence Snopes as victim; if they feel they are being imposed on, "a switch knife with a six-inch blade" appears out of thin air. Flem packs them off to Frenchman's Bend, but since they destroy everything and everyone in sight there too, Flem, defender of civilization, is forced to ship them back to Texas and liberate himself and the town of the last of the ineducable Snopeses: he has run the others out or they have gotten rid of themselves. As they are about to be deported, Ratliff says, "Would either of you gentlemen like to go down with me and watch what they call the end of a erea, if that's what they call what I'm trying to say? The last and final end of Snopes out-and-out unvarnished behavior in Jefferson, if that's what I'm trying to say."

If the reader feels that this doesn't sound quite like Ratliff, he has come upon one of the major issues in Faulkner's literary development. The Ratliff of *The Hamlet* is one of Faulkner's most admirable creations, a subtle, ironic sensibility, a disinterested intelligence through which the problems of a corrupt yet civilized society in the process of being infiltrated by Snopeses—not foreigners, but home-bred products of that corruption—are voiced. It is largely through Ratliff that *The Hamlet* achieves a poise and control unequaled by any other of Faulkner's works. He was to Faulkner what Marlow was to Conrad, and when we say that we again recognize the distinction of Faulkner's accomplishment in *The Hamlet*. Itinerant sewing-machine agent, carrier of news, repository of local history, Ratliff, who has known the Snopeses from boyhood and can even sympathize with their predicament, wages a long-drawn-out campaign against them. He represents the novelist's conviction that if civilization and sanity are to be preserved, they must be fought for constantly, even if one has to fight with one hand tied behind his back, since to beat the Snopeses by their own methods would be to forfeit the values one wishes to defend. Ratliff appears in *The Town* in a more limited and constrained way. He is one of three characters who tell the story, and his part is the smallest, amounting to only thirty of the novel's 370 pages. This reduction of Ratliff's role is partly a result of the shift in time and place of the novel. We are to understand that he does not possess in Jefferson the decisive knowledge that he and no one else possessed in Frenchman's Bend.

Because of this, two other characters take over the bulk of the narration; Gavin Stevens and Charles Mallison are the Jeffersonians, and we are meant to see them as inheriting in some degree Ratliff's insight into the Snopes character and activity. Each of them is supposed to personify a successive generation with a particular awareness: Ratliff, born shortly after the Civil War; Stevens, Faulkner's own age, born near the end of the century; Mallison, Stevens' nephew, born around the time of the First World War. I say "supposed" because Faulkner's intention here is not fulfilled, is in fact overridden by the persistent failure of Gavin Stevens as character, intelligence, and moralist: that part of the novel in which he is the dominant figure—the working out of the Flem-Eula-de Spain triangle—is absurdly sluggish, involuted, and opaque. Although whenever he is juxtaposed to Ratliff, Stevens seems silly and in a sense impotent,[2] Faulkner is still too involved with him personally to admit that Stevens never was and never could be that fountainhead of moral enlightenment and of a gallant, embattled tradition which in the crisis of his culture and therefore of his art Faulkner needs to portray. In *The Town*, Stevens is the same windbag he has always been, and his character continues to reveal what one can only call the coarseness and vulgarity of moral tone that have been so ruinous in Faulkner's more recent writing. "Harvard M.A. and a Ph.D. from Heidelberg and his hair beginning to turn white even at just twenty-five," Stevens is the most transparent of lay figures; he embodies an undisguised personal wish. It is he who goes along with what Leslie Fiedler has termed the frozen and ossified grandiloquence of Faulkner's later style—and it is he who wrote the speech Faulkner delivered at Stockholm.

In *The Town*, however, Stevens is put to an additional use. Since his is the mind and the rhetoric with which Faulkner feels the strongest affinity, it is largely through him that we get a glimpse of Ratliff—his ruminative, melodramatic consciousness is the complicated filter through which Ratliff's clear intellect is allowed to trickle. Mallison, a decent

---

[2] Faulkner suggests that impotence only in the most literary and highfalutin manner: "... now only the afternoon remained: the interminable time until a few minutes after half past three filled with a thousand indecisions which each fierce succeeding harassment would revise. . . . And I was in time but just in time." The echo of Prufrock is clear enough, and a case for its relevance might even be made. It is a comment, however, on Faulkner's sense of Stevens that he has to resort to literature itself to attain the very frailest impersonality or irony in his relation to him.

and perspicacious young man, affords an even further rare-
fication of this device; he is less obfuscating than his uncle,
but further removed from the events of the narrative, and
often we reach Ratliff only through Mallison, who has gotten
to him through Stevens. This extreme refinement in point
of view is inherently undramatic and indicates how exiguous
Faulkner's direct grasp on experience can become. Yet it
indicates, too, how insistently he feels the necessity of re-
establishing that grasp, and how strenuously he labors
toward it.

At moments *The Town* does somehow get to Ratliff, and
thus to Snopes, and whenever it does we seem to have come
upon life and intelligence again, for in *The Town*, Ratliff
spends a good part of his time retelling the stories that made
up *The Hamlet*. They are not, however, quite the same
stories. The order of narration and even the facts are different. "Spotted Horses" is related for what must be the third
or fourth time now, but as a compressed and anecdotal
aside to another larger story. The story of Eula Varner and
McCarron is retold with interesting variations. In the first
version she gives up her virginity on the front porch after she
and McCarron have returned from being ambushed by the
country bucks, and after her father has set McCarron's
broken arm. As Ratliff recounts the story in *The Town*, they
fall upon each other "on the still-hot field of the triumph;
right there on the ground in the middle of the dark because
somebody had to hold that skeered horse, with the horse
standing over them and her likely having to help him up too
off that broke arm." The murder of Houston by Mink Snopes
is retold with the details of time and place slightly different
from those in *The Hamlet*. In fact, the whole treatment of
time, of dating the events in the narrative, becomes a part
of our response to the novel; on the evidence of both *The
Hamlet* and *The Town* it is possible, for example, to locate
"Spotted Horses" in 1891, in 1900, or in 1908.

Someone is bound to say that these repetitions are compulsive and a sign of Faulkner's waning invention; that the discrepancies of detail are a sign of his forgetfulness and carelessness as an artist; and that it is pedantry to pause over them or view them in other ways. This might be true, but for me these variations and recurrences reveal something worth noting about Faulkner and his art: he is moving back in the direction of his singular genius. The analogy I should like to make in this regard is to the post-Homeric fragments; in those almost entirely lost cyclic poems the stories of *The Iliad* and *The Odyssey* were re-created and amplified with the same character of variation that one finds in *The Town* and in parts of Faulkner's other works. As one reads about them one gets a renewed sense of how one of the primal powers of literature is to raise mythology to the level of history, to treat the material of the imagination as if it were indistinguishable from the actuality it invades and transcribes. Faulkner is the only contemporary American writer who has a faculty for this; perhaps he is the only modern writer who has it at all. The stories he wrote over twenty-five years ago have become part of the given; he takes a past which he has created himself and deals with it as received reality. It is "out there," independent of his ministrations, waiting for him to record and re-create rather than invent. And as the degree of Faulkner's conviction about the historicity of his imagination seems positive, so, too, does the degree of his conviction about the authenticity and necessity of society, and the degree to which he seems able to represent concretely the deterioration in American life of those institutions and values which allow for the cultivation of the imagination and the spirit.

To have achieved this is to have achieved classical status. In *The Town*, however, we do not have the major achievement so much as we have the impulse to discover the condition in which that achievement is again possible. We find that impulse in Faulkner's effort to come at Ratliff and the Snopeses again, as we find the contradicting impulse in his continued attachment to the obscuring sensibility of Gavin Stevens. In his sense of the motives of Flem Snopes, for instance, Ratliff is sharply distinguished from Stevens. For Ratliff, Flem and the Snopeses are primarily *objects*, animals (rabbits, snakes, rats, ants are his metaphors for them), which are to be understood as phenomena of nature. Their intense spirituality, their passion and rapacity are a direct animal response to the values of money and power which control society. Their spirituality is depraved just because their response to society, their instinctive understanding of power, is so untrammeled and precise, so unfettered by the hypocrisies of form and manner with which society disguises from itself the facts of its life. Some Snopeses, like Mink, the murderer, and Ab, the old man, are destroyed by their uncontrollable animality. Others, like Ike, the idiot, and like Eck, the good-natured fool, are destroyed because they aren't sufficiently endowed with the Snopes passion and shrewdness for survival. Still others, like Byron, like I. O.'s son Montgomery Ward, and like I. O. himself, expose their rapacity too nakedly and are driven out of society. One Snopes, Wallstreet Panic, even turns his passionate endowment against Snopesery, becomes a mortal enemy of Flem, and dedicates himself to a fanatic honesty. Only Flem has made the perfect adjustment: he sees how much of the Snopes is hidden in almost everyone, in the men who possess money and power and in the men who do not, and it is upon their secret charge of resentment, avarice, and aggressiveness that he works. He is successful because he understands society so completely and because he is willing to submit himself to the terms that it demands.

As Gavin Stevens contemplates him, however, Flem Snopes undergoes a transformation; he becomes part of that viscous ooze of rhetoric which flows from Stevens' mind like sap from a wounded tree. He ceases to be an object and becomes primarily a consciousness. Nothing could be more fatal to his integrity as a Snopes. He is "humanized" by Stevens; his motives are understood as almost unexceptionable—they become the motives which move Everyman. Stevens even begins to pity Flem when he considers his origins in underprivilege and his plight as cuckold. The Old Heidelbergian's rubric reads *nihil humanum alienum est*, and under his spell Flem and Eula become articulate and begin to speak in those orotund cadences with which Stevens—and Faulkner when he is Stevens—inflates all reality and makes everything in it a duplication of himself. Stevens is a true solipsist—here is, I think, one of the clearest indications of the central imbalance in Faulkner's art— the kind of monster who effaces the actuality of others by imposing on them his own. By apologizing for or denying their animality, he not only misunderstands the Snopeses but dehumanizes them too. It is this misunderstanding and dehumanization that Ratliff tries to withstand, insisting that Flem's motives will not be understood if they are sociologized, that his desire for respectability is simply another form of his desire for power, that his success is a result of having beaten the Jeffersonians at their own game, a game few of them admit they play.

Out of this contention a third and broader understanding begins to take shape, through which we begin to make out the connections between the success of Flem, the impotence of Stevens, and the destruction of Eula and de Spain. Charles Mallison, educated by Ratliff and Stevens but uninvolved with the Snopeses, expresses it, and it is, it seems to me, one of the most explicit and critical statements Faulkner has made about his culture. It is a negative judgment, a judgment of failure upon a culture being devastated from within by its own values—values it has always had, even in its palmiest days when there were giants in the Southern earth. It is a judgment that is rigorous and self-denying:

. . . ours a town established and decreed by people

neither Catholics nor Protestants nor even atheists but incorrigible nonconformists, nonconformists not just to everybody else but to each other in mutual accord; a nonconformism defended and preserved by descendants whose ancestors hadn't quitted home and security for a wilderness in which to find freedom of thought as they claimed and oh yes, believed, but to find freedom in which to be incorrigible and unreconstructible Baptists and Methodists; not to escape from tyranny as they claimed and believed, but to establish one.

There is no other living American novelist who can write with this authority, the authority of truth lived with for a lifetime. The tyranny which the passage describes and which the novel enacts generates both the fatal, desperate passions of the Eulas and de Spains, and the meanness of spirit against which they batter themselves and which finally, meanly, extirpates them as it tends to extirpate most impulses toward sensibility, vitality, and style. It is utterly appropriate that a Snopes should come to power in this culture; he is no harbinger of something new and alien, something out of the North, or part of the "coastal spew of Europe," but the fulfillment of a tradition, its native, purified, stripped-down product. Once again Faulkner has cut the ground out from under his apologists, for this too, he is telling us, belongs to the South, to an abiding and in the end perhaps dominating tradition.

Coming from someone as intensely implicated in the fate of his culture as Faulkner is, we must, I think, recognize again what a force for truth art can be, and how an artist who is faithful to his art is likely to be faithful to his intelligence and humanity as well. With all its imperfections, *The Town* represents a great novelist's dedication to those values—seriousness, wit, style—toward which his art aspires and by which it will again immortalize itself.

(1957)

Sinclair Lewis

I

After finishing Mark Schorer's immense biography,[1] one feels confirmed in all one's apprehensions about Sinclair Lewis He remains a writer about whom it is peculiarly difficult to speak with intelligence. He is still more a phenomenon than a man, and his books are still facts of American history and reports on American styles and attitudes more than they are novels. He was himself fitfully aware of this. On the occasion of his physician father's death, he found himself staring into a mirror and anticipating the time when he would

[1] Mark Schorer, *Sinclair Lewis: An American Life* (New York, 1961).

41

resemble somewhat a dignified old gentleman of the old school, but actually I shan't be. It takes three genera-tions, and I'm only the second. My son Wells is the third. I think he *is* a gentleman, and perhaps he may create literature—as I have not.... The best of what I'll ever have produced will bear the same relation to true literary achievement that a jacket blurb does to the text of a really great book.

The combination of callowness and cliché with forthright-ness, of provincial snobbery and bottom-doggery with the ability, at a certain level, to speak plainly and honestly are altogether characteristic. The same qualities stand revealed on almost every page of his novels, where their effect is to cancel each other out by reducing everything to a dead level of contradiction and thus to undo the critical intelligence. Mr. Schorer's book is itself evidence in support of such an observation: in more than eight hundred pages he is unable to deliver himself of a single critical analysis of one of Lewis' novels.

Yet for an American this recognition amounts less to a dismissal of Lewis from the ranked choirs of those who sing with such doleful joy in our literary empyrean than it does to a firm reseating of him in the place from which he has never moved. That place is not at the precise center of America's general idea of itself but it isn't far from it. Lewis' novels are still likely to be among the first "serious" books that adolescent Americans turn up for themselves. And the shock of recognition that then occurs is almost certain to be ineffaceable. These works are part of the mythology that in America has always tended to take the place of history.

Take, for example, this typical passage:

But a village in a country which is taking pains to be-come altogether standardized and pure, which aspires to succeed Victorian England as the chief mediocrity of the world, is no longer merely provincial, no longer downy and restful in its leaf-shadowed ignorance. It is a force seeking to dominate the earth, to drain the hills and sea of color, to set Dante at boosting Gopher Prairie, and to dress the high gods in Klassy Kollege Klothes. Sure of itself, it bullies other civilizations, as a traveling salesman in a brown derby conquers the wisdom of China and tacks advertisements of cigarettes over arches for centuries dedicated to the sayings of Confucius.

This comes from *Main Street*, of course, and was written more than forty years ago. In the face of such a text one is inclined to say that liberal-radical criticism of America has in that interval advanced about an inch: the brown derby has given way to the gray-flannel suit, and the Lucky Strike poster that once adorned the Great Wall of China has been displaced by Coca-Cola signs in Africa. That represents half an inch. And the unearned snootiness about Victorian England has expectedly fallen by the way. That's the other half. At the same time it would be frivolous to disregard the truth in such a charge or to disregard the fact that what in 1920 appeared to be wild-eyed, irresponsible criticism of America has been assimilated to the permanent liberal consciousness of things. Indeed, the problem today has to do with discriminating such truth from the generalized, lifeless, ritualistic reiterations of it which often seem here to be a substitute for personal virtue. (The equally ritualistic denial of that truth, I might add, has failed to sustain itself at the level of intelligent discourse.) Part of Lewis' importance has to do with the fact that he was among the earliest figures to give this new phase of consciousness an articulate form; and part has to do with the fact that he was the first in whom that consciousness became a popular institution.

The very ease with which the new awareness was accepted and ratified was ominous. And on this side, too, Lewis was a premonition of things to come. His sole unwavering desire was success, to do "something in the writing game," he wrote in 1910, "which shall be comparable to, say, the work of the Mayos, in the medical game." The unexceptionable vulgarity of this statement comes into significant focus when we recall that Lewis achieved his colossal success by satirizing the very values expressed in it. We cannot understand the importance of *Main Street, Babbitt, Arrowsmith, Elmer Gantry* and *Dodsworth* if we think of them merely as social satires: they are satires that made their author a millionaire. And the profound and thoroughgoing equivocation of values which both constitutes their charm and vitiates their power was the "secret" of Lewis' success.

In these novels he managed to roast the eaters of flesh while filling the fleshpots, to chase the moneylenders from the Temple in order to conduct a tidy business of exchange outside. He deplored advertising from every billboard he could cover—when the General Conference of the Methodist Church assembled in Kansas City, *Elmer Gantry* was advertised "on forty-nine billboards including, in the center of the city, thirteen that were illuminated"—and denounced the evils of publicity in an endless stream of press releases and gossip-column interviews. Main Street's idea of art he summed up this way: "Harold Bell Wright is a lovely writer, and he teaches such good morals in his novels, and folks says he's made prett' near a million dollars out of 'em." *Mutatis mutandis*, he was predicting his own career as a writer.

This naturally tells us something about the quality of Lewis' attack, but it also tells us something about the society which was ostensibly being beaten about the ears. America's new ambition of seriousness and self-criticism found its perfect object and expression in him. It was a seriousness perfectly compatible with a contempt for all things "highbrow," and a self-criticism so pleased with itself that it became frequently indistinct from self-congratulation. If you can't beat 'em, join 'em, goes the native adage; but in the case of Lewis and America it is difficult to say who joined up with whom. In the long run, however, it is plain enough who lost out. The history of Sinclair Lewis' life as both a man and a writer demonstrates again what everyone knows but no one ever really learns—that in America, at least, nothing fails like success.

Such remarks may seem to imply more than the commonly held view that Lewis and Babbitt were the same person, or, more charitably, that Lewis had a Babbitt in him. On this account Lewis might be understood by Max Weber's formulation that

> when the imagination of a whole people has once been turned toward purely quantitative bigness, as in the United States, the romanticism of numbers exercises an irresistible appeal to the poets among businessmen.

He was, in other words, a Babbitt of genius. The creation of Babbitt, of course, was neither an accident nor a minor episode in the history of American literature and culture. *Babbitt* and Lewis' other better novels are *documents* of exceptional importance. How current that importance remains may be gathered from this passage in Babbitt's memorable address to the Zenith Real Estate Board:

> In politics and religion this Sane Citizen is the canniest man on earth; and in the arts he invariably has a natural taste which makes him pick out the best, every time. In no country in the world will you find so many reproductions of the Old Masters and of well-known paintings on parlor walls as in these United States. No country has anything like our number of phonographs. . . .

The power of observation in this speech reveals what one would be happy to call a large sociological gift had not modern American sociology in considerable part dedicated itself to a denial of it. Indeed, one of the minor ironies of recent years lies in the fact that the sociological commentators on American culture who began by denying, quite reasonably, that America was still and forever unchangeably the America of George F. Babbitt have come in the course of their defense to sound strangely like Babbitt themselves. And what in the light of recent pronouncements from Washington are we to say to this utterance of Chum Frink, Zenith's advertising-poet:

> Culture has become as necessary an adornment and advertisement for a city today as pavements or bank-clearances. It's Culture, in theaters and art galleries and so on, that brings thousands of visitors to New York every year.

The new American Augustanism has announced itself in accents which, if they don't exactly echo Pope's numbers, poignantly remind us of Chum Frink's tetrameters:

> *And when I saw the jolly bunch come waltzing in for eats at lunch, and squaring up in natty duds to platters large of French Fried spuds, why then I'd stand right up and bawl, "I've never left my home at all!"*

And so one feels about Lewis. That he could, alternatively, diagnose Babbitt's values and then repudiate the diagnosis, or create Babbitt and then affirm the moral superiority of that creation to the intelligence that created it, seems characteristic of a culture which continues to express its vital principles almost exclusively through self-destructive contradictions.

When we ask what kind of a man and what kind of a life produced these documents which are at once so broad in their representativeness and so shallow in the depths they choose to penetrate, we are confronted with an utterly dismaying vision. Lewis' central experience of life was to be humiliated, rejected, and overborne. Extremely ugly and graceless, he was as unblessed in his family as in his person; his parents, particularly his father, were desiccated and degenerate inheritors of the Puritan ethos. Apart from a dedication to work and professional responsibility, his father seemed to embody no other positive living values. "Cold, rigid, parsimonious, almost compulsively mechanical, absolutely without self-questioning," he expressed neither affection nor regard for his son. When Sinclair Lewis was a boy his father remarked that his son had no future; when Sinclair Lewis won the Nobel Prize he remained unimpressed. He passed on these attributes to his son, though as often happens in such passage, they were weakened in some respects and more severely distorted in others. What in the father was recognizable as the Puritan virtues in an advanced stage of ossification became in the son incoherent honesty, impotent rebelliousness, rootless independence, and finally something close to chaos and madness.

Unlike most novelists, Lewis made almost no reference to his boyhood, and apart from certain external details, Mr. Schorer's biography has almost nothing to tell us about the first fifteen years of his life. As for the remaining fifty years, they, too, are almost without exception a matter of relentless external detail, of trivia, chitchat, and gossip. For the truly terrifying thing about Lewis' life was its entire want of inwardness. At the critical moments in his life, one looks for comments from him on what is happening or what he feels, and nothing, literally nothing, is forthcoming—neither concrete response nor abstract idea, neither reflections in private nor confessions in public or to friends, neither self-examination nor the refusal of it. And from the evidence of Mr. Schorer's book we must conclude that Sinclair Lewis was that modern nightmare, a man whose life had no essential idea, not even an idea of himself. His consciousness was as good as without content; and as for his unconscious mind, he was so estranged from it that it might have belonged to another man.

His passion was to record and catalogue everything, immediately, as he experienced it: apparently unable to believe in the authenticity of anything he might recollect, he made a virtue of noting things down automatically— "& in each instance I will really be in the place as I say 'I am now in This or That.' " And he went on to become a novelist whose method of writing was equally mechanical. It was all a matter of preliminary work: a "field" to research and master; "full biographies of all the leading characters . . . elaborately detailed maps of the setting . . . floor plans and furnishings of houses; a complete scenario of the action, step by step"; and often "collaborators," assistants, or researchers. When all this was done the novel would, he said, "write itself." There is about this something more distressing than the fact of Lewis' idea of writing as mechanical; he thought of *himself* as a machine, something into which data was fed and out of which, after he was filled up and the proper levers manipulated, would come a novel. Nevertheless, Lewis was all his life nothing if not a writer—one uses the term here neutrally—and one of the pitiable things about that life is that long after he has anything to say or anyone to say it to, long after his relation to the world and to other people has ceased to have a semblance of meaning or coherence, in the midst of collapse, alcoholism, delirium tremens, insane restlessness, mindless fears and furies, he goes on writing, writing, writing in a kind of wild, endless masturbatory frenzy. Writing was a symptom of whatever malady constituted Sinclair Lewis, but it was also his principal and finally his only connection with life.

Mr. Schorer's book is, I believe, far too long for what it at last encompasses. So much of it, given Lewis' person, is itself mechanical cataloguing of trivia that one often wonders whether Mr. Schorer has not been infected by the deadly virus which he expertly describes. On the other hand, the last 250 pages of this biography are, in their own ghastly way, worth waiting for. They chronicle Lewis' decline and fall, and I can recall nothing in modern literature more appalling in its presentation of human emptiness, squalor, and agonized nullity. There is, for example, the picture of Lewis coming to his second wife, Dorothy Thompson, in the dead of night, "drunk and demanding," and exuding an odor, she recalled, "like rotting weeds." Or there is Lewis in the paroxysms of the d.t.'s, suddenly beginning to speak in his wife's voice, delivering to himself an insane parody-lecture on his dissipations. These pages amount to a kind of monstrous cautionary tale, though it is difficult to make out what it is warning us against. It certainly can't be the evils of drink, or the dangers of deracination, or the consequences of rebelliousness or leaving home. Perhaps we are somehow being told that this is what being an American writer can be like, and going on what has happened since Lewis' time, one is hard put to deny the application.

There is one large point about Mr. Schorer's work with which I must take issue. When one is finished with it, one wants to ask: How could this man ever have written *Main Street* and *Babbitt?* No connection seems to exist between Sinclair Lewis, an automaton who could suffer, and the mind that created his best books. The anarchy and devastation of Lewis' life have, I am afraid, managed to dominate Mr. Schorer's view of him; Lewis' consciousness may have been inchoate and his life a shambles, but that is not sufficient reason for surrendering up unconditionally to those terms any understanding of his life and writing and the connection between them. He was, after all, a human being, a fact which, in the course of Mr. Schorer's disturbingly unpoised account of him, the reader must periodically force himself to remember. But the cause of this may be no more than what I proposed at the outset—that there is something about him and his work that resists intelligent comment. That we must think of him, generically, as a writer rather than a novelist, and that he emerges from Mr. Schorer's pages as something other, if not something less, than a recognizable human being, indicate again the essentially phenomenological nature of his interest. Like the America he represents, he seems on the one hand to fall below the level of generalization and on the other to invite the fanciest metaphysical speculations.

One of the primary American disabilities is that America continues to be thought of as an idea, a state of mind, rather than a place, a piece of geography, a country. However true or false this notion may be, every American drinks in with his mother's milk the myth that "America is here or nowhere." Lewis' wretched life was mortified by it, and Mr. Schorer's biography is its cenotaph.

II

One of the oddest things about Mark Schorer's biography of Sinclair Lewis was that its hero's name was Dorothy Thompson. She gave Mr. Schorer full access to her papers, he reported, and permission to use any of them as he pleased; and before she died in 1961, Mr. Schorer was in return able to offer her an uncorrected copy of the typescript of his immense biography. Mr. Schorer tells us that "she read it with approval and finished it in tears." She had reason to, since the story of her marriage to Sinclair Lewis was recounted essentially from her point of view. It isn't difficult to understand why this should have been so. The chief characteristic of Sinclair Lewis' life was its incoherence, its want of form, direction, or even idea. In comparison to the pitiful and self-destructive chaos into which his life at length dissolved, Dorothy Thompson's appeared to have been a model of shapeliness, order, and proper self-preserving self-regard. She was at any rate anything but incoherent.

Now we have another book about the Sinclair Lewis-Dorothy Thompson marriage. *Dorothy and Red*, by the memoirist Vincent Sheean.[2] Mr. Sheean was a close acquaintance of both partners in the marriage; he traveled with them in Europe, stayed with them as house guest in America, and partied with them wherever the party happened to be. Mr. Sheean is more or less explicitly a partisan of Dorothy Thompson; he, too, has had access to her private papers— which are now deposited at Syracuse University—and his account of the marriage, in large part based on these documents, features her as its central character, and is also told from her point of view. It should be said at once that Mr. Sheean is in no way capable of satisfying the intellectual requirements that his subject demands. One sentence will serve to diagnose his standards of judgment. "It is a misfortune," he writes, "that the greatest of American journalists should have been married to the greatest of American writers." The irrelevant or inappropriate attribution of greatness in the first instance combined with the exaggerated or inflated attribution of it in the second fairly indicates Mr. Sheean's values: they are the values of café society or of advertising—it does not matter which, they are the same thing. By "greatest" he means of course most famous, most newsworthy, most talked about. Nevertheless, this dismissive judgment of Mr. Sheean cannot be extended to his book or to what it contains. He has chosen to publish a good deal of material which Mark Schorer either had to reject or did not see; this material is in itself of considerable interest. And in a curious way Mr. Sheean's very incompetence and naïveté allows his subject to reveal itself with a clarity which Mr. Schorer's infinitely superior work was denied.

Dorothy Thompson and Sinclair Lewis first met in July, 1927, in Berlin. Lewis was then forty-two years old and was by far the most famous and successful living American novelist. Dorothy Thompson was thirty-three and was employed as the Berlin correspondent for the Curtis news-

[2] Vincent Sheean, *Dorothy and Red* (Boston, 1963).

papers, a chain which included the Philadelphia *Ledger* and the New York *Evening Post*. Dorothy Thompson's first marriage had just ended in divorce; Lewis' first marriage had long since been on the rocks. The occasion of their meeting was a birthday party Dorothy Thompson gave for herself, to which she spontaneously invited Lewis—they had been casually introduced the day before. At this party, so the story goes, Lewis waited until dinner was over and then asked her to marry him. She was naturally in no position to accept such an offer from a man whom she did not even know. This difficulty was remedied by their starting something that has to be called an affair, and Lewis obligingly continued asking her to marry him. They followed each other around Europe; occasionally they even caught up with each other; and in May, 1928, they were married in London. The marriage ended in divorce in 1942, but it had been over for years before that. It was in some sense over before they were even married. Even in the earliest period of the marriage they spent more time apart than they did together. They had nothing to say to each other, and after a certain point had nothing to do with each other—and wanted to do nothing for each other. Their intimacy was such that they were both able to speak more freely and openly to strangers or casual acquaintances than they were to each other. And yet it would be gross ignorance to write off the marriage of these two extraordinary persons as lacking in content or significance. On the contrary, their relation is almost too exemplary to be true.

Lewis was that remarkable modern phenomenon, a man who had apparently no inner life; he was incapable of reflection or self-examination, and was virtually guiltless of ever having said anything in confrontation with himself. He was fated to experience humiliation and rejection throughout his life. That endless suffering and the fact that he was a writer are the two most authentic things about him. It is altogether typical, however, that the suffering did not get into the writing, that he was quite unable to express his anguish in the one form of expression available to him. Furthermore, his conception of himself as a writer was entirely external and mechanical; he thought of himself as a machine into which facts were fed; when all the material was there, out would come a novel. His well-known methods of writing were equally mechanical. Though she did not carry matters to such an extreme, Dorothy Thompson was herself a thoroughly externalized person. As Mr. Sheean puts it, "for the most part she dwelt outside, resolutely outside herself." The daughter of an upstate New York Methodist minister, her first work after college was with the Woman's Suffrage Party; from there she gravitated naturally into the spacious and pseudo-personal world of journalism. Her style of thought ran generally to grandiloquent cliché: women, she would say, "are, somehow, closer to biological verities." And when it did not run in this direction, it turned into abstract, liberal claptrap: what she wanted from a marriage, she wrote, was "a home which will be a center of life and illumination for people who can really contribute to the development of the humanities." There is something here that is even deadlier than Lewis in his most clownish vulgarity; compared to this, George F. Babbitt seems a true hero of the passions.

Such facts help us to begin to understand one of the most interesting questions this book raises—namely, why Dorothy Thompson married Lewis. Certainly it was not for love, as most of us understand the idea; there is hardly a shred of evidence in this book to suggest that Dorothy Thompson was able to experience love in relation to men or had any pressing need to experience it. Her conception of marriage, as we have seen, was wholly abstract. That there were certain opportunistic elements in her decision to marry Lewis cannot be doubted. In 1928 he had just about reached the height of his great fame and success; at the same time he was just about going over the hill both as a man and a writer. Putting her acute sense of journalistic timing to use, she chose precisely the right moment to marry him—the moment which turned out to be of largest advantage to her, out of which she got the greatest leverage. Our sense of this is confirmed by what happened subsequently; soon after the marriage, as soon as her own career really began to rise, she left him like a shot, without second thoughts, without regrets, without explanations, indeed without explicit awareness or acknowledgment that she had even done so (not that she hadn't abundant reasons on other grounds to leave him, and not that he wasn't doing exactly the same thing as well).

Moreover, she married Lewis with her eyes open. Long before the marriage Dorothy Thompson knew all about him. At forty-two Lewis was a violent and complete alcoholic; when he was not drinking himself into a stupor he was drinking himself into wild and mindless rages. When he was not drinking he was writing. When he was not withdrawn he was holding forth in endless monologues and imitations—he was almost incapable of conversation or being what, for want of a better word, must be called himself. More things were wrong with him—he embodied more unattractive, disagreeable, and unfortunate qualities—than can be numbered. Dorothy Thompson knew all this at once; there was nothing for her to learn, for Lewis hid nothing, was unable to hide anything—and there was in any case miserably little to hide. Yet she married him, and the nature of that decision accurately expressed the character of their relation. Shortly before the marriage she wrote him a letter in which she took an oath of loyalty: she was giving herself, she asserted, "not to a man who can stir me to excitement with his kisses, or comfort me with his caresses," but to "a life-ideal"; this ideal was at that moment represented by Lewis, in whom she saw "some call to be the expression of the discontent and aspiration of your country." The marriage bore out the sense of this dedication. It was so exterior an affair that it seems more like a treaty or trade agreement between two minor nations than what is usually thought of as a marriage. Both Sinclair Lewis and Dorothy Thompson naturally tended to think of themselves as large corporate institutions with collective goals and representative destinies. This is particularly true of Dorothy Thompson, who, as the thirties wore on toward their ghastly climax, became what she was called upon to be—a public figure, celebrity, and personage, one of the leaders in a national cause, and a familiar of the great and powerful. Her advice and good opinion were courted by presidents and chancellors; she helped waken America to the menace of Hitler; she became what every journalist wants to be, a maker and unmaker of kings—and even more. Some time during that decade she began, like royalty, to go about without carrying money.

Yet even two such highly abstract and depersonalized people must have been possessed of motives of a deeper and less generalized kind. Lewis' motives, from what we can know of them, seem to have been fairly simple, or minimal. He was losing his grip on life and himself, and he, as well as his friends, looked to Dorothy Thompson as his last hope of salvation. He could not have made a more ruinous choice—not that a fortunate one would have "saved" him either. Dorothy Thompson closely resembled the most important person in Sinclair Lewis' life, his father. Like Lewis' father she was extremely competent, utterly self-confident, absolutely incapable of self-questioning or self-doubt. She was, again like the elder Lewis, virtually impregnable to personal emotion; a "vitally important element in Dorothy's greatness," writes Mr. Sheean, was that "she could always step over the corpses and go on, steadily, resolutely, right to the end." All through his life Lewis was to reexperience the emotions of humiliation and impotence which he first sustained in relation to his father; in marrying Dorothy Thompson he made certain of their perpetuation.

Dorothy Thompson's motives were of a different kind.

Her first marriage, to Josef Bard, a Hungarian-Jewish journalist, had been a fiasco. Bard seems to have been something of a Don Juan, and began having affairs and spending Dorothy Thompson's money on them as soon as they were married. It is also clear that he found Dorothy Thompson sexually inadequate and unresponsive, reproached her for what she calls her "erotic failures," and talked about these shortcomings to women known to both of them. While admitting to the truth of the charges he brought against her, she seems not to have been particularly disturbed by them; what troubled and angered her was the gossip and disloyalty (though she was to do something of the same during her marriage to Lewis) and the fact that she had been "defeated" by a man. It seems perfectly evident that in marrying Sinclair Lewis she was both avoiding the possibility of another such experience and taking revenge for what had happened in her first marriage. Her idea of marriage was that the male partner should do "creative" work and that she would be "the wage earner of the household." In a genuinely good marriage, she believed, a woman finds a man "whom she can fertilize with her own spirit," and she went on to declare that she would only "give my body, soul and spirit to a man who can use it up to make a Damascene blade." What women need, she continued, "is not to find the man who completes ourselves . . . what we need is to create a man *in* ourselves." The unconscious configuration of these remarks is poignantly revealing.

Lewis earned his own wages, but apart from that he must have seemed to fit her bill of particulars. (In fact, he was a parody of it.) He was a "great" and "creative" man, but he was also weak and in trouble and in need of being delivered from himself. Moreover, he represented no sexual threat to her, since he seems to have been impotent a good part of the time and was continually haunted by fears of impotence. And Lewis always behaved so badly, with such self-annihilating intentions and with such preposterous and irrational cruelty, that any woman who undertook a relation with him occupied perforce a position of unassailable moral superiority. Sinclair Lewis made it extremely easy for any woman who had a need to feel self-righteous or who thought of sexual relations in terms of moral victory and defeat. Dorothy Thompson had such needs; she was also determined to triumph over life, and Sinclair Lewis may be justly accused of having encouraged her in this illusion.

Such intimate details along with a host of others make up the three hundred and some odd pages of *Dorothy and Red*. Yet almost none of them is really convincing; almost nothing that we read in this book makes us feel that we have touched upon the literal truth or been in the presence of the authentic. There are several reasons for this. In the first place, the state of Dorothy Thompson's papers makes it nearly impossible to tell when or whether she is ever telling the truth, not merely about her emotions but about anything at all. It would take a trained scholar, some kind of literary cryptographer, to order, make sense of, and authenticate this material, and Mr. Sheean is not equipped to do such work. Throughout her life Dorothy Thompson was accustomed to write letters "which she never sent; they were kept in her own files and sometimes she rewrote them or parts of them. Occasionally we have two or three versions of the same letter, without any indication if any of them had been sent." For example, Mr. Sheean reports that her long letters to her first husband, written while their marriage was breaking up, were never sent; we know this to be true, he states, "because she says so." But how do we know that this is true? Mr. Sheean guesses that such and such a letter was sent and that such and such was not, but he clearly has no way of knowing. Some of her longest and most important letters to Lewis seem never to have been sent, and she wrote these, Mr. Sheean conjectures, "as if there were some thought (conscious or unconscious) that eyes other than his might some day see them." She was also in the habit of making carbon copies of some of her most personal letters, but again Mr. Sheean has found no way of telling whether the original was sent or destroyed. In her later years she went through her papers with the idea of an autobiography in mind. She made notes and deletions, we learn, but of course we do not know what she destroyed. A similar thing can be said of her diaries; whole years are unaccounted for. Interestingly enough, the one diary that Lewis probably read, the "Honeymoon Diary," which is an account of a tour they made of England, and which she inscribed "to us," is, with the exception of one remark, altogether impersonal in tone and manner and reads very much like advertising copy.

What we have then in *Dorothy and Red* is neither a biography nor the account of a marriage; in a sense we do not even have the materials for either. What we have is a construction, a fantasy, a work of fiction. And insofar as all biography and autobiography are selective and conjectural and rely on memory and other uncertain kinds of evidence, a work of this kind renews our awareness of how unreliable is the line of distinction we draw between fact and fiction. There is, however, an illustrious precedent for such a performance; with its combination of letters, diaries, and marginal editorial commentary, *Dorothy and Red* often read astonishingly like Richardson's *Pamela*, and Dorothy Thompson is unmistakeably one of Pamela's granddaughters. Like Pamela, she uses her letters and journals to control and manipulate the reality of others. Like Pamela, she is a master of duplicity and calculation without apparently ever being quite aware of it. Like Pamela, she is relentlessly high-minded and a remorseless moralizer. Her principal mode of address is self-congratulation; she shakes moral hands with herself all day long. Like her great predecessor, she sets out to overcome the masculine world by means of her moral virtue, personal superiority, and intellect. But Dorothy Thompson was not Pamela, and what in the mid-eighteenth century amounted to a whole new range of self-consciousness and inwardness, a new fullness of account in rendering one's responses to life, has two hundred years later become cliché and avoidance and palpable self-deception. These qualities are even present in what has already become a widely publicized section of this book, Dorothy Thompson's confrontation of her homosexuality. It is a truly touching passage and does represent at attempt at honesty. At the risk of appearing ungenerous, I must say that it, too, struck me as tainted. It is, to begin with, rather cheaply literary, a sad little effort to imitate the style of D. H. Lawrence. And it is, in the end, not self-confrontation, doubt, or examination but one more self-assertion, one more exertion of the abstract will to prevail over experience.

None of this demonstrates that Dorothy Thompson was a bad or wicked person, or that she was even what is ordinarily thought of as a liar or coiner of falsehoods. It does demonstrate what can be thought of as the lie of consciousness. She and Sinclair Lewis probably belonged to the last generation of Americans who were able to believe that one could give a full and reliable account of oneself in strictly conscious terms. They were both considerable figures, but we must understand them as coming at the end of a line of development rather than at the beginning of one. Lewis was among the last of the external, realistic school of novelists; the strength of his sociological-mythological images of American life lies in their breadth of representativeness, a breadth which is somehow inseparable from their shallowness. Dorothy Thompson was among the last of the original "new women," whose intention in life was to impose themselves and their wills on the world in the way they thought men do, and who therefore imagined the world as a wholly exterior place and themselves as externalized. They did not, in other words, think of themselves as we have come to do. They did not think of themselves as having unconscious minds which were overwhelmingly powerful, largely uncontrollable, and a central part of themselves. They were the last generation able to do so, and the strain of the effort is everywhere visible —as it is not in figures of an earlier period who did not have this new knowledge to deny.

This is what makes them so different from us, this simultaneous lack of consciousness and lie of consciousness. But it is also what endows them with their awkward and crude yet genuine force, vitality, and magnitude. For they were creatures who inhabited a real external world, a world which they took as the only reality, which they wanted to conquer and possess, for which they created themselves and felt they had been created. And they could live in this world without suspecting that its value or existence might be problematical, without doubting it or themselves as part of it. For all the unreality of their inner lives, for all their poverty of inwardness, for all the naked evasions, flights, and self-deceptions, they had an undeniable reality. They had the reality of large figures engaged in a large, strange, substantial world which had actual objects in it. Out of Sinclair Lewis' belief in that world came those remarkable fictions which confirmed and enlarged its existence. In *Main Street, Babbitt, Arrowsmith, Elmer Gantry,* and *Dodsworth,* Lewis was able to make a considerable contribution to the mythology that, as I have suggested earlier, in America has always tended to take the place of history and society. Dorothy Thompson was not nearly so sizable a presence, but she, too, has been rewarded. She believed in and committed herself to the quasi-fictional world of journalism and the official American democracy represented in its utterances. If she was not privileged to make a lasting contribution to the mythology that is America, she remains herself as a figure in its folklore. It is their reality in this sense that makes these two still meaningful for us.

(1963; 1964)

Stalky & Co.

Stalky & Co. is a fantasy and a celebration. It is an idealized recollection and re-creation of Kipling's experience at school. It celebrates a period of life and a way of life, or culture. The period of life is what was once called boyhood. The way of life or culture is that of the English public school, in this case the United Services College, founded in 1874 by a group of army officers who wanted to provide their sons with an education suited to their class and family, but who could not afford to send them to the more expensive schools. Most of the boys who attended the United Services College were soldiers' sons, and many of them had been born in India. At the College the boys were prepared for the Army Entrance Examination, for most of them were, in their careers, to follow in their father's footsteps. By extension, then, *Stalky & Co.* celebrates the way of life of the British Army —of its officer class—and of the Empire which it helped to administer and rule. This Empire and its way of life have ceased significantly to exist (and there is reason to doubt whether they ever existed in the manner that Kipling would have us believe). As a result, *Stalky & Co.* is the celebration of a dead culture, a culture that may seem to many Americans as remote and strange as that of Sparta or the Roman Empire.

Whether the period of life—boyhood—which *Stalky & Co.* celebrates still exists is perhaps something of an open question. It is certain, however, that our modern conceptions of childhood and adolescence are very different from Kipling's and the nineteenth century's conceptions of boyhood and youth. The very change in the words we use to represent those years of life indicates a change in our idea of them—and a change in ideals and values as well. One of the many uses to which a book like *Stalky & Co.* may be put is that it helps us define and understand ourselves by showing us what, in part, we no longer are. No reader of this book will need to be convinced that in our time the period of adolescence is undergoing a crisis and disturbance of peculiar intensity; or that this crisis is nothing if not one of value and of the authority of value; or that what is being registered so painfully, explosively, and honestly in adolescence is expressive of a general social condition. Among its many other qualities, *Stalky & Co.* will be understood to possess the quality of speaking with intimacy and relevance to this situation.

No doubt this is weighty significance to place upon a book that has for generations been an almost exclusive possession of schoolboys. And there can be little question that its appeal will continue so long as readers enjoy jokes, gags, japes, comic plots and revenges, and the life of free-wheeling fantasy. Yet we should note that if *Stalky & Co.* has been a much loved book, it has also been much hated. The strong word here is accurate, and we should not mistake the matter: it has been hated precisely for its values, or what its values have been taken to be. The school life that it describes is harsh, cruel, and often brutal, and Kipling has been accused of siding with the cruelty and justifying the brutality. The boys are being trained for a life in which force and violence are to be met every day, and Kipling has been charged with affirming the domination of the weak by the strong. The boys are to become part of the governing caste of the British Empire, and Kipling has been accused of uncritically supporting—and as being the propagandist of—the moral values of imperialism and the imperalist system.

These accusations are in one degree or another substantially true. It would be pointless to deny them and almost equally so to try to mitigate them. It might, for example, be argued that although the British Empire was a bad thing, it was still, as George Orwell once remarked, a great deal better than the younger empires that have supplanted it. However true and useful Orwell's remark might be, to introduce it into a discussion of *Stalky & Co.* would act more to distract the reader's attention than to extenuate Kipling. The point to be grasped is that among and alongside all these bad attitudes which seem calculated to outrage the values that most educated persons today affirm—values which can be roughly summed up in the term liberal democracy—there exist other attitudes and values whose absence from contemporary life we all feel and are probably the worse for. These values are described by old, obsolete words like honor, truthfulness, loyalty, manliness, pride, straightforwardness, courage, self-sacrifice, and heroism. That these virtues exist as active and credible possibilities in the world of *Stalky & Co.*, and that they seem not to in ours—or if they do, appear almost solely in corrupted forms—must give us pause. Such a fact may serve to remind us that the moral benefits, conveniences, and superiorities of modern democratic society have not been acquired without cost. Part of this cost seems pretty clearly to have been paid by a diminution of the older masculine virtues. These virtues were felt to exist in the societies of the past, and that they existed in conjunction with the injustices of class, the inequalities of inherited privilege, and with all the offenses against human dignity of which the social past is grossly guilty, should act to increase our awareness of the tragically paradoxical character of social progress. In the moral life of history, there are apparently no gains without losses. Few books urge us to confront this contradiction more barely and boldly than *Stalky & Co.*

Yet it would be an oversight to consider *Stalky & Co.* solely from the point of view of social comment and in isolation from its place in literature. It belongs to a genre of literature peculiarly characteristic of the modern era. This literature is concerned with the discovery, examination, and commemoration of childhood and boyhood—especially one's own. It begins with Rousseau's *Emile* and the poetry of Blake and Wordsworth and is carried forward in the English and American novel, most notably in Dickens, George Eliot, and Mark Twain. Although a serious concern with childhood is a common feature of all modern culture, in no other culture has that concern been so central and intense as in the culture of the English-speaking world. In no other language does the word for boy have the kind of resonance that it does in English. *Garçon, Knabe, muchacho* are good enough words in their way, but they do not take away the winter of desolation or make the buds unfold or cause one's moral being to rejoice in the way that the word boy does. In what other language is there such an epithet as "Oh, boy!"—an expression of the very essence of spontaneous delight. Or in what other language are lines such as

Shades of the prison-house begin to close
Upon the growing boy

thought of as expressing the very essence of sadness and of
the human condition. In *Stalky & Co.*, when the triumvirate
are publicly rubbing in their revenge on King's house, one
of the masters who is being mercilessly imitated overhears
what is going on and murmurs to another " 'It's not brutality,' . . . as though answering a question no one had asked.
'It's boy; only boy.' " Clearly, the word is being used here
in a metaphysical sense and as descriptive of a metaphysical
state. In short, boy is one of the sacred words of the English
language; boyhood is, or for one hundred and fifty years
was, a priestly state or condition; and the literature of boys
and boyhood has had, for a secularized era, something of
the aura of doctrinal or holy writ.

One of the chief characters in which the boy appears is
as a schoolboy. English literature is particularly rich in the
literature of school (as opposed to America, where the boy
tends more often to be regarded in his relation to nature).[1]
This unique richness is in accord with the unique importance that education has been given in English tradition
and history, and with the unique English feeling for the
experience of education—a feeling which may be summed
up in D. W. Brogan's epigram that England is the only
country in the world where being a schoolboy is an end in
itself. This does not mean that going to school is not also
a means to an end, or, as we say today, a preparation for
life. It does mean, however, that school is first and foremost
an experience, like all other experience, and that it is to be
thought of, judged, and respected as such. It also means that

[1] And of course one ought not to overlook the fact that in America the
word "boy" has also been used in a dishonorific sense, most notably
in relation to blacks.

the best way to ensure the success of educational means is to insist upon them as ends; conversely, the surest way to destroy belief in the value and reality of any effort is to make clear that it is not self-justifying or autonomous. Finally, the statement implies that since being a schoolboy has such a special weight and significance, much of one's later experience as a man will itself be justified in the degree that it bears out or is in accord with the values of one's earlier experience. As we see in *Stalky & Co.*, the names that the boys give themselves at school are the names by which they greet and recognize each other for the rest of their lives. And for the rest of their lives—no matter what their age—they think of themselves as "Old Boys," not graduates or alumni, as we think of ourselves, neutralizing the sex in one case and fleeing from the language in the other. The brute emotion, the unabashed sentimentality of that phrase "Old Boy" is still another indication of the fierce importance with which the English experience of school has traditionally been felt. Such a phrase also reveals the direction in which character will be distorted by an unremitting application of its idea.

Stalky & Co. is a classic of this sub-genre of literature. That it emerges from and refers to a literature which deals with life at school we learn from the book itself, where such popular works as *Eric, or Little by Little* are mentioned only to be held up to comic contempt. These tales, as the reader might suspect, were largely didactic and moralistic in purpose. They dealt with good little boys from home who fell prey to the infinite temptations to immoral behavior at school and who, on the very brink of irredeemable corruption, were saved only by an intervention of moral reform, corporal punishment, or religious conversion. Usually it was a combination of all three. Odd as it may seem today, these books probably served a purpose in their own time. But by and large they served it badly and falsely, and one of the intentions of *Stalky & Co.* is to alter the picture of life at school presented in these books and to set the record straight.

One of these books, the most famous of them, is significantly not mentioned in *Stalky & Co.* Thomas Hughes's *Tom Brown's Schooldays* is a work of considerable historical importance. The story of a boy's experiences at Rugby during the early years of Thomas Arnold's headmastership, it records with sharp realism the terrible, inhumane life of an English public school before Arnold's reforms were instituted, and the salutary effect on mind, spirit, and morale that those reforms had when they took hold. It is a work of high Victorian seriousness and moral earnestness, dedicated to the liberal, humane, responsible, and intelligent values which Dr. Arnold's educational ideas and reforms were founded on and which it was his purpose to instill among his students. In its own minor way, *Tom Brown's Schooldays* is a distinguished book, and though it is carefully not mentioned in *Stalky & Co.*, it is always there in the background. Kipling could not in fact have written his work without the precedent of *Tom Brown's Schooldays*; and *Stalky & Co.* may be described as both anti-*Tom Brown* and *Tom Brown* revived. Kipling may have had this in mind when he once referred to *Stalky & Co.* as a moral tract.

All ideals become corrupted in practice, by application to practical life, and the longer any practice persists unchanged, the more corrupt it will grow—this, incidentally, is one of the sounder arguments for the necessity of constant criticism and reform. By the late Victorian period— 1875–1900—the high ideals of Arnold and *Tom Brown* had succeeded in penetrating and reforming much of English thinking about school and school life. They had succeeded so well and had been so thoroughly assimilated that they seemed well on the way to turning into their own corrupt opposites. And the forms that cruelty, injustice, pettifogging, and hypocrisy take in *Stalky & Co.* are, by and large, the forms of corrupted Victorian idealism. In such a context, the anti-*Tom Brown*ism of Stalky, M'Turk, and Beetle takes on meaning. The boys' disdain of organized games, their refusal to be moved by petitions in the name of "the honour of the house," their systematic flouting of appeals to their sense of moral decency and honesty (as in the "combined" work that goes on in their study), their contemptuous disregard for the entire prefectorial system, even their inconsistent anti-clericalism, are in considerable measure a result of their revulsion from what today we would call the phoniness into which these ideals and values had descended. That the boys are not opposed to these ideals in themselves, that their rebelliousness is in fact intuitively directed by their feeling for them, is among the major burdens of the message which *Stalky & Co.* communicates. It is in this sense that we must think of it as a *Tom Brown* revived.

It should be clear by now that in *Stalky & Co.* we are faced with a moral situation of some complexity and probably of deep-seated contradiction. This situation is represented most forcefully in the variety of attitudes we find both Kipling and the boys taking toward authority and institutions—that is, institutional authority—and toward the social system which the institutions serve and whose nature they express. That a writer's attitude toward social and institutional authority should be complex, ambivalent, and even contradictory is no more than what we, in the modern world, have become accustomed to expect. But to find this attitude in Kipling may be something of a surprise, since the side of his writing that has drawn the most conspicuous attention in the last thirty years is the side that maintained a friendly or affirmative, not to say submissive, attitude toward authority. And if we use the word authority, then we must also use its derived form, authoritarian, for almost all criticism of Kipling boils down to the accusation of authoritarianism. That there is an impulse toward it and a streak of it in him, no open-minded reader will deny; but that this impulse is checked by other and opposite impulses which, working together, make for a condition of moral stress and ambiguity the open-minded reader will also see. Why these countering impulses should have been overlooked is a historical question of some complexity. The fact of their having been overlooked, however, may serve to indicate the distance that separates our own age and attitudes from Kipling's.

We find these attitudes represented in the boys' relations with the various masters and with the Head. The modern reader may find the open and mutual antagonism between the boys and masters disturbing because of the book's assumption that this antagonism is natural and proper, and because of the directness, intensity, and ferocity with which the antagonism is enacted on both sides. We don't believe in the propriety or inevitability of such antagonism today; we believe in the cooperative and conciliatory virtues, and distrust the powers of our own aggressiveness so thoroughly that we have almost forgotten how to deal with them—and in the forgetting, we have, among other things, palpably increased the likelihood of the world's being blown up. In addition, we are troubled by the kind of freedom that a situation of outright and assumed hostility provides for both sides. All questions of fantasy notwithstanding, the free-wheeling aggressiveness and baiting by both boys and masters in *Stalky & Co.* would today undoubtedly be regarded as pathological conduct. And with a certain justness, for such behavior made sense only within a certain context. This "context" is the Head, and what he stands for. He represents, for both boys and masters, an authority which can be believed in and trusted. He is a court of appeal to which one resorts with faith, and a source of justice whose verdicts one accepts with trust. He represents experience humanized into wisdom, benevolent intelligence, and responsible power. We may think of him as a surrogate for God, as the perfect substitute father for all his orphaned charges, as the idealized voice of society—for he is all these, at least in the eyes of the boys. Whether he or anyone could ever actually embody such qualities and powers is not immediately to the point; what matters is that the boys believe he does, and that, through his conduct toward them, he is able to sustain their belief. Because of this he is able to sustain in them the belief that life itself has certain values, and that one's career in life may have as its legitimate purpose the extension and enlargement of those values.

With this we come to the secret life of *Stalky & Co.*, and to the secret which Kipling, like all distinguished writers about boyhood, has grasped. It is that boys live a life which is passionately moral. Half of the intensity, difficulty, and refractoriness of boys may be traced to the fact that their passionate moral demands on life seem, in the sad course of things, bound to be frustrated and betrayed. As the reader of *Stalky & Co.* will soon discover, boys are by nature moral casuists of genius; they are religious fanatics for justice and the last true believers in the divinity of law. Boys slavishly worship tradition, blindly reverence ritual, and are the untamed partisans of precedent. They are individually and in aggregate the most naturally conservative, if not reactionary, social grouping—they *want* to believe in the doctrines and ideals that have been officially handed down to them. And we can, without exaggeration, say that every liberal or radical has within him a boy who once found out that "they" were telling him lies, who discovered hypocrisy, sloth, and double-dealing in his elders and superiors. The failure of conservatism has always been a moral failure.

This is not to say that boys devote all their time to inspecting each other's moral fingernails, or that they are not naturally disobedient and do not chafe at discipline and restrictions. That they are and do is written large on every page of *Stalky & Co.* Neither can one say that their ardent moral life can be approached directly and in morality's own terms. When Beetle once complains that King has been unfair, Stalky reproves him: "You've been here six years, and you expect fairness. Well, you *are* a dithering idiot." And after they have exacted retribution on the school bullies, Stalky dryly remarks, "If I knew anything about it, I swear I'd give you a moral lecture." Living in an age and atmosphere in which they have been shot at with moral bullets since infancy, the boys are preternaturally gun-shy of all the cheapened and canting terms of value. (The great creative genius of the Victorian age, Dickens, was almost unable to use the word "moral" in any but an ironic sense—so debased had its currency become.) When the Head chooses to punish the boys, he tells them he is about to perpetrate a howling and flagrant "injustice." Only in this way can he distinguish his moral decisions from those of the lesser masters, which are always of course "just." At a later moment he makes this characteristic distinction in regard to the boys' misbehavior: "I can connive at immorality, but I cannot stand impudence." Given the world of 1880, the Head can make sense only by standing these terms on their heads; and only a man who has the intelligence and courage to do that can reach the moral world in which boys live. Today a gifted teacher of youth would be forced to do something very similar with words like tolerance, cooperation, equality, getting along with the group, and love.

Kipling understood that the moral life of boys is at once extremely primitive and simple, and extremely sophisticated and complex. The virtues to which boys most avidly give themselves are the primitive, ancient, classical, masculine ones—what were known in the past as the heroic virtues. The boys in *Stalky & Co.* are being prepared for an arduous military life, and there is no mistaking the connection between their fantastic exploits at school and their heroic exploits on the Northwest frontier—such is clearly Kipling's intention. But we should realize that there is a heroism in *Stalky & Co.* superior to physical conquest and martial prowess, though it co-exists with them. By common consent, the most heroic deed in the book is the Head's saving of a boy's life by sucking the membranous film of diphtheria from his throat. The point of such heroism is in its disregard of self, in its self-sacrifice. And we might recall that the ideal of self-sacrifice is not foreign to the soldierly tradition —at least in its older style. It was this ideal which moved Don Quixote to assert the superiority of the profession of arms to the profession of letters. By means of it we can in part account for the extraordinary affection in which the English still hold Nelson. It was this ideal that Ruskin—the same Ruskin read by M'Turk—had in mind when he declared that the soldier's trade is not slaying, but being slain. In an age like our own, in which the military tradition has suffered a degradation which has put it almost beyond redemption, it might be useful to recall that in the past, intelligent men were able to see something noble and humane even in this most destructive mode of human behavior.

Yet these values and ideals, though they are a constant presence in the lives of the boys in *Stalky & Co.*, are never to be discussed, as we learned in the episode "The Flag of their Country." There the brash, vulgar, and jingoistic Conservative Member of Parliament violates the reserve and offends the soul of every boy in the school by speaking about patriotism and waving the flag in their faces. "In a raucous voice he cried aloud little matters, like the hope of Honour and the dream of Glory, that boys do not discuss even with their most intimate equals; cheerfully assuming that, till he spoke, they had never considered these possibilities." The complexity and sophistication of the moral life which Kipling depicts in *Stalky & Co.* has to do with the fact that the values which inform it are precisely those which are never to be explicitly referred to—like the true name of God, they are too sacred to be spoken—except in parody, joke, or absolute understatement. "Don't you want to die for your giddy country?" M'Turk quizzes Stalky. "Not if I can jolly well avoid it," is the ritual answer.

This quality of indirectness leads us to observe that

modern readers will find a certain obscurity and difficulty in reading this book. The obscurity exists in the speech of the boys and is a result of the fact that they speak elliptically and in code. All companies of boys have an argot, a lingo, a code by which they exclude others and help to identify themselves. The code of speech in *Stalky & Co.* is exceptional because of its severity, economy, and power of compression —all of these, attributes of Kipling's prose as well. The danger and weakness of any code is that it tends to become excessively limiting, rigid, and self-referring, and to exclude the user from large areas of experience. In *Stalky & Co.*, however, the code in which the boys speak resonates and is confluent with the life for which they are being trained and with its code. What used to be known as the life of an officer and a gentleman was regulated by a strict and complex code. The mastery of this code of living is the object of the education described in this book. By means of it the boys were to learn, supposedly, to rule a vast, primitive colonial Empire, successfully and with relative decency; they were being taught to play what Kipling elsewhere called "the Great Game." The weaknesses of such a conception are manifest: to think of life as a Great Game is to run the risk of never growing up; it is also to run the risk of thinking that there are, in the end, winners and losers in life—a more subtle and profound moral danger. But the strengths of such a conception are too easily by-passed: if life is a Great Game, then there are certain rules of play or conduct which are not to be violated; to violate them is to do worse than lose—it is to put oneself out of consideration altogether. The history of the twentieth century has seen the steady attrition of this ideal; and one of the bitterest accommodations that thoughtful and feeling persons, especially young persons, have had to make is to a world in which this ideal possibility of human conduct is not merely violated and flouted, but made to seem irrelevant, foolish, and naïve.

Kipling's consuming interest in a code of life brings us

finally to the two modern writers in whom his influence is largest—Ernest Hemingway and Isaac Babel. Both were permanently preoccupied with the heroic code; both took as their central concern the problem of how man is to confront with honor the tragic life of violence that has been his inescapable fate in modern civilization. Like Kipling, both were strongly involved with the life and ideals of boyhood, with conceptions of masculinity and manliness, and with adventure, and the life out-of-doors, these latter our twentieth-century equivalents for the nineteenth century's idea of nature. Both were deeply influenced by Kipling's style as well, with its incisive force, speed, and dramatic economy. Hemingway's indebtedness to Kipling is unmistakable and important. Babel's is less well known but in its way even more interesting.

In his "Reminiscences of Babel," the Russian writer Konstantin Paustovsky tells of their first meeting. It took place in Odessa, shortly after the Revolution. Paustovsky was working in the editorial offices of a magazine called *The Seaman* which had recently published one of Babel's stories. One day Babel was brought to the magazine's offices to meet the editors. He arrived carrying a volume of Kipling under his arm, which he put down on the table but kept looking at impatiently throughout the polite general conversation. At the first opportunity, Paustovsky remarks, "Babel switched the conversation to Kipling. Writers, he said, should write in Kipling's iron-clad prose; authors should have the clearest possible notion of what was to come out of their pens. A short story must have the precision of a military communiqué or a bank check. It must be written in the same straightforward hand one uses for commands and checks. Kipling's hand was just like that." He then concluded with this unexpected statement. "Here in Odessa," he said with a note of irony, "we don't produce any Kiplings. We like a peaceful, easy life. But to make up for it, we'll have our home-grown Maupassants." He then left the office. Paustovsky watched him from the window. The moment Babel was out in the street, he "opened his Kipling and started to read as he went. Now and then he stopped to give passers-by a chance to go round him, but he never once raised his head to look at them."

It is, of course, a charming story. Babel's remarks about Kipling are very much to the point, and the discrimination he makes between Kipling and Maupassant, and the choice implied in it, has the same kind of force that in an earlier generation Joseph Conrad's decision to write in English rather than French had. But there is something wonderfully ironic and apt about the entire incident. That Kipling, the arch-imperialist and reactionary, should wind up in the hands of a Russian-Jewish revolutionary writer is curious and paradoxical, though not unprecedented: literary influence, fortunately, is not bound in by politics. But that the values of Kipling's prose style—and the moral values which that style embodies and implies—should be precisely the values Babel desired for his own radical and revolutionary writing cannot fail to be a surprise. But when one thinks about it for a while, there is something very right about it all.

(1962)

Mt. Everest and the
British National Spirit

He who ascends to mountain-tops,
  shall find
The loftiest peaks most wrapt in clouds
  and snow;
He who surpasses or subdues mankind,
Must look down on the hate of
  those below.
Though high *above* the sun of glory glow,
And far *beneath* the earth and ocean
  spread,
Round him are the icy rocks, and
  loudly blow
Contending tempests on his naked head,
And thus reward the toils which to those
  summits led.

—Childe Harold

In the nature of the case, the climbing of Mt. Everest was an extraordinary event. And the vague sentiment of cultural uplift that such achievements always evoke was augmented by the fact that the news came just in time for the coronation of Queen Elizabeth. Not only had a mountain been climbed; England had reasserted her glory. The film *The Conquest of Everest* reinforced one's feeling that somehow

gle. But perhaps there is a technological cause
ions as false and gratuitous as this. Who can
rence between a white man and a Sherpa when
aring bulky down suits, balaclavas, and oxygen
famous snapshot of Tenzing on the summit
een a picture of almost anyone. But not merely
arel of mountaineers been transformed (the
rs of Everest were clad in "tweeds, felt hats,
Alpine boots"); the idea of climbing itself has
eded by the general idea of "teamwork." There
with a "job to be done," and while the job may
ders or administrators, it cannot tolerate
like the French mountaineer Maurice Herzog,
imbs an actual mountain and not a metaphysical
e mountain is in a way *too* actual, coming often
ose to being merely a problem in the tactics of
and supply.

ntirely, of course. The "team" did have its hu-
ments, unwilling to yield entirely to the logic of
ut if humanity did insist on asserting itself, the
was in many ways on a pretty low level. The
Darjeeling and Katmandu kicked up a sordid,
circulating a heroic story about Tenzing dragging
anoxic Hillary up to the peak. The British, when
he point, awarded a knighthood to the "Sahibs"
Hunt, but could not find it in their hearts to do
Tenzing, basing their reluctance on a ludicrous
er Tenzing's citizenship. When Tenzing was in-
inner at the Explorers Club in New York, India's
eign relations somehow got involved, and the
ved for Tenzing remained empty. And when Sir
from his apologetics about being a "Sahib,"
in what must be even for the British Army a
unexampled stupidity, that Tenzing was a good
ithin the limits of his experience," the atmos-
ocial uncertainty and embarrassed liberalism,

a larger significance did inhere in the triumphant climb; one came away from the film half prepared to contribute to the Alpine Club's next outing, for never before had anyone been able to demonstrate what an extremely difficult and complex thing it is to climb a mountain. It comes then as something of a shock to read Sir John Hunt's book *The Conquest of Everest*.[1] In every way it so little fulfills our expectations —whether these expectations are founded on experience of the literature of travel and exploration, on the dispatches published in the *Times* of London, or on the film itself— that one begins to feel that something has happened both to the fact and to the idea of exploration, and in particular to the English tradition of exploration, whose unexpected climax this book may well be.

I suppose there has never been an expedition more· prosperously fated than this one; nothing went wrong. Appendix III of *The Conquest of Everest*—"Memorandum, 'Basis for Planning,' " which was drawn up in London before the expedition's departure—offers some indication of the completeness of the expedition's success: the differences between what actually happened in the Himalayas and what was foreseen in the Memorandum of London are negligible.

Perhaps Hunt's most significant remark is that "on Everest the problems of organization assume the proportions of a military campaign." And if one should ask *whose* military campaign, the answer, after reading the book, is inevitably, General Eisenhower's. For the surprising truth about this most recent expedition to Everest is how much it was "Americanized." It is true that the attempt to climb Everest had taken on the shape of a military battle for earlier mountaineers too—even for George Mallory, who disappeared into the mists with a volume of romantic poetry in his pocket—but it was an older kind of battle, the kind, for instance, that began with the recitation of Gray's "Elegy

[1] Sir John Hunt, *The Conquest of Everest* (New York, 1954).

in a Country Churchyard" at the foot of the Plains of Abraham. Hunt's expedition seems to have prided itself especially on those qualities of social or industrial organization, cooperation, and "teamwork" which, in their most refined forms, have come to be appreciated as singularly American.

Hunt himself is obviously a genius at planning and logistics, and *The Conquest of Everest* is more an engineer's report than a book about climbing a mountain. Almost the entire text is given to detailed accounts of how so many tons of supplies were moved from one camp to another in so many hours at the expense of so many foot-pounds of energy. "It was a routine which became increasingly monotonous by its constant repetition. . . . The scheduled ferries ran to an almost clockwork time-table." This is like reading a report of one of those famous Productivity Teams the English used always to be sending here to discover why American industry is so efficient—except that this time it is the English who have established the production figures, and they are bursting with pride at having beaten us at our game. But they have done so at the expense of depersonalizing the activity of exploration. What else can one conclude about an account of an expedition in which almost no notice is taken of how its members behaved, or how they talked, or what they read (or at least took along to read)?

The appendices are more interesting than the text; only there does one find a little of what one particularly looks for in books about travel and exploration: detailed description of some of the equipment and how it works, the report that men's appetites and tastes go wild at great altitudes (in 1952 on Cho Oyu, Hillary had a terrible craving for pineapple cubes), or that the Sherpa cooks invented a pressure cooker out of a "biscuit can with the lid forced on and a small hole stoppered with a stick acting as a safety valve." There, too, one discovers with delight that the sausages for the trip were provided by the Société d'Alimentation de Provence, that the Indian army presented the expedition

with—of all things—a
razors were considere
since an oxygen mask
heavy beard. These th
cal" appendices, are ir
book. To assume, as tl
done" was the only im
to lose sight of what
place what has always l
calf of America: success

Of course, the Briti
nology. But the truth i
in his book *Made in /*
adapting and improving
of the last century. And
hoven; an inspection of
ings produced in Engl
skeptical that "ironmon
culture where standardi
tue, the lengths to whicl
absolute interchangeabil
British oxygen company
German firm Dräger of
tion of adaptors for so
Everest by the Swiss in
of professional efficiency
domain of the British am

One is troubled also,
recurrent uneasiness of
called the white men "S
to account for such a "
word, denoting superior s
dition, when necessary, si
bers of the party and tl
written by a colonel in t
of service in India before

the mind bo
for explanat
tell the diffe
both are we
masks? The
could have b
has the app
early climbe
and ordinar
been supers
is a "team"
require lea
"Sahibs." U
Hunt still cl
idea, but th
perilously c
engineering

Never
man compo
the "job." I
assertion w
Nepalese in
comic row,
a helpless,
it came to
Hillary and
as much fo
wrangle ov
vited to a d
touchy for
chair reser
John, fresl
remarked,
moment of
climber "
phere of

consorting with the cheapest political exploitation and the remnants of imperial insularity, reached its full expression.

Perhaps the unkindest comment on the expedition was provided by the exploit of the correspondent from the *Daily Mail* who had been ordered to "get the story" despite the carefully guarded agreement to give the *Times* exclusive coverage. The *Daily Mail* reporter, who had never climbed anything steeper than a flight of stairs, walked off in the direction of Everest—accompanied by five natives and epuipped with such odds and ends as two pairs of sneakers, an old pup tent, an umbrella, and a few pots, but no map or compass—and simply turned up on the mountain one day, 19,000 feet up, not only to the embarrassment of the party in general, who were ordered to give him no information, but to the particular embarrassment of the expedition's doctor, who seems to have thought it an affront to science that the man was even alive. This, one feels, is something like it: the unorganized and merely human sometimes does survive, even if it must find its last refuge in journalism (accompanied, to be sure, by those same old inevitable Sherpas).

All this, of course, does not alter the fact that the expedition did get to the top of Everest, a "job" which presumably had to be carried out sometime. If the success of the expedition demanded a subversion of some of the older values of exploring, it is pointless to repine. What is troubling is the pretense that this subversion in itself represents the fulfillment of the older tradition; one does not like to see a great nation forced in its decline to insist upon the empty symbols of greatness—as the British have done, not only in their slightly spurious excitement over the climbing of Everest and, slightly later, the four-minute mile, but most distressingly in the coronation itself, that elaborate inauguration of a "new Elizabethan Age" which only emphasized more painfully the fact that the old Elizabethan Age can never return.

I think we can get a clearer idea of what has been lost by comparing Hunt's account with another account of a large British effort in exploration. A little more than forty years ago, the British sent out an expedition that was assumed to be as prepared, as modern, and was as loudly heralded, as this recent one: Scott's last attempt to reach the South Pole. From this expedition came what is probably the finest work about exploring of our century, Apsley Cherry-Garrard's *The Worst Journey in the World*, a book which has received practically no recognition in this country.

If Hunt's expedition was a flawless success, Scott's was virtually a total failure. Everything went wrong, all the misfortunes and mistakes culminating in the death from starvation of the five men of the Polar party, locked in their tent in a blizzard, only eleven miles from the next depot of food —this after having been beaten by Amundsen, who had had the bad taste to turn the whole business into a race and reached the Pole thirty days ahead of Scott, getting there and back without the loss of a man or even any serious hardships. Scott himself seems to have been as unreliable and inept a leader as Hunt is a steady and knowledgeable one. He was prone to neurotic anxiety (Cherry-Garrard says he wept more easily than any man he had ever met), and had no trust in his own decisions, often reversing them at inopportune moments—at the very last minute he chose to take five men to the Pole, when all along plans had been made for only four; this in the long run brought about the shortage of food and supplies which proved fatal to the returning party. He chose his equipment short-sightedly, bringing expensive and almost untried motor tractors to the Antarctic, none of which performed at all well, and he didn't take along nearly enough dogs. What his men went through with the equipment—their sleeping bags were perpetually frozen, their boots gave them almost no protection, their food was hopelessly deficient, they hauled their supplies

thousands of miles harnessed like dogs to their sledges—
is excruciating to read.

In almost every way, Scott's men were unfit to be explorers, and this radical unfitness constitutes one of the
reasons why their story remains so moving. They were
picked men, but one feels that they had been picked for
their personal qualities more than for their usefulness to
the "team." Cherry-Garrard himself, for example, spent two
years in the Antarctic virtually unable to see his hand in
front of his face; he was extremely near-sighted, and the
cold made it impossible to wear glasses. But this serious
disability did not prevent Scott from taking him along; it
was assumed that the extra risk belonged to him alone.
Indeed, half the time the polar explorers seem to have been
not quite aware of what they were doing, though they had
worked out what seemed to them a very substantial idea of
why they were there: it was for Science. Three of them—
Cherry-Garrard, Wilson, and Bowers—took a six weeks'
journey through the midwinter darkness to get some eggs
of the Emperor penguin. The temperature was frequently
at 70 below zero; the surface of the snow at such temperature made hauling so difficult that they often progressed no
more than three miles in a day; their bodies were continu-
ously covered with a thin layer of ice next to the skin, from
frozen perspiration; it took an hour each night to get into
the frozen sleeping bags; several times they were nearly
killed (Wilson and Bowers later died with Scott on the Polar
trip); Cherry-Garrard's teeth all cracked and fell out. They
returned, finally, with three eggs.

Cherry-Garrard reprints in his book—as evidence that
it had all been worthwhile—a dry little paper on the embry-
ology of the Emperor penguin written by a scientist to
whom the eggs were eventually delivered for study. He also
tells us of the day when, as sole survivor of the three men
who made the winter journey, he brought the precious eggs

to the Natural History Museum in South Kensington. His reception at the museum was so offensively indifferent that he is forced to relate the story in parody. Apparently he was taken for some kind of messenger—though by that time, presumably, he must have been already equipped with a set of false teeth—and responded by demanding a receipt for the eggs, which he obtained only after several hours of cooling his heels in an anteroom. He did not even meet the director of the museum. The point of this display of British bad manners is that if Cherry-Garrard wanted to risk his life and sacrifice his teeth for three penguin eggs, that was strictly his own business; nobody at that time mistook the eggs for a symbol of the greatness of England. In 1910, reaching the South Pole, or climbing a great mountain, or even discovering the source of the Nile, was still conceived as one of the appanages of national greatness, rather than as the fact of that greatness itself. It probably seemed natural for the men of a nation that had subdued one-quarter of the world's surface and population to attempt these strenuous, heroically absurd things, but it was rarely suggested that the actuality of national greatness rested on such performances. That greatness, everyone knew, was perpetuated in the shops and the factories and the trading posts, and the achievements of individual endurance and courage were only the panoply, the decoration, just as a coronation at that time was too. It has come to pass, however, that such events as the ascent of Everest or a coronation have devolved into the principal facts of the national sentiment of greatness.

This alteration in the terms of national self-esteem is what compelled the kind of expedition—the grimness, the fierce engineering, the dehumanizing "teamwork"—that Hunt led. Scott's men went to the Antarctic for their own sakes, not for the nation and not even for adventure (though the idea of adventure was certainly not absent), but primarily, as Cherry-Garrard indicates, with the idea that to have gone

with Scott would advance their careers as scientists or journalists or soldiers. Certainly they were very much aware of
themselves as Englishmen; indeed, the qualities of national
distinctness, or at least an awareness of the ratifying importance of nationality to exploration, attenuated in Hunt's
book, are constantly present in Cherry-Garrard's; the men
on Scott's voyage could have walked right off the cricket
field onto the Polar Ice Barrier, and they possessed and
sometimes flaunted all the virtues and shortcomings of the
education and way of life which rested on the culture of
the cricket field.[2] But it was their own safety and success
that hung in the balance, not England's. For this reason
their failure holds a meaning that Hunt's success cannot.
The deaths and disappointments of this journey remained
personal, and it was the failure of the expedition, the collective effort, that was eclipsed. Hunt and his men climbed
Everest "for England," and if their success is taken as a
testimony to England's greatness, the inference is inescapable that her greatness would have been less had Everest
remained unclimbed, or had some Amundsen climbed it first.
The Nepalese, in their ungentlemanly attempt to claim that

[2] Cherry-Garrard writes: "The truth was that Amundsen was an explorer of the markedly intellectual type, rather Jewish than Scandi-
navian, who had proved his sagacity by discovering solid footing for
the winter by pure judgment. . . ." Amundsen, that is, was a better
explorer than Scott, extremely shrewd, and had the confidence of his
intuitions. Scott's crew were unashamedly furious at Amundsen for
racing against them, turning south at the last moment when everyone
had been led to believe that he was going to the Arctic: this was not
playing the game. On the other hand, although Everest was regarded
as a "British mountain," Hunt studiously avoids accusing the Swiss
or the French of poaching on English preserves; the manners of the
explorer seem in some ways to have improved as an international
political style has deteriorated. Perhaps it would be more accurate to
say that Hunt is not sure that his objecting to such encroachment
would carry the kind of weight that the men on Scott's expedition
felt their censure of Amundsen carried.

Tenzing and not Hillary was the hero of the climb, showed that they had got the point all too clearly.

Despite all their pride in manufacture and industry, the Englishmen who traveled with Scott in 1910 were fundamentally not technologists but entrepreneurs who retained that fierce trust in the unalterable grace of their individuality and whatever that individuality might compel them to do which distinguishes the entrepreneur from the technologist. A visit to the Scott Polar Research Institute in Cambridge verifies this impression, for there one is able to examine the ridiculous equipment with which, only half a century ago, these men expected to reach the South Pole, and with which, in fact, five of them did reach it; if there were any ideas about rational technology then, they took appallingly little cognizance of them.

Of course, they also paid the price of individualism. One cannot conceive of any museum official today treating one of Hunt's men as Cherry-Garrard was treated when he brought his penguin eggs to South Kensington. And today Cherry-Garrard could count on getting the finest set of false teeth the National Health Service could provide. When Scott lay dying in his tent in the Antarctic, he thought of his family and the families of his companions, and made a final poignant entry in his diary: "For God's sake, look after our people!" The plea was necessary, and the old procession of images passes before one again: the children in the mines, the Indian mills, the general strike. . . . Had disaster fallen on any of the men with Hunt, no such plea as Scott's would have had to be made. But one must return to the fact that the Polar expedition had for Scott and his crew a personal significance that was different from the significance which the Everest expedition seems to have had for Hunt and his men. The decreased possibility of this older kind of significance is associated with the passing of an extraordinary imperial temperament which, now that it is defunct, even the Socialists elegiacally, if surreptitiously, consent to celebrate. They celebrate it because they can hardly escape assenting to what an elderly Englishman, unconsciously echoing Talleyrand, recently said to me—"You will never know how fine life can be, if you haven't lived in England before 1914"—any more than I could escape assenting to it in spite of my having Scott's last words fresh in my mind and in spite of my disinclination to mourn anything as complex and mythologized as the English idea of the English past. The irretrievable "fineness" of that life accompanied its prodigality and indifference, and all three were contained in the reality of England's great wealth and power.

Nevertheless, we do injustice to Hunt's trip if we do not see that it was a distinguished achievement. That is not difficult if one has seen the film; from it one knows that George Lowe's eleven days on the Lhotse Face and Bourdillon and Evans' first assault were very remarkable performances, and having watched Hunt's embrace of Tenzing, one can never doubt the full humanity of the triumph. Ironically, however, it is a characteristically American technique that permits us this knowledge; only through a movie camera are we allowed to glimpse what really happened, and beside it the supreme English gift, the articulateness of the written word, seems inadequate to its task. The neutral camera has preserved the personalness of what happened; it is the explorers who have lost the ability to apprehend and communicate their experience in human terms.

(1954)

Evelyn Waugh and the
Art of Entertainment

It is almost certain that Evelyn Waugh is the finest entertainer alive. It is certain that both Waugh and the kind of book he writes are supremely distasteful to many of the most serious people. One of the most intelligent men I ever met told me that life was too short to waste any of it on Waugh. Another replied to my recommendation that since he never read for pleasure anyway, there wasn't much point in his reading something that didn't at least *pretend* to offer more. Waugh has been variously characterized as nasty, hateful, snobbish, trivial, reactionary, vindictive, fawning, immature, pompous, and rude, ascriptions which are substantially true yet somehow beside the point. The general repugnance of the contemporary intellectual for the litera-

ture of entertainment is, I think, related to his dislike of
Waugh; one cannot applaud either without sounding dan-
gerously like some "smart" radio book-reviewer, or like a
superannuated Oxford don feebly praising the delighting
power of art. Our culture has to an unprecedented degree
succeeded in dividing our entertainment from our elevation.
Today most of us find our real entertainment in the movies
or television or by watching sports. We read, on the other
hand, with an heroic seriousness: we bring great expectations to literature, and although we are pleased by our ability to discover and follow the subtle dialectic of it, we are
quick to mistrust any piece of writing which does not seem
immediately to challenge profound assumptions or elicit the
most delicate moral choices. Our less ponderous relations
to literature have suffered an attrition, and it is possible
that a certain kind of literature—the kind I assume Waugh
to represent—is losing the capacity to express anything
significant, just as about a hundred years ago the personal
essay and the art of verse lost theirs.

An entertainer is a writer who does not press upon us
the full complexities of life, who does not demand from us
a total seriousness in making moral judgments, and who
does not necessarily bring to experience a mature and
searching form, though his works may be rich in individual,
internal patterns and correspondences. When he is inspired
he may produce a work of art, but most often he is content
with being artful. His writing charms us because it is clever,
observant, and sprightly; the appearance of his prose is
nearly always immaculate. Yet because we no longer feel it
unobjectionable to give ourselves to these virtues unless they
seem to promise greater significances residing within, we try
to justify our affection for some of our entertainers by passing them off as serious artists. One of the minor annoyances
of recent years has been the steady flow of essays about
Henry Green, Graham Greene, and Joyce Cary; repeatedly
it has been "demonstrated" that each of them is a consider-

able and important novelist. They have, it is true, sometimes aspired higher than Waugh, but their larger efforts generally display lack of clarity, patterns that correspond only to each other, and a murky portentousness which does little more than communicate the writer's will to express something beyond his understanding. Most of the time, however, these writers, like Waugh, are fundamentally and simply interested by what happens in society and how it happens; the surfaces and appearances of things, the styles in which men face the world, the ways they get around each other, and themselves, the rituals through which they pass each day, and the minute details of the crises they must endure— these, rather than the more inclusive concerns of the serious writer, make up their purview. The entertainer is primarily interested in the facts; he knows that the facts, if they are delivered with clarity and relevance, will delight and reward us. His stories are profuse in incidents and anecdotes. He lets us know that the most implausible things happen every day, and thus he makes us less skeptical and hard-bitten about the possibilities to which we are bound.

Waugh is one of these victims of our sanctions about the serious. I have frequently read that he is a brilliant satirist and that his early novels are a blistering, comprehensive satire of fashionable prewar society. If *Decline and Fall* and *Vile Bodies* are brilliant satires, I wonder what hyperboles should be reserved for *The Dunciad* or *Pride and Prejudice* or *Don Juan* or *Our Mutual Friend*. Even if Waugh is juxtaposed to a less momentous satirist, Peacock, for example, or to a modern one, Mary McCarthy, say, it should be apparent that he is doing something else. For Waugh is essentially a comedian, and his early novels are celebrations of Mayfair, not satires of it. Nothing is more patent than that he loved the Hon. Agatha Runcible who disappeared in the company of a racing car and ended in drunken delirium in a nursing home, or that he loved Lady Metroland, proprietress of an international chain of brothels, or that he loved all the raffish, bored, useless, picaresque characters who fill the pages of his earliest novels. These novels, and *Black Mischief, A Handful of Dust* and *Scoop*, are successful because of the purity of their comic vision—they are elaborated spoofs. Remarking the absurdity and waste of a particular social life, they omit its real consequences. The worst fate that overtakes anyone in them (besides, of course, being bored) is being eaten by cannibals, or reading Dickens aloud to a madman—grisly consummations, but merely grisly. Although Waugh understood that the assumptions his "bright young things" lived by were preposterous, he was honest enough not to deny that, with certain qualifications, their standards were sympathetic to his own. They were thundering snobs, xenophobes, opportunists, ignoramuses, and thoroughly cultivated ladies and gentlemen. Like Waugh they were more outspoken than an American can easily imagine, and like Waugh they accepted with an abandoned equanimity their misfortune in being three hundred years too late. In his early novels Waugh was able to sustain a tone of bemused mournfulness over a society bent on smashing itself to pieces, while at the same time depicting the feckless innocence of both those who were most active in the smashing and those most hurt by it. The matrix of his comedy is this conjunction of the most abrupt and violent events with the most innocent villains.

Waugh's initial vein was a shallow one, though, and sometime in the late thirties it began to run thin; Basil Seal, who had once blithely survived a meal made of his sweetheart's flesh, could not survive his own self-pity, and Waugh's repining over the evanescence of his generation soured his appetite for comedy. He wrote a couple of slim, adequate satires, *The Loved One* and *Scott-King's Modern Europe*, and he wrote two pretentious novels about his religion, *Brideshead Revisited* and *Helena*, his most conspicuous failures. They failed because Waugh's snobbery and growing biliousness could not accommodate themselves to humane, religious impulses; indeed, they overrode his Christianity and made it seem just slightly disreputable. He recognized this at the very beginning of his next novel, *Men at Arms*, in which he diagnosed his hero's religious peculiarities: "But Guy had no wish to persuade or convince or to share his opinions with anyone. Even in his religion he felt no brotherhood. Often he wished he lived in penal times when Broome had been a solitary outpost of the Faith, surrounded by aliens. Sometimes he imagined himself serving the last mass for the last Pope in a catacomb at the end of the world." Even Catholocism, most hierarchic of religious dispensations, is too democratic for Waugh, whose admiration of "blood" and class will always compromise his obligations to the poor in heart and spirit and pocketbook. The unpleasant atmosphere of *Brideshead Revisited* was directly a result of the far-reaching disagreement between Waugh and his religion.

In the last few years, however, Waugh has found himself again, and has just published the second part of a novel in two volumes, *Men at Arms* and *Officers and Gentlemen*.[1] These volumes belong with his finest comedy, and they show a surprising maturity, for in them Waugh has been able to poke fun even at his Catholicism. But their excellence derives principally from his having found something that again exhilarates him: the Army. Waugh fell in love with the Army in much the same way, and for the same reasons, that he fell in love with Mayfair twenty years ago. The Army, Waugh finds, is more interesting in its distinctions of position and privilege (and in its ability to harbor the pretenders to them) than a society which has been "democratized"; it is the final repository of the remnants of class and tradition, of unlimited pride in inheritance, of true values, and of

---

[1] Evelyn Waugh, *Men at Arms* (New York, 1952); *Officers and Gentlemen* (New York, 1955). These two volumes are the first parts of a trilogy. The third part is *The End of the Battle* (New York, 1961).

honor. It is also very funny. Through its ranks move some of the phoniest, most brazen picaroons in English literature, and in its infinite, inefficient reaches lurk the grotesques, fossils, and fantasts of all good burlesque.

Guy Crouchback, the hero of these volumes, is the last male heir of an ancient Catholic family which, though obscured by time and fortune, is of unchallenged honor; it has had its share of martyrs, saints, and madmen, and recognizes no English king after James I. At the beginning of *Men at Arms*, Guy, middle-aged and much diminished from his ancestors' glory, separated from his wife, who has since remarried three times, sulks in feeble melancholy at the family villa in Italy, in despair about himself and the lack of purpose in his life. At the outbreak of World War II he returns to England and manages to join a "good regiment," the Royal Corps of Halberdiers. The Halberdiers are so historic, so distinguished and decorated that they can afford to look down their noses at the Guards. Here, amid the congenial setting of antiquity wedded to service, Guy—the forlorn gentleman, the withered "flower of England"—comes to life again. "It seemed to Guy that in the last week he had been experiencing something he had missed in boyhood, a happy adolescence."

The Halberdier officers take part of their training in a boys' school, and Waugh is at pains to draw a detailed analogy between life in the Army and life in school. "The curriculum followed the textbooks, lesson by lesson, exercise by exercise, and the Preparatory School way of life was completely re-created. They were to stay there until Easter —a whole term." Boys' schools, like Regular Army officers, are survivals of a happier civilization, "where differences of rank were exactly defined and frankly accepted." In England, of course, both the Army and schools are very different from what they are here. Somehow, and with a minimum of transmutation, the values that inform the life of a decent English school tend to inform the life of English

Regular Army officers. The character they ideally produce is the same, "salty, withdrawn, incorrigible." As I have noted on another occasion, D. W. Brogan once remarked that England is the only country in the world where being a schoolboy is an end in itself. The standard by which this end is justified is the gentlemanly character, a still most highly cherished trophy of English social life, the *raison d'être* of "people who had represented their country in foreign places and sent their sons to die for her in battle, people of decent and temperate life, uncultured, unaffected, unembarrassed, unassuming, unambitious people, of independent judgment and marked eccentricities." These are the people whom Waugh has more and more come to value above all others. Although very much aware of how crusty these ideas must seem in modern England, Waugh's faith in the goodness and trueness, if not in the efficacy of this ideal, is unwavering. In fact, his conception of the life and character of an officer and a gentleman is virtually Kipling's.

The reader may recall how in *Stalky & Co.* all the aggressive pranks and escapades of the boys in school seemed actually to be dress rehearsals for the high destiny of directing the course of a great Empire and keeping the peace on the Northwest frontier, and how in the extraordinary last chapter of the book when all the "Old Boys" meet again Stalky's exploits with his faithful natives and his Martini rifle are attributed to the values exemplified in the life of the school. Waugh is slightly more skeptical about the possibilities of heroic success in action than Kipling, yet his great hero, Brigadier Ben Ritchie-Hook, understands his profession as Stalky did his and as countless good English gentlemen did theirs. "For this remarkable warrior the image of war was not hunting or shooting; it was the wet sponge on the door, the hedgehog in the bed; or, rather, he saw war itself as a prodigious booby trap." There is a good deal about this boyish ethos that we can envy and admire: it may enable men to maintain an audacious gaiety amid

the circumstances of modern war, to experience the erosive-
ness of Army life as a series of comic misadventures, or to
keep their sense of purposiveness intact amid the fumblings
of military recalcitrance and stupidity. It may even tend to
mitigate some of the horrors of combat. The schoolboy takes
his grisliness lightly, and Waugh's sense of sudden violence
and terror is tinged with a schoolboy's fascination for the
bloodcurdling.[2] Stalky's dead cat planted in the ceiling of
a dormitory is in its effect much like Basil Seal's feasting
on his fiancée's carcass at the cannibal's banquet, or Agatha
Runcible's crack-up, or all the hopeless and bloody fiascos
of the Halberdiers and Commandos in Norway, Dakar, or
Crete. The conventions of the school and of a gentleman's
war are often fortunately congruent—they are both exten-
sions of the "prodigious booby trap" that life and the Head-
master have set for all boys.

Waugh unhappily grants, however, that the world allows
increasingly fewer opportunities to the kind of gentleman
he most admires. *Men at Arms* and *Officers and Gentlemen*
cover that period of modern history when, he believes, acts
of honor were still feasible—the period from the signing of

---

[2] I recall once hearing Henry Green expostulate on this topic at one
of those embarrassing and aimless "discussions" that university English societies convene for visiting dignitaries. He apparently was content with saying very little in a very gnomic way until he hit upon
the subject of humor, whereupon he suddenly became expansive. He
didn't try to define what he believed to be funny, but illustrated his
sense of the comic by telling a number of his favorite stories. It
struck me then that almost every one of them concerned life at school,
and a great many of them were gory. His favorite (it set him howling
while he told it), the humorous gist of which I cannot for the life of
me remember, involved a schoolmaster who is enticed into a room
whose ceiling is bathed in blood. This particular genre of hilarity
struck me as more curious than funny, and I think it is valuable to
point out that the singularly English interest in the bloodcurdling—
we find it regularly even in E. M. Forster—has its profound connection
with school rather than family life.

the Russo-German Alliance to the German invasion of Russia. Guy Crouchback had read of the Russo-German agreement with joy: "a decade of shame seemed to be ending in light and reason—the Enemy was plain in view, huge and hateful, all disguise cast off; the modern age in arms." By the end of *Officers and Gentlemen*, Guy is ready to concede that he was suffering from an hallucination, and he wakes again "in the old ambiguous world, where priests were spies and gallant friends proved traitors and his country was led blundering into dishonour." The dishonoring accident of Russia's becoming an ally is contemporaneous with Guy's loss of faith in the purely aristocratic character, for he discovers that the officer he considered to be the epitome of gentlemanly honor, Ivor Claire, deserted his men at Crete in unforgivable circumstances. The modern world, "bounded by barbed wire and reeking of carbolic," triumphs, and the loss of the older values is dramatized when Guy's former wife, an athletically promiscuous beauty, goes off with Trimmer, a one-time beautician on the Cunard Line, now the trumpery hero of a trumpery Commando victory. The Holy War has become merely another scuffle among the dishonored, and Waugh now views the war's larger purposes with blunt contempt.

Nonetheless, devotion to duty is always a virtue, and Waugh continues to love the Regular Army types in all their sacrosanct and irrepressible oddness. The most marvelous of these, and to my mind among the finest comic characters of the century, is Brigadier Ritchie-Hook, a perfectly Dickensian conception, a man whose life is spent in dramatizing the idea he has of himself. Ritchie-Hook is the incarnation of the warrior, the one-eyed, battered, indomitable exponent of the art of "biffing." "The years of peace had been years of unremitting conflict for him. Wherever there was blood and gun-powder from County Cork to the Matto Grosso, there was Ritchie-Hook. Latterly he had wandered about the Holy Land tossing hand-grenades into the front parlours of dissident Arabs."[3] In such buoyant and indestructible characters as Ritchie-Hook, as Jumbo and Tommy Blackhouse, in the less honorable but no less comic Apthorpe, Hound, and Trimmer, and of course in the rich accumulation of anecdotes about the eternal mismanagement of war, is the charm of these novels to be found. The qualities that make them interesting and worthy are not organic to their structure or their moral implication, but are there in the things that exist before the reader's eye, in the events arranged and acted out.

These outward, superficial virtues can be sustained only by a professional writer, and the remarkable attractiveness of Waugh and his fellow entertainers, Graham Greene, Henry Green, and Joyce Cary, is inseparable from the unobtrusive rectitude, the professional style, of all their writing. What we feel in them is a kind of superb efficiency in expending their talents. They seem most of the time to have been able to calculate just what they can do, and they do it with the strictest economy of effort. By fully exploiting their comparatively modest talents they rise above their

[3] Ritchie-Hook's original, Lieut. Col. Alfred Daniel Wintle, retired, sometime of the Royal Artillery, First the Royal Dragoons, and Eleventh Hussars, recently turned up in the news. He has been sentenced to six months in prison for assaulting an aged solicitor whom he believed to have swindled him out of an inheritance. Wintle ambushed the man, knocked him about, stole his trousers and was about to fly them from his flagpole in triumph when he was arrested. He was, naturally, wholly unrepentant, and declared, "It will be a sad day for this country when an officer and gentleman is not prepared to go to prison when he thinks he is in the right." As to his failure in completely "biffing" his foe, he said, "One must expect some casualties. . . . I have been accustomed to meeting the enemy and trying to trap him wherever I met him. Wintle's career, like Ritchie-Hook's, is as improbable as the foregoing remarks. As is the case with Dickens' novels, when the original of a character who seems unlikely or outrageous can be discovered, one is always struck by the strict realism of the comic artist's observation—sometimes even by his understatement.

rank and demand comparison with America's more serious writers, writers of demonstrably finer intelligence and fuller seriousness than these entertainers but less gifted in their capacity for articulating the intelligence they have to communicate. In America we don't have anything quite like them. Our entertainers are either the potboiling, unreadable historical novelists, or the quiet, pretentious *New Yorker* story writers, or else they are like J. P. Marquand or John O'Hara, writers equipped by their faculty of observation and the circumscription of their gifts to be good entertainers, but who for several reasons, not the least of them an irritation at not being first-class writers, seldom realize their powers with unequivocal success. Nevertheless, the English knack of producing brilliant figures of the second rank has more to it than plain unpretentiousness or contentment with doing a limited job expertly. It is connected with the Englishman's relation to writing, to the naturalness and ease of his prose compared to ours.

When a writer sits down to write he hears a voice speaking in his ear. This voice is not his own, nor is it the voice of someone else reciting or making a speech. It is a kind of ideal voice he hears, as if it were he, with all the halts and clumsiness, and all the lapses of vocabulary and discordances of rhythm finally expunged or resolved, speaking as he has always desired to speak. The effort of writing is to transcribe this voice, to capture its tones and cadences. On the other hand, this ideal voice is not wholly unlike our speech; it is after all only the refining in our minds of our usual voices. This refinement has been accomplished chiefly through our reading of literature; the tones of rhetoric and style that we retain from our reading infuse this voice more fully than they ever can our speech—there is no organ like the tongue for them to get past. It is apparent, of course, that difficulty or ease in writing will be in proportion to the dissimilarity or resemblance our actual speech bears to the silent voice that is heard when we write, and that the qualities of our prose will be the outcome of this communion. It is also true that the relation of our actual speech to the tradition of English speech and prose is an essential component of whatever difficulty we may face in writing—what may be most alive or immediate in our speech may not easily find its way into the usual forms of expression. But for the English, the living connection between speech and traditional prose has not altered radically, as it has for us, and in writers like Waugh the transition from cultivated speech into clear, elegant writing requires a minimum of artifice. Take a passage like this:

> The Isle of Mugg has no fame in song or story. Perhaps because whenever they sought a rhyme for the place they struck absurdity, it was neglected by those romantic early-Victorian English ladies who so prodigally enriched the balladry, folk-lore and costume of the Scottish Highlands. It has a laird, a fishing fleet, an hotel . . . and nothing more. It lies among other monosyllabic protuberances. There is seldom clear weather in those waters, but on certain rare occasions Mugg has been descried from the island of Rum in the form of two cones. The crofters of Muck know it as a single misty lump on their horizon. It has never been seen from Egg.

Aside from the comic talent embodied in it, it has a naturalness and a propriety with the language that can only be owing to a perfect assurance about the way it ought ideally to sound. The conversational tone—in general the objective of all English prose—can be preserved only if speech retains its affiliations with the complex language of literature.

In America this has not happened, and some of the extraordinary things that have taken place in our writing are the result. What voice does William Faulkner hear when he goes out into his barn with his jug of white lightning and begins to write? It's certainly not anything we could recognize as his own. It has something in it of an angry preacher, and something of an unregarded soothsayer, and something of a slightly swozzled lawyer too, but it is not a voice that could ever speak—it can only write. Or when Mary McCarthy writes, what does she hear? Something, I suppose, like an argument between several splenetic philosophers, a lengthy dialogue of retorts and contradictions, a dialectic of ironic equilibrations; but again, it somehow, despite all its intelligence, does not issue as a prose commensurate to the talent we feel behind it. What do the editors of *Time* hear when they sit down to amend their articles? They hear, I expect, what other editors of *Time* have written, which is like nothing ever heard before on land or sea. What we feel in Faulkner—and in Thomas Wolfe, and Robert Penn Warren, and Saul Bellow, and others—is more than a writer's natural impatience with the prevalent conventions of the language. Rather, there is a barrier between them and the existing tradition of prose; their sense of what is most relevant in their speech—their ideal voices—seems inappropriate to the more ordinary and essential locutions of writing. When they try to express themselves fully or eloquently they sometimes are compelled to write in a manner that, apart from the vocabulary, seems to have remote and oblique relations to spoken English. This condition of strife between our speech and our writing is present everywhere in America; it is a condition of our democracy, and the list of writers whose talents have been constricted by it includes almost every one of us.

Perhaps this is one of the reasons why writers in America have often shown so little capacity for development. It is a truism of our culture that the majority of serious American novelists are "one book" writers; they either write one large good book and then almost nothing else, or spend their careers writing the same book over and over again. It is possible that the disjunction of American speech from the living tradition of English prose has poorly disposed us for taking advantage of some of the most accessible resources of the language, and that this disjunction has often worked against our talents. Certainly it might account for the impression that some of our most interesting writers make. What we sense in the typical American "giants" who fail is an enormous talent that is dying unexpressed, a latent richness that can find no means of articulating itself. We regularly produce novelists who seem just on the point of writing really first-class works, while what we get from them are large, unwieldy failures, evidences of an inability to harness or express themselves with adequate grace or economy. Naturally, this condition has everything to do with our culture and its effects on the mind, but it also has to do with our sense and use of the language. The modern American style of language, for instance, is rich in picturesqueness and humor but lacking in the kind of wit and terseness that ordinary good English prose presupposes. Why our language has developed in this way is a study in itself. It should be noted, however, that we have generally maintained wit and terseness in our best poetry, perhaps because the poet's relation to the language is ultimately more stringent, more resistant and conservative than that of the writer of prose. In the meantime we look to England for the kind of excellent, unstrained delight that the professional entertainer can give us. There, in writers like Waugh, the irreplaceable intimacy of speech and prose has been preserved.

(1956)

Three Obsessed Critics

Some years ago, in an essay which soon became famous, Randall Jarrell argued that our age is an age of criticism. Subsequent events have tended to verify Mr. Jarrell's notion, and epithets like "critical industry" and "critical racket" have become commonplaces in literary and academic conversation. In England, the phrase "American criticism" regularly evokes a response once reserved for the lower middle class; there is something depressingly brash, energetic, ambitious, professional, engineered, about this large-scale undertaking; its intense gravity and self-consciousness seem especially suspect and are very likely bad form, slightly vulgar. But then, the English have seldom taken kindly to formal discourse of any sort, and their judgments of our cardinal literary discipline must be discounted as largely defensive and self-justifying. The three volumes[1] under discussion do much toward explaining the English discomfort. These books simply outface anything our transatlantic cousins are able to do. Coming from diverse points of the intellectual compass and having in common little besides the common pursuit of true judgment, they may be fairly taken to represent the solemn dedication, the devoted single-mindedness, and the proud service of the absolute which are characteristic of the American critical enterprise.

Hugh Kenner is one of the most remarkable critics writing today. Mr. Kenner has a subtle, supple intelligence and a genuine gift for developing and enlarging other people's ideas. One of his sentences has long seemed to me a touchstone of this talent. In his book on Wyndham Lewis he writes: "It hasn't been safe for men of letters to think since the seventeenth century, when ideas were substituted for things as the accredited materials of thought." One can trace the progress of this notion from the dogmatic coarseness and crudity of T. S. Eliot's "dissociation of sensibility" and certain vaguely metaphorical statements by William Carlos Williams to the complex, definitive clarity of Mr. Kenner's formulation. What a vista of history this sentence opens up for us: happy John Donne with his brain full of real compasses safely wrapped in real hair; poor, empty-headed William Blake who could only have perilous ideas about London or Newton's atoms. Mr. Kenner handles many ideas in this instructive fashion.

Mr. Kenner is also an editor of considerable skill, though in his modest way he doesn't advertise it; and he is not afraid of rejecting lines or statements which do not

[1] Hugh Kenner, *Gnomon: Essays on Contemporary Literature* (New York, 1958); Maxwell Geismar, *American Moderns: From Rebellion to Conformity* (New York, 1958); Harry Levin, *The Power of Blackness* (New York, 1958).

seem authentic to him or to his clear sense of the writer's purpose. The opening essay in *Gnomon* is about Yeats, and Mr. Kenner unveils Yeats's secret, hieratic intention, which was not to write poems but to prepare a "deliberated artistic Testament," in which all things were to make sense only in relation to other things within the volume.

> The book, then, is (by a Yeatsian irony) self-contained, like the Great Smaragdine Tablet that said, "Things below are copies," and was itself one of the things below; a sacred book like the Apocalypse of St. John, not like most poetry a marginal commentary on the world to be read with one eye on the pragmatical pig of a text.

One of the poems that Mr. Kenner uses to demonstrate this assertion is "Ego Dominus Tuus," in which the following appears in my edition: "I seek an image, not a book." Mr. Kenner neither reproduces nor refers to that statement, and I conclude that he has discovered that Yeats never wrote it: like most sacred books or apocalyptic visions it has probably passed through porcine, pragmatic, and irreligious hands, and Mr. Kenner has done us all a service by his excision.

Mr. Kenner's ideas about literary and social history are no less curious and exciting than his editorial manipulations. For him, "Chaucer is the last thoroughly civilized English writer." (This is, isn't it, infinitely more accurate and useful than saying that Chaucer was the first thoroughly civilized English writer?) Under the impact of this remark I returned to Layamon and Minot, reread "The Battle of Brunanburh" and peeked into *The Pearl*. Of course Mr. Kenner is right; compared to these, *Measure for Measure* or *King Lear*, say, are indeed the products of a barbarous and dehumanized sensibility. But, gentle reader, let us not despair over the ravages of history—for Fenellosa has saved the day! "What

Fenellosa does is install us once again in a universe where intelligibility does not need to be imposed by the mind. . . ." The grasp of philosophy and of the history of ideas that this statement indicates is staggering, but no more so than Mr. Kenner's remarks about Whitman, "the democracy snob." Whitman, "a corrupted prophet" who had "an intermittent Blakean talent for naïve perception," is the chief instrument in a conspiracy organized against the real America and its true history, "The conspiracy to suppose that American political history begins, effectively, with Lincoln. . . ." This baleful plot has as its object the suppression of "the whole novel tradition of an aristocratic government deriving authority from a popular franchise," the central, vital tradition of American politics. It is directed by men who believe, perniciously, that it is "for some reason important to present an America dominated by an image of itself as egalitarian paradise"; these are, *mirabile dictu*, the same bigots who rigged up the new interest in Henry James, for "one notes as an overlooked feature of the James revival that it is only to a neurotic James that it has been thought safe to entrust the aristocratic tradition"—which is just about the most persuasive argument for the soundness of Ezra Pound's mind I have yet to read. Furthermore, the worst result of these subversive machinations against America is the "notion of an American consciousness diffused across the sidewalks of Manhattan." We must, I think, pause here to sympathize with this *cri de coeur*: someone seems pretty lonely.

The sidewalks of New York lead us to Mr. Kenner's essay on Freud, that "Sinaitic will-specialist." This essay, a review of the first volume of Ernest Jones's biography, is a little classic of ignorant and conceited certitude, and I cannot hope to do it justice here. To Mr. Kenner, Freud "is already as dated as William Archer or *Trilby*," and was "continually the victim of bright ideas." Mr. Kenner strikes through the mask and finds that in Freud's work "the illusion of being conscious, and of intending and willing, is represented as no more than an indispensable self-deceit," revealing here not merely his encyclopedic understanding of that work but his mastery of tautology as well. The world Freud created, moreover, is one "in which, ultimately, nothing possesses any interest at all, except for the sort of tumid interest people can always derive from themselves"—which is, I suppose, not only a direct hit at Freud, but a shot that ricochets down the corridors of history, felling, among others, Jesus, St. Paul, and St. Augustine, all of whom, one suspects, Mr. Kenner must by implication be concerned to deny.

What is all this? Is it, as crusty Christopher once said, "a narcotic dose administered by a crazy charlatan"? It's hardly that simple. Praising Lessing as a critic, Kierkegaard remarked that he possessed "an exceedingly uncommon gift of explaining what he himself had understood. There he stopped. In our age people go further and explain more than they have understood." Mr. Kenner's special gift lies in explaining more than he has understood in ways that few others will ever care to understand. He is more like an alchemist or a mathematician than he is like a critic; in his most typical essays he tends to conjure up a totally autonomous, self-referring universe, whose terms have virtually nothing to do with experience, and which functions according to some arcane concoction of rules whose unintelligibility is the safeguard of their inconsequence. Mr. Kenner's writing about Wyndham Lewis thoroughly exemplifies this practice. Once that machine of mystification is set going, once one assumes that a work of literature is an entirely self-enclosed system, then all questions of judgment or justification are impertinent (how else, after all, *could* one write about Lewis?) and Mr. Kenner can come up with things like this: "Perfection, it seems, implies an exclusivity of function which leaves no room for the self-knowledge which in Lewisian terms is the ground of intelligence, and so intelligence is as rare among angels as among men." Mr. Kenner's new essay on Lewis in *Gnomon* is in fact, an achievement in itself—it manages to have about as much relation to literature, to experience, or to Lewis as the binomial theorem. He is similarly successful in his discussion of Pound's *Rock-drill* cantos, from which I have extracted this representative passage of prose:

> the interaction between heaven, prince, and people paralleled by that between the descent of light, the refractive processes of dented water, and the substantiality of the water-bug, which results in a radiant unforeseeable entity, the spectral flower on the stone. This metaphysical image effects a blending of the moral ambience of the *tê* ideogram with the motifs of the Paradiso proper in the latter half of the book.

Pity the poor English! How can we expect those sad and exhausted empirical souls to continue to withstand this engine of organized inanity? They have not, they have given in, surrendered unconditionally: in 1956 Mr. Kenner was invited to address the Royal Society of Literature. *Eheu fugaces!*

Meanwhile, from the antipodes speaks Maxwell Geismar, although it does not seem quite credible to imply that he and Mr. Kenner inhabit the same universe. His new book, *American Moderns*, is subtitled "From Rebellion to Conformity" and is largely made up of reviews reprinted from *The Nation, The Saturday Review* and *The New York Times*. Mr. Geismar stands for the tradition of "social protest," or, as he felicitously puts it elsewhere, "the social realism school." We are, he tells us, in desperate shape, for most of our writers have "repudiated their heritage and their link with a central literary tradition of the past," have lost contact with the 'atheists,' the radicals, the immigrant dreamers of social justice in the late nineteenth century, who mainly inherited and preserved our true cultural heritage." With Mr. Kenner, Mr. Geismar believes that a damnable plot is afoot to betray the true America and its history, traditions, and literature; and they both agree that the same powers are masterminding the operation. Those who, in Mr. Kenner's eyes, have subverted the tradition of an aristocratic government and who are not disciples of Pound or Lewis, are, strangely enough, the same recreants who according to Mr. Geismar have intrigued seditiously against the "central tradition of American conscience" and have "almost blackened [it] out of the national consciousness today." The measure of their perversity can be gauged by their deplorable refusal to worship in Mr. Geismar's Pantheon, where the works of "Stephen Crane, Frank Norris, Jack London, Ellen Glasgow, and Theodore Dreiser," the great writers of our century, and our true cultural heritage, lie enshrined.

As befits his conception of himself as critic, Mr. Geismar is explicitly prescriptive: he *knows* what novelists need and want and is generous with his advice. Thus, what is essentially missing in Hemingway is "a sense of that 'ordinary' life, in all its variety and mystery, that had always been the core of the great novels, at least." He locates the center of Sinclair Lewis' failure by perceiving that nowhere did he "attempt to project a single working-class figure of any dimension" or "an effective or even attractive social rebel." He reproves Norman Mailer for similar lapses: "Mr. Mailer leans rather heavily on the sexual experiences of his lower-class figures, too. These may be a solace for the common man, and even a source of strength, but they don't constitute his only achievement." These two sentences are, I think, a miracle of the picturesque—they summon up an image of the Worker, striding from the whorehouse to the factory, while his sense of achievement swells to a crescendo of moral triumph, like Tamburlaine in Persepolis.

And what ought novelists to write about? Like a Philadelphia lawyer, Mr. Geismar comes well prepared:

one would welcome a new generation of novelists who would look into such things as McCarthyism, or the white-collar equivalent of Nixonism, or the loyalty oaths and security dismissals, or the large-size looting of our natural resources, or the marriages of the corporations, and the rise of the stock market while small business and farming declines; or the hostility of Asia and the alienation of Europe while our public mind is both intimidated and dazzled by a series of shifting advertising slogans.

Mr. Geismar's tastes and interests are truly catholic, and his voice is as mild as the sucking dove's. It is always rewarding to read so genial a critic—it justifies one's confidence in the pleasure principle and in the richness and possibilities of experience. Moreover, I wish that Norman Mailer would take some of this advice, and instead of leaning on the sex life of lower-class figures, would describe just how Anaconda coils herself around National Gypsum when they get into bed together.

Yet Mr. Geismar knows that novelists are not currently interested in the things that interest him, that they are not dedicated to finding "self-expression . . . in the movements of social reform or social revolution" as they once were and ought still to be. And he knows why they aren't, too; they are being misled, they are the dupes, the front-men in that old conspiracy against Geismar, home, and beauty. In an epiphany called "Higher and Higher Criticism," Mr. Geismar identifies the brutes, these literary counterparts of McCarthy and Nixon. They have established the "New Criticism," which is

surprisingly well organized, with its chains of communications running from the colleges to the dominant literary magazines (*Kenyon, Hudson, Partisan* reviews, etc.), to the foundations and fellowships. It could be

> called a literary monopoly . . . it has been developed in this country [like fascism, it is international] mainly by romantic Southern conservatives. . . . Another branch of what is almost an interlocking directorate includes the literary ex-Communists seeking refuge in pure criticism; and such hesitant humanists as Lionel Trilling, who now represent the "Liberal Mind."

Still another subsidiary wing of the cartel is run by "bitter ex-radicals like Sidney Hook." Having clarified things so thoroughly, Mr. Geismar goes on to speculate about "the amount of fascism in this general movement and the poetry it advocates," since what binds all these power-mongers together is at once "a bland authoritarianism" about literature and a lost ability "to keep their human values intact"— that is, if they ever had human values, for the only people whom Mr. Geismar seems to allow as having them are those who were once radicals (Mr. Geismar's favorite euphemism) and who have not repudiated their heritage and commitment. That we are in imminent peril from this movement is Mr. Geismar's constant message: "Isn't it odd that our English departments, which yielded themselves to the racist concept of the Anglo-Saxon 'gentleman' at the turn of the century, now flaunt the defiant banner of the Old South?" It would take, I believe, a bitter ex-radical like Sidney Hook to analyze properly the relations between the two parts of this proposition: I would merely like to point out the exquisitely modulated resonance, the delicate suggestiveness, in the word "odd" (herewith qualifying as a New Critic and bland authoritarian) and call to the reader's fancy a vision of John Crowe Ransom wrapped in a Confederate flag at the bloody angle called Ambiguity, while Cleanth Brooks, mounted on his dappled charger, Paradox, leads his irregulars around to the rear to cut off Mr. Geismar and his embattled, decimated, yet loyal, crew. At the same time, up north, Phillips and Rahv are at work in the munitions factories, sabotaging the big dialectical guns, Trilling is making hesitant speeches about conciliation on the corner of 116th Street and Broadway, and Hook is instigating draft riots in Washington Square.

In the latest issue of *December*, a little magazine published in Iowa City, Mr. Geismar reviews his own book. He gives himself a very good notice, but is slightly troubled that he should do so, even in "this obscure little western publication which I hope and pray will never reach our eastern shores." Well, Mr. Geismar ought to have known better; he ought to have known that in this age of witch hunts and mass persecutions no liberal or progressive is safe, that the literary FBI has a full dossier on him—our agents in the Midwest notified central headquarters long before *December* ever hit the newsstands. I would like, however, to linger over one statement in that review: Mr. Geismar declares that he "writes, on the whole, as if reading books was a pleasure." I have compiled a modest thesaurus of Mr. Geismar's edifying remarks about writers, and would in this connection like to set down a few extracts from it here. To Mr. Geismar, Heimingway "has always refused to understand the nature of his own private orbit of anguish"; Fitzgerald, Hemingway, T. S. Eliot, and the other writers of the twenties "were masters, not of life, but of a kind of romantic enchantment; wizards of illusion," who were "as ignorant of their real heritage as they were indifferent to their future"; John Dos Passos lacks "an interest in people as such, a knowledge of possible experience, a curiosity about life simply as life"; Faulkner "doesn't seem to understand the South," and is "completely bound in by the class and caste concepts of his ancestry and origins"; James Gould Cozzens is deficient in "primary feeling; he is a cold writer who has needed a recharge, say, of human sympathy"; Steinbeck's work contains "a certain malice and hostility toward human life itself"; *The Deer Park* has "no human center"; its social values "are based on a biological void"; Saul Bellow is struck off as "the Herman Wouk of the academic quarterlies"; J. D. Salinger's later stories prove that he fails "to understand his own, true life experience and to fulfill himself"; in James Jones's novels, people are "so odious and sterile, so lacking in affection or sympathy" that Mr. Geismar doubts whether Jones is "capable of describing ordinary human relationships at all." These are representative specimens of Mr. Geismar's critical vocabulary, of his tact and tone; and it is clear that the pleasure that he gets from reading seems to be exceeded only by his sense of the intelligence, honesty, and seriousness of the subjects of his reviews. And if one feels that the coo of the sucking dove is occasionally drowned out by the whine of the bottom dog, one should recall that many of these reviews were published in *The Nation*, because, as Mr. Geismar says, "*The Nation* was the only magazine that would publish them."

Finally there is Mr. Geismar's prose, which is as distinctive in its way as Mr. Kenner's. It is lively and precise, and scouts all stale or fuzzy metaphors—thus, "Our writers do indeed lack a spiritual purpose, which in former generations was accompanied by a broad social base. . . ." Mr. Geismar must here be referring to the pedestal on which Ozymandias' feet remained. And there is this:

> The theme of sibling rivalry is recurrent and dominant in the Old Testament itself. It is subject to many levels of interpretation, from the moral, ethical, or social import, to the deepest levels of psychology, where both Mann and Freud found it so fascinating.

I find something wondrous in the picture of Mann and Freud skin-diving together in the unconscious, searching for "imports," Mr. Geismar's metaphor for Spanish gold. Or there is this, my personal favorite:

> As in almost all of Dos Passos' fiction, the human core

of his philosophical concepts is absent. Perhaps the central deficiency in his political thought rests, after all, upon a psychobiological failure.

Only an impenitent radical would have the courage publicly to rebel against the reactionary dictates of style—no one but a deeply committed progressive could deal so progressively with sense and metaphor, would refuse so loyally to conform to the repressive class and caste concepts of the English language.

If Mr. Kenner speaks from the right and Mr. Geismar from the left, then Harry Levin is at the center, the dead center. Mr. Levin, however, is really beyond party strife, and the political metaphor is not very pertinent. Mr. Levin lives out in the great world. He is a kind of literary Christian Dior, dealing almost exclusively in current, high-priced fashionable ideas; and his literary creations are like Dior's models, objects, devices, for putting on and taking off these attitudes as if they were no more than garments. *The Power of Blackness* traces the images of blackness—and of whiteness, shade, shadow, dusk, and night—as they appear in Hawthorne, Poe, and Melville. The origin of this pervasive image lies in Calvinism and the involvement of the American imagination with its notion of original sin. To this extent, Mr. Levin's book is substantially like Richard Chase's remarkable *The American Novel and Its Tradition*, which V. S. Pritchett recently called, without exaggeration I think, "decisive." But Mr. Levin has a fatal attraction for pretentiously going the best one better and for resonant and classy new terms: he wants to write a "literary iconology"; his icons become "archetypes," "elemental shape[s] assumed by the collective imagination," and are expressed through "fabulation," which is a process no less singular than "man's habit of telling stories as a means of summarizing his activities and crystallizing his attitudes." Mr. Levin also likes to speak about Hawthorne's "general vision of evil," a phrase one might hesitate to use even about a theologian, much less a novelist, but which in its vague inflation is pretty clearly current and *chic*.

Mr. Levin has never shaved with Occam's razor, and he is hirsute with self-proliferating entities. Of Hawthorne, again, he writes, "he balanced the rival claims of Eros and Thanatos, love and death in their universal phase." If we take Eros and Thanatos in their modern acceptation and with all their modern associations, which, one assumes, Mr. Levin has in mind, they scarcely seem "love and death in their universal phase" but something a shade more complex and precise, and which, when draped upon Hawthorne in this context, simply produce, like the chemise, an attractive blur. Or, Mr. Levin has this to say about Thoreau's idea of the fable: "Since it could pass from one environment to another without essentially changing, in a process which folklorists would call diffusion, it could become a constant factor, an irreducible unit of what Jung would call the collective unconscious"—which is the intellectual equivalent of traveling from the Bronx to Brooklyn via Chicago. The allusions take us on a long and dull and gratuitous—though not really unpleasant—trip, and having arrived at the end of the line we find that after accumulating all this mileage we haven't gotten anywhere.

But Mr. Levin is not merely a high-flyer in the empyrean of vagrant generalities. With heroic assiduity he has read through an entire literature, and ferreted out, noted and counted every reference to blackness that occurs in it:

> Statistical investigation has shown what the common reader might expect: that blackness predominates, equaled—and slightly eclipsed—by whiteness, when the latter is taken together with grayness. Actual colors are not much in evidence, except for lurid yellow and various shades of red; "The Masque of the Red Death" is the polychromatic exception that proves the rule.

The pedantic innocence of these remarks is rather touching. Mr. Levin's solemn assumption of significance, the total absence from his prose of any hint of irony about the fragility, the tentativeness, the dubious and peripheral importance of evidence of this order, his very use of the term "statistical investigation," disclose his failure to conceive of literature in an essentially critical, discriminating way. Writing about *Typee*, for example, he stops to remark that the narrator is welcomed by Polynesian women "with jet-black tresses," as if this had some special meaning, as if there might be blond Polynesians hiding in the coconut trees, or something exceptional about dark-haired ones. Or, referring to Hemingway's *The Old Man and the Sea*, Mr. Levin portentously extracts a passage in which the old man speaks of how the sun's reflecting off the sea hurts his eyes and how he welcomes the relief of dusk—as if literature never came near the naked irreducible facts of experience and there were nothing in it that should not be assimilated to this chromatic metaphysics. With perfect seriousness he finds this to say about Hawthorne: "Why should this blackness, which lifted for the philosopher, have settled again so heavily on the romancer? The year he spent measuring coal in the port of Boston will not suffice to explain it." In short, Mr. Levin appears to have lost his sense of what is relevant or irrelevant. Had Hawthorne ever shoveled snow in a blizzard, measured flour in a grocery, or dieted on black-eyed peas or black-strap molasses we would have been informed of that too. For to Mr. Levin all things are of equal, indistinguishable weight and cogency. Like Polonius' cloud, which was humped like a camel, backed like a weasel, and very like a whale, the blackness he discovers is amiably protean; a black horse, a black night, a head of black hair, all or any of them, regardless of the context in which they appear, have a uniformly powerful authority of value. There is no surer way of reducing a thesis to absurdity.

But one more example ought to be enough:

The symbolism of terror is universal. Otherwise, Death would not ride a pale horse in Scripture, and the Ancient Mariner would never have been bedeviled by an albatross. The glitter of Antarctic snow and ice . . . was the single mystery that Poe had left unresolved. W. H. Hudson would explain it as animism, "the mind's projection of itself into nature," our predisposition to be terrified by the exceptional. This may account for the stimulus it lends to visions or hallucinations like that of Hans Castorp in *The Magic Mountain*. One effect of taking mescaline, Henri Michlaux has recently testified . . .

And so on into the night. It is one thing to have an organic sensibility, to apprehend that correspondences between the outward and physical forms of things often mark inward and spiritual similarities; it is another to be at the same time incapable of seeing that certain words, images, or ideas which resemble each other from a verbal or mechanical point of view are in fact incommensurate. By the time one finishes Mr. Levin's book one has lost all confidence in his formless organicism, and feels that his conception, which initially seemed quite plausible, has been inflated out of existence. A literary critic is not a Hegel; his job is not to tie up the world in a pink ribbon—or a black and white one for that matter—to describe everything as a function of everything else. And had Hegel himself read Mr. Levin's book, he would, I think, have found himself once more in that night in which all cows are black.

Although Mr. Levin's failure is a failure of intellect, his book, unlike those of Mr. Kenner and Mr. Geismar, is not solely a curiosity. He does make interesting comments, but these are mostly by-blows and incidental, bits of insights that fly out from the whirring centrifuge of his method. Could he have managed to suppress about half of his "evidence," could he have restrained the pedantic impulse to set down everything that came to mind, to drop names as if they were hot potatoes, and to make as many associations as possible all the time; could he have remembered that great literature is not written by dormitory metaphysicians, that its systems, though real, are partial, fragmentary, and full of cross-purposes and contradictions, and that criticism is neither a detective agency nor a census bureau; could he have done all this, it is conceivable that his particular intellectual gifts might not have drawn him so irretrievably into the failures of method and manner which make his book so finally unenlightening.

Though these three books represent the current outer limits of American criticism and are so different from each other, they share one quality: they are all excessive and extravagant. Each suffers from an unbalancing commitment to a radically distorted and distorting point of view—from an obsession. And the very fact of such books expresses something about our society and culture. We are still, as Matthew Arnold said of us seventy-five years ago, a provincial and decentralized society, a society without a center of cultural intelligence and sanity; and that Mr. Levin should write his deeply eccentric and provincial book from a "center" like Harvard is exactly to the point. It is not that our kind of culture, out of its violent oppositions and devastating obsessions, cannot breed a distinctive literature—it can and does, which is precisely the thesis Richard Chase has argued commandingly. But the dissipation of talent, the desolation of intellect, the regard for trivia that are so notable in these three books are equally facts of its existence. These books are not so much comments on the state of our literature and society as they are expressions of the permanent conditions within them against which centrality of intelligence, balance of mind, and maturity of value must continue to make their way.

(1958)

An Ideal Reviewer

The publication of a new collection of essays by V. S. Pritchett serves as a reminder of the degree to which educated readers are in his debt.[1] The present volume combines a welcome reprinting of the thirty-odd essays of *The Living Novel*, first published in 1947, to which the author has added twenty-seven new pieces, written and published, presumably, during the interim. These pieces, like their predecessors, first appeared in the columns of the *New Statesman*. Pritchett is not merely a fixture (and director) of this institution; in retrospect, the distinction of its famous "back of the book" appears, as a practical matter, to be inseparable from the distinction that Pritchett can claim as his own. However imprecise or unfair it may be to both parties, one

---

[1] V. S. Pritchett, *The Living Novel and Later Appreciations* (New York, 1964).

thinks of the two in the same breath; and both, one may add, have been enhanced by the association.

In the title of this volume, Pritchett refers to these pieces as "appreciations." In another place he calls them "essays." Most of them seem to have been in fact written as reviews, yet one feels a certain hesitation in continuing to think of them as "mere" reviews, since most of them effortlessly transcend the form as it is commonly regarded. A similar ambiguity exists in Pritchett's relation to his office or function. To think of his writing essentially as journalism does honor to the trade, not to him. He is of course a critic, but his essays have neither the weight, ambition, nor presumption of most modern criticism, nor do they seem to provide the occasion for that special kind of spiritual anguish by which modern literary criticism characteristically announces itself, and through which the modern literary critic recognizes himself and his brothers-in-blood. Pritchett's pieces are all "re-views" in the simple radical sense of the word: they are general surveys and conspectuses of a field; they cast a glance once again over an author's writings or a genre; they sum up what is to be said in short compass about a particular subject. As much as he is anything else he is a reviewer; and how often has one caught oneself thinking of him as an "ideal reviewer."

In order to be an "ideal reviewer," however, one has to be other things as well. Pritchett is both a man of letters, in the older sense of the term, and a writer. He has spent a lifetime with literature, and is the master of all English prose fiction. He has read just about everything, and is particularly inward with the range and possibilities of the English novel. And he has the gift of communicating to the reader the continuing and unalloyed pleasure he finds in the act or pastime of reading. His essays on minor English novelists are models of their kind. In his pieces on Arthur Morrison or J. Meade Falkner or Sheridan LeFanu he does the rare thing—he discusses unimportant works one has not read with such warmth, lucidity, and interest that one wants to go out and read these books at once. He adds, in other words, to our possibilities and our experience; no work or writer that he undertakes to consider is not augmented by Pritchett's discussion. In this general enlargement of both his subject and his readers Pritchett fulfills the traditional role of the man of letters.

No one who has read Pritchett's work can fail to have been impressed and charmed by his skill as a writer. Only rarely do we find him faltering. He writes of George Eliot: "Hers is a mind that has grown by making judgments—as Mr. Gladstone's head was said to have grown by making speeches." Here his gift for epigram has become mere epigrammatism, a bit of belle-lettristic superiority in the lesser tradition of English weekend reviewing. For the most part, however, the freshness, vigor, and directness of his mind prevent him from such self-indulgences. When he says of E. M. Forster that "he has indeed been a haunting absence in the English novel," we feel that the truth and edge of the epigram have not been gained at Forster's expense, that the compression and wit of the statement do not exist apart from its substance and weight. Another of his essays typically begins: "The English humorists! Through a fog compounded of tobacco smoke, the stink of spirits and the breath of bailiffs, we see their melancholy faces." Here again the energy and gaiety of the prose are directly connected with the perception of a real object. Much of the time, in addition, we are aware of the fact that this distinguished reviewer of fiction is a writer of fiction himself, and that his critical essays are often as much "composed" or "observed" as they are "thought out."

> For, east of Aldgate [he writes in his essay on Arthur Morrison], another city begins. London flattens and sinks into its clay. Over those lower dwellings the London sky, always like a dirty window, is larger; the eyes

and hands of the people are quicker, the skins yellower, the voices are as sharp as scissors. Every part of London has its smell, and this region smells of little shops, bloated factories, sublet workrooms and warehouse floors; there is also the smell of slums, a smell of poverty, racy but oftener sour; and mingling with these working odors, there arises an exhalation of the dirty river which, somewhere behind these streets and warehouses and dock walls, is oozing toward the flats of the Thames estuary like a worm.

Yet these extracts of description and epigram do not sufficiently convey the general, unorganized intelligence and the disciplined powers of perception that illuminate with a kind of random regularity every one of his essays. If we feel that such a remark as "the great Russian novels of the nineteenth century arose from the failure of a class, whereas the English sprang from its success" loses by its not being located in an adequate context of qualification and elaboration what it gains by its ease and facility of statement, we can always balance it against such a telling formulation as the following. "The price of progress may be perversion and horror, and Wells is honest enough to accept that. Shaw appears to think we can evade all painful issues by a joke, just as Chesterton, the Catholic optimist of his generation, resolved serious questions by a series of puns." The depth of reference to a whole literature which such remarks indicate has its counterpart in Pritchett's hard-headed view of experience and of the society which the novelists to whom he addresses himself both represent and exemplify. "The acerbity of a novelist like Mrs. Wharton," he writes, "is *mondain* before it is intellectual; it denotes a positive pleasure in the fact that worldly error has to be heavily paid for spiritually. Her sense of tragedy is linked to a terrifying sense of propriety. It is steely and has the hard efficiency of the property market into which she was born." On the other hand, his critical parsimony does not lead him to demand from literature what it cannot possibly give. "One thing scientific culture has done for us," he writes in his excellent essay on Dostoevsky's minor novels, "is to give us a desire for order and for intellectual propriety, and I hope we are beginning to see again that egging readers on to personal conversion is not one of the functions of the novel." Yet he will also write of Gorky that he has "a memory, we say, that allows the world to have existed to the full, without first having to ask a tacit moral or intellectual permission from himself." Every one of Pritchett's essays is lit up by such insights, and the depths to which they penetrate are often disguised by the lightness with which they are thrown forth and the unobtrusive corners in which they are, almost literally, dropped.

The casualness with which Pritchett offers his insights makes clear his difference from the major contemporary critics—from, say, Edmund Wilson, Lionel Trilling, or F. R. Leavis. In this connection, his use of the modest term "appreciations" to describe his writings is altogether precise and just. His essays are not merely brief, but they have no discernible analytic structure, and often almost no argument. His gifts have not developed in that direction which leads toward the logical organization and deployment of large masses of material. It is one of his virtues as a reviewer that he brings no pre-formed critical theory to the novel; but it must be added that he also takes none away from it. Although his powers of generalization are evident in his natural epigrammatic style, he almost never rises to a large, outgoing, or quasi-systematic generality of statement. And if he is happily innocent of ideology in his criticism, it should also be noted that he is not interested in ideas in the fierce, distinctive modern way. His chief talent is for rendering up the immediate workings of his own mind, for laying out before us the finely connected tissues of his educated sensibility as it takes new material into it and handles it in a fresh but familiar way.

Such absences—in particular the absence of analysis—lead to the observation that on one side Pritchett does not respond to literature as modern criticism has taught its readers to do. He does not regard literature as a mode of cognition; he does not see in it some implicit form of metaphysical or ontological structure which can claim for itself the intellectual autonomy of the other humanistic disciplines. He largely responds to literature in terms of its moral and social force or efficacy. At its best, his essays say, literature reminds us of what we know and tend to forget; it keeps us morally vivid and prevents both boredom and meretricious excitement by putting us again in touch with what is most human in us. These considerations are in a direct line with De Quincey's "The Literature of Knowledge and the Literature of Power." And though Pritchett's essays have all been brought forth by specific literary occasions, they are in the direct tradition of the general English essay as much as, if not more than, they are in the line of more recent developments in literary criticism. One need only compare them to those most overrated volumes of modern writing, Virginia Woolf's Common Readers, to gain a clear sense of their eminence as examples of this form. It is, therefore, no accident that Pritchett's most favorable references among other modern essayists are to E. M. Forster and George Orwell. In both, as in his own writing, one hears once again the firm, vigorous, personal—and in Orwell and Pritchett, masculine—voice that is a touchstone of the genre.

For all their looseness of form, their reliance upon sensibility, impression, and association, Pritchett's essays do in fact make reference to a coherent body of opinion, to a set of intellectual coordinates and a tradition. His judgments are grounded in a deep-seated preference for the eighteenth century, that time which seems to him, as it does to so many other Englishmen, a center, a norm, to which literature and life and the judgment of both can be referred.

"Man is not yet trapped in our later prefixes and qualifications," he typically writes. "He is not yet industrial man, economic man, evolutionary man, civilized man, mass man, or man in transition. He is simply himself, a wonder ordained, like a tree watched in a garden . . . when we look back upon that world we cannot but suspect that half our present miseries date from the dissipation of the common feeling and philosophy that ensured the sanity of the age." When he wants to praise a later writer he often thinks of him as a kind of refugee or displaced person from the Enlightenment. He compliments Samuel Butler by calling him "a throwback to the eighteenth century," and says of H. G. Wells's "best narratives" that they "go back to the literary traditions of the eighteenth century, the highest traditions of our narrative literature." And he sees in this period of English history and literature "a coherent and integrated mind, a mind not deeply divided against itself." We cannot be certain from these statements whether Pritchett is endorsing the *ideals* of the eighteenth century or whether he is saying that during the eighteenth century these ideals were actually realized. In certain other passages there is a similar uncertainty of specification: one is never quite sure whether he is not identifying the ideal or idea of a norm for literature and life with the notion that such a standard was in fact realized. One of the consequences of such an error would be a tendency to regard all later developments in history as deviations from that hypostasized ideal. It seems to me that Pritchett does fall into this error, but his remarkable tact and feeling for all literature of any age prevents him from making the barbarities of judgment that such a logic, if he really followed it, would commit him to. In any event, what he finds in the eighteenth century is a combination of notions, standards, or values to which he can give his personal allegiance: the skepticism, empiricism, humanism, and feeling for comedy that he takes away from the Enlightenment are by no means the wrong equipment for a literary critic.

Pritchett's tastes in prose fiction follow a corresponding arc of development. His favorite writers are Fielding and Swift, and he remarks and emphasizes again and again in his essays the feeling of the great novelists for "normality" and "sanity." For example, he praises Arnold Bennett for "his patient and humane consideration of the normal factors of our lives: money, marriage, illness as we have to deal with them. Life, he seems to say, is an occupation that has been forced on us, not a journey we have chosen, nor a plunge we have taken. Such a view may at times depress us, but it may toughen us." He is most at home with "the accents of the brusque and off-hand sanity" which is for him "in the central tradition of English comedy." Yet he can also say that although at first we define Trollope as "one of the masters who enables us to recognize average life for what it is," on second thoughts "we change the phrase: we recognize that he has drawn life as people say it is when they are not speaking about themselves." The brusqueness and sanity of the tradition have also expressed themselves in such a judgment.

That line of growth in the novel which Pritchett most regularly thinks of is what he calls "the masculine comic tradition." Here is one of his characterizations of it:

It is intelligent rather than sensitive: it is prosaic rather than poetic; it is sane rather than extravagant. It is egocentric and not a little bullying. It has a manner, and that manner is ruthless and unkind. To stand up to the best manners of English society one has to be rude, exclusive and tough. One must be interested in behavior, not in emotions; in the degree to which people hold their forts—and how much money the forts cost—not in what human beings are. The tradition begins with Fielding: it is there, minus the animal spirits, in Jane Austen. Its values are bound to the social class the writer belongs to. . . . Hard-headed, often gifted, snobbish—for the most part—appreciative of other people's disasters and evasive about their own, self-oppressed and taking it out in horseplay and libertinage . . . [the] characters are a sort of club. They can listen unexhausted to gossip about each other, but their faces become suddenly masked if an outsider comes up. Their privacy is phenomenal.

This is of course a wonderful passage of prose. It should be added that Pritchett is the master of this tradition of the English novel, that he moves about in it with incomparable familiarity and expertness, and that, locating himself within it, he does indeed encompass a good part of the range of English fiction.

But something else has to be said. For it seems unlikely that a critic with such a group of preconceptions might respond fully, sympathetically, to the modern world and its literature. It is a measure of Pritchett's disinterestedness of mind that he does, that his presuppositions do not interfere to any seriously disabling extent with his openness and susceptibility to what currently comes before him. He does not, to be sure, deal at any length with the major modern figures, and one of the more striking things about this volume, which is after all about the novel, is the sparsity of references it contains to Joyce, Kafka, Gide, Proust, Mann, Hemingway, and Faulkner (and even to Lawrence, though Pritchett devotes an ambivalent essay to him). Sometimes he misses the boat altogether, as when he inveighs against certain unspecified "modern tough writers," who "lose their effect because they are tough all the time. They do not allow us to have the homely, frightened, law-abiding emotions. They do not allow us the manly fear, and they lose the interest of moral conflict." There is, I am afraid, a good deal of self-defensive bluster in such a statement; yet when Pritchett subsequently compares this literature with that of an earlier period, which could pierce one "with human fear and horror, without once cutting adrift from probability and an identifiable daily life," we see the point in a new light.

His great skill lies in his dexterous assimilation of contemporary literature to the tradition of which he has so firm a grasp. Occasionally he uses a writer from the past in order to comment critically on the current state of fiction—as he does in a superb essay on Vigny's *The Military Necessity*. Most of the time, however, he regards contemporary fiction as falling naturally within the context of an enduring and continuing convention. He can thus write easily, shrewdly, and without troubled second thoughts about such writers as Anthony Powell and Lawrence Durrell. In my opinion he overestimates both of these novelists, but whether I am correct or not, such overestimation is part of the appreciator's art or gift. For it is just such endowments of interest and sympathy which permit Pritchett to make the minor Victorian novelists live for us in his essays; and his pieces on Powell and Durrell discuss these writers as if they were what indeed they are—minor figures of curious interest. Pritchett's critical view, then, is naturally a very far-sighted one, and sometimes he is rewarded handsomely for this distance—as in his remarkable essay on Dostoevsky, in which he turns the great modern icon inside out by emphasizing Dostoevsky's "realism and sanity," and remarks on how his major works are "festive with experience of human society."

The long view has its limitations, naturally. And when Pritchett derides the "modern alibi" of saying "it is beyond the power of the imagination to grasp," he is doing more than scolding contemporary sloth or puncturing a fashionable cliché. He reveals at such points his unresponsiveness to the radical unstructuring of experience which is contemporary literature's obsessive subject. Similarly, Pritchett deals with the novels of Samuel Beckett by connecting them with the Irish tradition of talk, of interminable garrulity. This assimilates Beckett to something we understand, and in this measure Pritchett does very well by him. At the same time, one must remark that such a service also tends to underestimate the radical break with tradition that such writing represents, or that the break is its intention and *raison d'être*; it is more alien to the literature of the past, even of the Irish past, than Pritchett indicates. Yet this particular absence of indication lies at the very center of Pritchett's strengths, his command of the traditional and his generous impulse to extend it and to assimilate to it even the most aberrant contemporary efforts. If the modern seems slightly tamed by such a critical procedure, it should also be added that to tame and make accessible has always been regarded as one of the tasks of humane civilization.

Finally one must mention a quality that does not fall within the logical terms of this discussion—Pritchett's natural gift of critical temperament, and its remarkable persistence in time. V. S. Pritchett was born with the century and is still going strong. He remains not merely generous and open-minded in his attitudes toward literature, but he has managed to stay genuinely interested in things outside himself without going soft or becoming cranky. Although he has through years of performance and achievement earned the right, so to speak, of being self-insistent or idiosyncratic, he has become nothing of the kind. He does not play the power game of cultural generations; and his literary tastes, preferences, and judgments never become the nasty instruments of snobbery, moral superiority, or personal domination. The closest he comes to self-praise is his essays in celebration of E. M. Forster, and to this we can add that Pritchett's virtues and accomplishments are in their own way and place analogous to Forster's, as is, all differences being allowed for, his intellectual temperament. Perhaps the best way of celebrating this highly estimable writer and critic is to say that he, too, can be looked to as an example.

(1964)

The Limits of
Literary History

Who does not recall, as a student, having been assigned to read certain large sections in volumes of "literary history." One opened those heavy tomes—their multiple authors running down along the spines like a series of professorial hiccoughs—with a sense of dread and read through them in a thickening twilight of stupefaction and intellectual melancholy. If this is what literature was, then why should anyone have an interest in it? But literature was not like this, one knew, and so one staggered on through David Hartley's influence on *The Prelude* (it may have been larger than Wordsworth's), tripped over a poem called *Whistlecraft*, which kept being proposed as the chief cause of Byron's *Don Juan*, and in the end did one's best both to remember that one had done this reading and to forget what one had read.

These commonplace reflections are called forth by the publication of the latest installment in The Oxford History of English Literature. Ian Jack's volume[1] covers just seventeen years of that history, and is much superior to the older kind of study I have been referring to. Mr. Jack has read just about everything there is to read, wears his considerable learning very lightly, writes with grace and dryness, and in the main regards his subject with sense and in depth. For all these virtues, Mr. Jack's book is somehow unsatisfying; one finishes it without the complex sense of gratification that the experience of a mind which has achieved a true historical mastery of its subject can render in us. One wonders whether Mr. Jack has chosen to write the wrong kind of literary history for the period in question, or whether there is something in the nature of the literary-historical enterprise itself—at least at this moment in its historical development—which breeds contradiction and inconclusiveness. For although Mr. Jack has read everything and covers a vast amount of ground, his book leaves the impression of a radical intellectual inconclusiveness.

Mr. Jack is at his best in dealing with specific historical material. The first chapter of his book, "The Literary Scene in 1815," is a virtuoso performance. In fifty pages it describes with clarity and in surpassing detail the growth, workings, and influence of the great reviews, the lesser magazines and periodical papers, the publishing or bookselling trade, along with changes in taste and in the composition of the reading public. That part of the last chapter, "The Literary Scene in 1832," which deals with similar subjects is equally impressive. In those chapters which concern the minor poets of the period—Clare, Beddoes, Darley, *et al.* —and the minor writers of prose and prose fiction—Pea-

[1] Ian Jack, *English Literature 1815–1832* (Oxford, 1963).

cock, John Galt, Theodore Hook, Leigh Hunt, Landor, etc.—
Mr. Jack writes with great assurance, authority, and wit.
Here is a typical passage of commentary:

> The most remarkable features of the *Poems* (1808) of
> Felicia Dorothea Browne (later Mrs. Hemans) are the
> precocity of the author (they were written between the
> ages of eight and thirteen) and the length of the list of
> subscribers, which begins with the Prince of Wales and
> includes a thousand names. In 1812 she published *The
> Domestic Affections*, while from 1816 another volume
> appeared almost every year until her death in 1835. . . .
> She took the pulse of her time, and helped to prevent
> it from quickening. Elaborate poems on the deaths of
> Princess Charlotte and of the King himself put her
> loyalty beyond question, while in *Modern Greece* (1817)
> she had succeeded in the remarkable undertaking of
> producing a sort of respectable *Childe Harold*. . . . Many
> of her better things, such as the line "Blend with the
> plaintive murmur of the deep," might be the work of a
> poetical committee. For her, we feel, poetry was a femi-
> nine accomplishment more difficult than piano-playing
> and embroidery but no less respectable. . . . What we
> miss in her work is poetic individuality. We read her,
> we commend, and we forget.

Such a passage almost makes the penance of having once
had to read Mrs. Hemans worthwhile. In it we hear the
cultivated voice of the author of the excellent *Augustan
Satire*, as we do in the following comment on the very popular poet Bernard Barton, "the worthlessness of [whose]
work is no longer in dispute. Yet he also serves as a reminder—a reminder of the fact that the English, who have
produced the greatest poetical literature in the world, have
a deep instinctive preference for the third-rate." Mr. Jack
himself does not share this preference for the third-rate,

although it must be added that the minor and the third-rate fit into the categories of literary history with supreme convenience. They are the figures who can be discussed as being wholly determined by the literary past, or whose work can be best understood as falling within the logic of the history of literary genres, and so, exhausted by that history. As long as he is dealing with such dependent sensibilities, the literary historian has it all his own way.

It is when he turns to the larger figures and issues of the age that Mr. Jack runs into trouble. His chapters on Byron, Shelley, and Keats, and on Hazlitt, Lamb, and De Quincey, are eminently disappointing; a discussion of Scott's fiction is only slightly less so. And as for problems of intellectual history, alterations in consciousness, developments in philosophy, and the relations of all these to literature, Mr. Jack meets such matters by what has to be called a studied avoidance. This volume deals with what is usually thought of as the second half of the Romantic period; and if one did not know about this from other sources, one would never learn from Mr. Jack's account that it was a time of enormous creative upheaval, or that during these years an astonishing congregation of major creative minds were suddenly thrust forth upon the world. No reader of Mr. Jack's work will be able to discover from these pages that in such immense circumstances as the French Revolution and its train of consequences, the growth of German philosophy, and the outburst in all directions of English literature a permanent revolution in human experience and consciousness was taking place.

The fact is that Mr. Jack is a revisionist historian, and his revisionist distaste for generalizations is extended so far that it makes most of the figures whom he discusses less interesting, less important, less meaningful than they in truth are. For example, at various moments Mr. Jack indicates that this period saw a remarkable increase in autobiographical writings, that writers suddenly became engrossed in their own childhoods. And at this point he stops. That this change: a) should have been caused, determined, or influenced by some thing or things; b) should have some large, manifold significance both in and outside literature; and c) should have changed our conceptions of both creativity and literature—not to say childhood itself—is a matter he resolutely avoids. That is, the interesting part is left out. Similarly, in dealing with a group of writers whose personal lives and experience not merely suffused their works but in whom personal experience was in the course of becoming a conscious principle of creativity, Mr. Jack has clung to the sturdy expedient of dropping all biographical matter into an opening footnote and then going on to discuss their careers as writers without reference to that experience. As a result, his chapters on the major writers tend to be chronological summaries of abstract literary careers; new works of literature are essentially caused by the writer's reading— that is, by other works of literature—and we find ourselves back again, though on a higher plane of intellectual competence, with our old friend, the history of literary genres. The major decisions in writing literary history have to do with contexts: how wide or narrow is the context in which you choose to regard a work of literature; how many influences are you willing to see playing on it simultaneously; how many relevant connections with the world outside literature are you willing to attribute and able to suggest. The revisionist historian, with his abhorrence of generalization, tends to choose the narrower, often the narrowest, context. For those figures or topics whose interest is purely "literary" and can be exhausted by purely technical and literary discussion, such a context is adequate, and, as I have suggested, Mr. Jack deals with them remarkably well. For those figures or topics whose interest transcends or goes beyond the purely literary, for those figures in whom we are interested by reason of what they have to say about their experience, or of how they engage the world about them, or of how they develop a vision or idea of the life of their own time—in other words, for the major writers—such a context is inadequate and indeed finally fails to make them either available or intelligible.

Such shortcomings are nowhere more evident than in those extended passages where Mr. Jack tries to dispute the idea that there was any substantial unity, coherence, or meaning in the period of English literature to which he has chosen to devote some years of his life. He attempts this by first declining to admit that there existed in England such a thing as the "Romantic Movement." He is naturally thinking of the situation in Germany, where certain writers discovered they had common ideas and goals, banded together and called themselves Romantics. In England, by comparison, there was less banding together and very little common ideology. But of course this sort of argument proves nothing. The absence of a consciously organized movement makes, in such matters, an interesting and important difference, but says nothing at all about the existence or nonexistence of the large phenomenon under examination—Romanticism. Mr. Jack has very simply tried to solve his problem by denying that it exists; his answer to the question of whether anything of peculiar significance "happened to English literature in the early nineteenth century" is that it all "depends on the standpoint of the observer." To which one can only reply, Come off it, old boy, you know better than this.

In his excess of revisionist skepticism, Mr. Jack has emptied his subject of general importance. In his refusals and denials he becomes a parody-in-reverse of those German academicians who solemnly insisted that only writers who explicitly declared themselves as Romantics could be considered part of the movement, related to one another, or part of the same general tendency of mind. They characteristically fell victim to a definition, mistaking an idea for a real thing; Mr. Jack, in a manner equally characteristic (if less hallucinatory), cherishes the discrete objects and is skeptical of all efforts to relate them to an idea. The only relations he will allow are those that go back to specific sources in the particular English literary past; and he rounds off his discussion by stating that "to me, at least, sources have always been more interesting than analogues." This is a bit of special pleading and doesn't even pretend to the rigor of argument. The answer to it of course is that neither of these alternatives, in either practice or theory, is exclusive of the other.

But Mr. Jack has already cited a conclusive disproof of his assertions. In the preface to *The Revolt of Islam*, Shelley writes: "But there must be a resemblance, which does not depend upon their own will, between all the writers of any particular age. They cannot escape from subjection to a common influence which arises out of an infinite combination of circumstances belonging to the times in which they live." The feebleness of Mr. Jack's position is indicated by the fact that he makes no effort to deal with this statement. The feebleness is of a general intellectual kind and is, paradoxically, reminiscent of nothing so much as those older and antiquated literary histories which Mr. Jack's volume and the companion volumes in this series are intended to supersede. Despite Mr. Jack's genuine sophistication and critical intelligence, his unmistakable superiority as a critical mind to those older historians, his work is in the end less supersession than substitution. And in the end it is the narrowness of his idea of literary history that does the most damage to his undertaking; in this connection it seems reasonable to ask whether it is literary history as a mode of discourse or intellectual discipline that is most questionable, or the current state—in our culture at least—of the historical disciplines in general. To those of us who understand the study of literature—including literary history—to be inseparable from the study of man, society, and civilization, Mr. Jack's book is a disappointment. It disappoints in the degree that we are led by its author's knowledge, scholarship, and intelligence, by his critical gift and humane wit to expect a great deal—and in the degree that those expectations are violated.

(1964)

Madness, Literature,
and Society

I

In July, 1959, Dr. Milton Rokeach, a social psychologist and Professor of Psychology at Michigan State University, entered the Ypsilanti State Hospital to begin a research project. He took along with him a group of assistants and a tape recorder. In Ward D-23 of the hospital were gathered three men, pseudonymously named Clyde Bensen, Joseph Cassel, and Leon Gabor. Each suffered from the same psychotic delusion: that he was Jesus Christ. Dr. Rokeach had several intentions in bringing these men together: he wanted to observe the possible results of a direct confrontation of their delusions, to conduct research into general problems of identity, and to explore "the processes by which systems of belief and behavior might be changed through messages purporting to come from significant authorities who existed only in the imaginations of the delusional Christs." For the next two years these three psychotic men lived together under the close supervision and observation of Dr. Rokeach and his assistants. They worked together, held frequent meetings, were set common tasks, and were subjected to a number of experiments. Tape recordings were made of their speech—soliloquies, their meetings together, interviews with Dr. Rokeach. After two years of this activity Dr. Rokeach concluded his recordings and experiments and left the hospital. His three delusional charges were returned to their abandonment in the wards.

On one side, Dr. Rokeach's work represents a further contribution to the study of how human beings behave in extreme situations and under extreme conditions; it is among the few such studies to have been cast in the form of an experiment. His three subjects shared a common systematic delusion about their identity, one that could not be broken into or changed from the outside, since it is in the nature of these delusions that they "cannot be effectively contradicted by another person because the deluded person will accept no external referents or authorities." Certain psychotic states derive their stability and power from their ability to sustain themselves without reference to the outside world. Their stability is also their horror; to the observer such psychotic states seem as impenetrable as a rusty safe to which the combination has been lost. At the same time, however, even a psychotic who has a mistaken belief about his identity retains another "primitive belief which is based on reality . . . the belief that only one person can have a particular identity." (Dr. Rokeach never explains why this belief cannot be given up too, but apparently it cannot.) In bringing these three Christs together, Dr. Rokeach "proposed to bring into dissonant relation two primitive beliefs within each of them: his delusional belief in his identity and his realistic belief that only one person can have a given identity." In other words, Dr. Rokeach undertook to create a severe conflict in each of these men, to bring about "as untenable a human situation as is conceivable." And his prediction was that "in a controlled environment wherein escape was not possible, something would have to give." His project may be thought of as an effort to disrupt a stable, if insane, identity; with three crazy men in hand, he set about to derange their craziness. The circumstances inevitably suggest a concentration camp run in reverse, or brainwashing administered by angelic commissars. Indeed it is in the literature on both these subjects that Dr. Rokeach's work in part takes its origins.

But *The Three Christs of Ypsilanti*[1] is more than the record of an experiment in the outermost reaches of social psychology. Among other things, it represents, in an unpretentious but remarkably vivid way, what institutionalized madness is like. Everyone knows the statistics which are supposed to define the mad scene in America today—that mental illness is our most common affliction, that more beds in institutions are given over to the care of the mentally ill than to any other disease, etc., etc. As so often happens, statistics like these blur our image of mental illness as much as they help to convey its reality. Dr. Rokeach operates on a slighter and more manageable scale: we learn from him that in Michigan there are more than 25,000 people confined to public mental institutions; that in the Ypsilanti State Hospital there are more than 4,000 patients; that to care for these patients there are *five* staff psychiatrists and *twenty* resident psychiatrists; that this ratio is typical as is its hideous inadequacy. Under these conditions, patients can expect to see a doctor "maybe once a year." It is no surprise that public mental institutions are places of detention and custody, not of treatment, rehabili-

---

[1] Milton Rokeach, *The Three Christs of Ypsilanti* (New York, 1964).

tation, or cure. The three delusional Christs of Dr. Rokeach's study are permanent inmates of the hospital. They have spent an appalling amount of time in the lock-up; two of them have been in mental hospitals for more than twenty years apiece; the third had, in 1959, already spent five years in "custodial confinement." However inadequate the treatment offered to mental patients who are public charges, the three Christs received more "sustained attention" than any other patients in the history of Ypsilanti State Hospital. Still, after two years with Dr. Rokeach they were as mad as ever.

Part of the poignancy of psychosis is that in some odd sense it seems to make no difference whether it is treated or not. The institutionalized psychotic has been abandoned by his family and to some degree by society too, even though he is its charge. But the saddest fact of all is that before his final desertion by society, a whole series of catastrophic abandonments, including the abandonment of himself, has taken place. As a document of the quiet hopelessness of psychosis, of its simple and dreary finality, Dr. Rokeach's book possesses a modest distinction. On a typical summer's day, for example, "Joseph often wore three pairs of socks—yellow, then pink, then yellow. He wore a pair of women's horn-rimmed glasses without lenses to which he managed to attach a lorgnette . . . he also threw towels and loaves of bread into the toilet and tossed magazines and books out of the window. When Leon asked him why he did this, Joseph replied: 'Everything's all right—the world is saved.' " Who is this character out of a movie or comic strip, this familiar figure from Major Hoople's boarding house? So long as one retains this comfortable distance, no further questions are necessary. But when one stops to consider that Joseph is a man sixty years old, that he has a family and children, that he worked and thought and lived for forty years before he took leave of the world for good—that he is still somebody's father!—all one's usual defenses against such terrible facts collapse. It is one of the virtues of Dr. Rokeach's book that it never ceases to represent these men as human beings, that it is faithful to their humanity, including the humanity of their psychoses.

To a large extent this fidelity is achieved by the device which created this book—the tape recorder. Dr. Rokeach's volume joins that growing body of works of quasi-art which the social sciences seem on the point of developing into a separate minor discipline. It may be useful to note that the first important practitioner of this art was Sigmund Freud, who spoke of himself as having been endowed with a phonographic memory: he was often able to record an interview in its entirety after a patient had left. More recently, in the works of a writer like Oscar Lewis, the tape-recorded interview has assumed considerable dimensions, and commentators have been quick to admire the literary quality of Lewis' books, as well as their scientific value. The outstanding qualities of the tape recording are immediacy and authenticity, qualities associated until recently with the art of fiction and traditionally regarded as among its functions or justifications. The fact that Mr. Lewis' volumes have been translated from Spanish augments the quaint impression that they might be novels by Tolstoy. Dr. Rokeach taped his interviews in English, and his book is of the greatest interest as a study of the relation of psychosis to language and literature, and in the way the unconscious mind expresses itself verbally. There is, of course, another modern work that uses a tape recorder as an imaginative device: in *Krapp's Last Tape*, a man hopelessly clings to a reality which has long ago given him up. The characters in Dr. Rokeach's study are themselves members of that company of images, spirits, demons, and devils which, for a hundred and fifty years since their first appearance in William Blake's prophetic books, have occupied an increasingly important place in literature. The mind of Samuel Beckett is only the most recent lodgings these familiar spirits have inhabited.

The psychotic has to express himself within the prison of a language; but his relation to language is itself partly psychotic, and his efforts to mediate his unconscious conflicts and fantasies through language produce that remarkable phenomenon which has been called the poetry of madness. Here, typically, is Joseph speaking:

> When I invented the world there was no paganism—just people who were helpers. Eventually when the world is on a firm basis there won't be any need for religion. . . . I'm God and I don't want anybody to worship me. The world was created by work and doing good, not by worshipping me and kissing me. I don't want to go to church. . . . What the hell is a cross for? It is simply a symbol of Christianity to hurt you. . . .

Here is a line from Leon:

> "To me, peace means ideology in the heart."

And one from Clyde:

> "Santa Claus represents God on assistance."

And yet another from Joseph:

> "There is only one God, and nobody seems to know where He is."

One is struck by the pithy, epigrammatic, and paradoxical quality of these statements, by their seeming to be so profound—just as one is struck by similar passages in the writing of Beckett. But these statements do not actually make sense; sometimes they suggest meaning, but most often they are merely syntactical elegies for a lost world of intelligible discourse. They are poetic and vivid because, in them, unconscious processes are given free enough play to force language into startling juxtapositions. Here, as in part of the literature from Blake to the present time, one has the sense that language is as much a barrier to expression as a means of facilitating it. For those modern writers whose use of language is of a radically regressive character, and for these psychotics whose relation to language shares this tendency, language itself tends ideally to become a transparent medium, without ordinary rules, density, or character. In such instances, language serves to point toward, rather than to express, certain gestures of the soul, certain flickerings of emotion—it is something *through* which we try to move in order to reach what psychoanalysts call the "primary process," that substratum of psychic energy from which the rest of our mental life is elaborated.

The Three Christs of Ypsilanti makes clear how intimately connected with this process are the most familiar turns, gestures, and locutions of modern literature. "Sir," Leon says, "since you are bringing up such pleasant memories, it reminds me of pleasant memories pertaining to my own wife. But that's in the future." What contemporary play or novel could not contain the following: " 'Why should a man try to be s-somebody else,' Joseph stammered, 'when he's not even himself?' " When Leon remarks that it is "better to live alone, relating to positive nothingness. . . . My love is for infinity and when the human element comes in it's distasteful," we must recognize that his insane speech is tapping the same resources of psychic energy and impulse as some of the most characteristic expressions of modern literature. When Leon at one point begins to wear a blindfold, "a neat rectangular affair made of dark green cellophane that fastened at the back of his head with rubber bands," we cannot be shocked. And we are not surprised when he adds blinders, "pieces of white cardboard at his temples which cut down his vision even further." When he shows up at the next meeting wearing all this plus a pair of earplugs, we know that what we see on the stage under the name of *Endgame* and what takes place on the stage of the Ypsilanti State Hospital are very much the same thing.

The analogy with Blake is equally revealing. "On March 29, Leon stated that when he was fourteen years old he had lost his heart and had not recovered it until November, 1959, when he married. . . . When he leaves for work, he said, his wife takes his heart away and puts a scroll of the Ten Commandments in its place." Or the following, as close a gloss on "The Mental Traveller" as one is likely to find:

> A woman bore me; she consented to having me killed electronically while she was bearing me, which is in itself a disowning of a child. And I disowned her after I put the picture together. And she also stated when I was eight and a half years of age that I'm nothing to her, and that was like a brick between the eyes. And after I died the death I told her she's nothing to me, and it's true what people say about her, she was a first-class fornicator . . . That particular woman, I call her the Old Witch. . . .

But one need not go so far as Blake. A figure as unlikely as Thomas Carlyle comes equally to mind. Of the Christs, the most accessible to influence was Leon, the youngest of the three. He usually spoke of himself as "Rex"—he was King Oedipus as well as Jesus and God—but under the pressure of daily confrontations with men who claimed to be the same person as he, he did not, as did the other two, refuse to recognize the conflict. After much contemplation, he discarded his identity as God, and revealed himself in a new incarnation as—who? none other than "Dr. Righteous Idealed Dung," Diogenes Teufelsdröckh himself. One has the sense, as one follows the various turns and developments, the shifts and dodges each of these men makes, that the history of Western culture is either invented anew in the psyche of every one of us, or—what may be worse—that

Western culture itself is like a broken-down and spliced-up newsreel composed of all the horror movies and black comedies ever made, which keeps playing over and over in the all-night theaters that exist behind the eyes of us all.

Moreover, to insist on the exclusive contemporaneity of Dr. Rokeach's Christs would be misleading. What has changed most dramatically is our conception of what is insane and what is not—I can think of no idea subject to greater fluctuation, more strictly relative and historical. The literature of the past contains, as part of its normal everyday world, eccentric behavior that today we would consider insane, suitable for institutionalization. For example, Leon had a ritual called "shaking off," an act "designed to get rid of the electronic interferences and impositions to which he believed he was continually subjected. He 'shook off' by sitting rigidly in his chair, pressing his fingers firmly against his temples, and vigorously massaging his head while holding his breath until he was red in the face." Think of any number of characters in Dickens for a moment—not to mention Ben Jonson or Shakespeare—Wemmick, the lawyer's clerk in *Great Expectations*, for example, who turns his face and mouth into a post office the closer he comes to his work in London and who walks through the city "in a self-contained way as if there were nothing in the streets to claim his attention." Or here is Leon describing his final passage into psychosis:

> I felt myself and it seemed real peaceful. It was so peaceful that I would have liked to remain dead, but God didn't call me.

One of the great passages in the imaginative literature of the past century occurs in *Our Mutual Friend*, when the crippled and visionary artist Jenny Wren, maker of dolls' dresses, looks down from the rooftop of a London hovel into the streets and cries out to a friend, "Come up and be dead!" The point is not that the past was unable to recognize madness and that we are able to do so today, but that in the past "normal" acceptable reality accommodated a larger amount of eccentric, odd, and peculiar personal behavior than it does now—and that different institutions existed for dealing with such behavior. Religion was able to accommodate part of it, and family life more of it (how many families did not have a crazy aunt or uncle who lived in a room upstairs for twenty years, ever since the day that—well, think of Miss Havisham). What we now consider characteristically psychotic behavior —depression, hallucination, and acute withdrawal—was thought of then as a part of life's expectations, something that had to be endured. Today we seem increasingly inclined to isolate such behavior even further by creating a large, separate, institutional world for it. I am certainly not suggesting that the doors to Bedlam be thrown open, but I think it may be useful to note again what has been noted abundantly in other places—that as our society continues to grow more complex, there seems to be a concomitant decline in the flexibility and range of behavior which we are able to tolerate. Yet even as we isolate such extreme behavior within our society, the very form and shape which society itself is coming to take seems more and more to resemble a re-creation, on a large abstract scale, of the condition it keeps locking away. Literature has been trying to say this for the last two hundred years in a thousand different ways, and it is the signal virtue of Dr. Rokeach's book that it makes the connection between these disparate realms palpable and clear.

II

There is much to be said in criticism of Foucault's study of madness.[2] It is written in a prose of an obscurity so dense

[2] Michel Foucault, *Madness and Civilization: A History of Insanity in the Age of Reason*, translated by Richard Howard (New York, 1965).

as to be often impenetrable. This is not so much the result of its genuine difficulty of thought as of the author's arrogance, carelessness, and imprecision. Helter-skelter he employs whole sets of technical philosophical terms which are only half assimilated to the matters he is discussing. Indeed he rarely bothers to define them, much less to use them consistently. The tone of the prose is high-flown and portentous. Foucault's powers of exposition are equally uncertain. Although his book is organized generally along chronological lines, and although each chapter focuses upon a distinct topic, reading through most of these chapters is like wading through several feet of water: paragraphs do not follow one another in logical and sometimes not even in associative order; great lacunae open up between what are apparently supposed to be consecutive parts of a discussion; conclusions are sometimes offered in advance of evidence, and sometimes they are offered in place of evidence.

The author's scholarship is to say the least irregular; one need only compare his discussion of seventeenth- and eighteenth-century medical theories of mental ailments with those contained in a recent standard work of medical history—Ilza Vieth's *Hysteria: the Histoy of a Disease* (1965), for example—to see at once how idiosyncratic is his use of sources. His scholarship is in addition surprisingly provincial. The subtitle is "A History of Insanity in the Age of Reason," but the book's conclusions apply in fact almost exclusively to France. Italy is pretty much ignored as being apparently outside history; Germany seems hardly to have made it to the Age of Reason; and of much of Foucault's material on England, well, the less said the better.

Such charges would be grave indeed if they were brought to bear upon another book. In Foucault's work they seem in the end hardly to matter. In spite of all the defects I have listed, it seems to me that Foucault has written a work of unquestionable originality and importance. It is certainly worth putting up with its flaws in order to get what it has to offer, and one's disagreements should be reserved for the arguments in the book itself.

Foucault begins his account with a discussion of leprosy. Throughout the Middle Ages leprosariums, or lazar-houses, had been established at the gates and margins of the towns of Europe. Within these precincts an immense number of sufferers were segregated, removed to a "sacred distance" from the world. It is revealing of the ambivalence with which medieval society regarded the leper that it simultaneously drove him out of it and confined him within it, at its very periphery which, as the cities expanded, was to become in turn a new center. As a figure in the religious consciousness of the period, the leper was invested with equally ambiguous qualities. Visible emblem of man's wickedness and God's angry punishment, his malady was at the same time a sign of his salvation—he literally embodied the grace of affliction, a grace whose visitation was accomplished by means of his very abandonment and exclusion. At the end of the Middle Ages leprosy mysteriously disappeared from the Western world. The lazar-houses were emptied but remained standing; these structures and the institutional structures of exclusion associated with them were to become the model for many of society's later efforts of segregation and confinement, including the confinement of the mad.

Foucault then turns to an examination of the variety of ways in which madmen were treated during the early Renaissance. One of the most interesting practices of the period was to pack madmen onto a Ship of Fools and send them sailing off into the beyond, in search, presumably, of the sanity they had somewhere lost. Part pilgrim, part vagabond, part exile, the madman on his *Narrenschiff* soon came to represent in the imagination of the times something more than himself, and the Ship of Fools became a central motif in the literature and iconography of the period. It is Foucault's thesis that during the fifteenth century a large change occurred in the consciousness of Europe: madness and the madman became "major figures," and from that time on, "the face of madness has haunted the imagination of Western man." The obsession with madness in the Renaissance displaced the medieval obsession with death, the mockery of the one replacing the solemnity of the other. "From the discovery of that necessity which inevitably reduces man to nothing," he writes, "we have shifted to the scornful contemplation of that nothing which is existence. Fear in the face of the absolute limit of death turns inward in a continuous irony . . . Death's annihilation is no longer anything because it was already everything, because life itself was only futility, vain words, a squabble of cap and bells. The head that will become a skull is already empty." And although madness had replaced death as a dominant theme, it nonetheless retained death's eschatological powers: the madness that sweeps through humanity reminds us of the chaos that is to come and of the imminent end of the world.

The figure of the madman did not, however, emerge at once in separate and defined clarity. He first makes his appearance in the company of other figures given over to the vices and faults that perpetually plague mankind, who are all gathered together under the rule or misrule of Folly, "a sort of great unreason for which nothing, in fact, is exactly responsible, but which involves everyone in a kind of secret complicity." The Madman, the Fool, and the Simpleton were often fused together and were always exemplary in function: if folly leads every man into "a blindness where he is lost, the madman, on the contrary, reminds each man of his truth." Folly was at work everywhere, even at the very heart of reason and truth, and the madman was beheld in juxtaposition not only with the drunkard, the debauched, and the criminal, but with the scholar, the pedant, and the lover as well. He was part of the moral universe of excess, irregularity, and disorder that at certain times are thought to be synonymous with the human universe itself. And he embodied the tragic essence of this universe. Mad in his excess, he was not insane in the sense we put to that term today.

During the sixteenth and seventeenth centuries this generalized conception of madness gradually declined. As a critical consciousness inexorably developed, as the powers of reason inevitably expanded, the idea of madness steadily lost its powers of reference, its significance as a commentary on experience. Madness became only the extreme instance of error and illusion—of reason suspended or gone astray, of human self-enclosure. Together with this intellectual development went a social change. Foucault calls it "the Great Confinement": the creation in the latter half of the seventeenth century of large General Hospitals, although General Prisons would be a more precise term. Into these great spaces of detention, the poor, the unemployed, the criminal, and the insane were indiscriminately herded. During the Age of Reason itself, society's characteristic way of dealing with its problems was by sequestering or excluding them. Indigence, idleness, moral irregularity, criminal license, and madness were all grouped together by a society that had begun to organize itself along consciously "rational" principles. The value of work was now thought of as ethically transcendent, and confinement was in part a punishment for idleness, sloth, and economic inutility, and in part a means of rationally "administering" the unreasonable. It was at this moment, too, that those confined were required to work, not simply in order to keep them occupied or even to add to the productive powers of society, but as "an exercise in moral reform," reason and morality now being used interchangeably.

The author then turns his attention, in several awkwardly organized chapters, to how the mad were treated during the seventeenth and eighteenth centuries, the various theories proposed to account for madness, and to how the varieties of madness were classified. Space does not permit me to comment upon all of this fascinating material, but Foucault's main point can, I think, be summarized. Even during the height of the modern "classical age" madness was still not thought to be a mental disease. The mad were sometimes considered men turned into beasts, and were exhibited in a freak show and beaten to tame their animality. Sometimes their disorders were considered physical irregularities, malfunctionings of the animal spirits or nervous fibers; and then the mad were shocked or soothed, boiled or frozen, bled or purged, gorged or starved—a variety of treatments, quite comparable in both humanity and effectiveness to those administered in numbers of our own institutions until very recently. And yet Foucault believes that all this battering was in some ways preferable to what followed. Throughout the eighteenth century the tendency increased to understand madness as strictly a condition of moral error, waywardness, or failure; in the degree that madness is progressively moralized, so is the madman charged with the responsibility for his condition—he is guilty of having freely chosen his escape into insanity—by the encompassing world of reason and order. To this accusation he must inwardly assent if he is ever to enter that other world again. From here, according to Foucault, it is but one step to the early modern theories of madness as a mental disease.

The era of confinement ended, both actually and symbolically, at the time of the French Revolution. But for the mad, it may be said, this juncture only marks the beginning of their deeper incarceration. During the eighteenth century objections had been made to the indiscriminate imprisonment of the insane among the indigent, the criminal, and the debauched. The point of these objections was that the mad were an annoyance and a danger to the other prisoners, who required protection from the moral contagion bred in the person of the lunatic. At the end of the eighteenth century humanitarian sentiment reversed this formulation; Pinel and Tuke struck off the madman's chains and demonstrated that as a rule the madman is harmless to others, and that it is he who requires protection—from himself. It was at this point that madness was finally separated out as an entity distinct from all the other forms of unreason. It was at this moment, too, that the insane asylum as we know it was brought into existence. Isolated as both a spiritual phenomenon and a physical reality from all other forms of aberration, insanity henceforth took on the shape we recognize today. Under the dispensation of the asylum the madman was no longer beaten, reviled, or punished for his guilt; but, according to Foucault, the asylum did something more, which was just as bad, if not worse: "it organized that guilt." It organized it by its concentration, its isolation, but most of all by its structure of authority, a structure modeled upon that of the bourgeois family. Under this regime the madman was treated as a minor or a child, and his keeper, and later his physician or psychiatrist, represented patriarchal authority. This circumstance, the fiction of the asylum-as-family, remains as true today as it was when it was invented more than one hundred and fifty years ago.

Thus as madness continued to be internalized, observed, circumscribed, and classified, it sank ever deeper into solitude and silence. What was once a dialogue between reason and unreason—even if that dialogue consisted only in delirium on the one hand and insults and punishments on the other—was disengaged for good. Madness became either a "monologue in a language which exhausted itself in the silence of others," or sank into final and wordless stupefaction. For the language or delirium was also rejected by the nineteenth century as non-language, and this rejection, this absence of language, has remained until today "a fundamental structure of asylum life." Since the end of the eighteenth century the life of unreason has, with two exceptions, withdrawn from view. It is manifest only in the work of the great half-mad poets and thinkers of the nineteenth and twentieth centuries, and in the work of Freud, who had the genius to "return to madness at the level of its language . . . he restored, in medical thought, the possibility of a dialogue with unreason." This dialogue is still only a possibility, and Foucault holds out little hope for its realization.

I have in the foregoing paragraphs tried to clarify a rich, complex, and frequently contradictory and incoherent account. Its implications seem to me very large indeed. On one side Foucault's work is a study of what is called "differentiation"—he shows how certain generalized intellectual and institutional structures of the Middle Ages split apart and became specialized, distinct, and isolated as the modern world emerged. In this respect *Madness and Civilization* has much in common with Philippe Ariès *Centuries of Childhood*, which follows the development of the ideas and institutions of childhood, the school, and the family along essentially similar lines. Unlike Ariès, however, Foucault deplores this process; in his mind "differentiation" is always the equivalent of "dissociation." For example, he judges later therapies for madness as "the impoverishment of the meanings which had richly sustained the therapeutic methods throughout the entire classical period." At this point it scarcely seems to matter to him that those older therapeutic methods were crazy themselves; what counts is that they made for rich metaphoric constructions. At another point he comments on the same development: "The unity of the symbols begins to break down, and the techniques lose their total significance." Foucault is extraordinarily astute at discovering the myths by which cultures sustain themselves, but in this connection it seems to me that he is putting forth a myth that may be more familiar to readers of English than of French literature. He literally believes in "the dissociation of sensibility"; he believes that the culture of the Middle Ages was possessed of a unified sensibility from which virtually all subsequent developments are fallings away. This is not only a myth, and a shockingly unhistorical one in the bargain; it is rather heartless as well, and in such passages Foucault momentarily forgets that madmen are human beings and not metaphors for poetry.

Madness and Civilization also follows the evolution in Europe of reason and self-consciousness and demonstrates how, in the course of that progress, madness was transformed from an objective to a subjective state. It demonstrates analogously how society internalized madness by confining it within soundproof walls. "Subjectivity," "self-consciousness," "internality"—these terms come to Foucault from Hegel, who used them to describe the growth of freedom. Foucault turns them inside out, and applies them with a quasi-Freudian twist; to his way of thinking Western society performed what amounted to an act of repression in an effort to rid itself of madness, and I suspect that Foucault hopes that the repression will be removed. He may not have long to wait.

Foucault's work is, in addition, a study of the growth of secularization. For the Middle Ages the madman was a sacred object. He was both cursed and inspired with demonic truths; he was a manifestation of God's judgment of the world and a symbol of things to come. History divested the madman of his holy rags and made him into what he is today, only a madman, a poor fellow who is very sick in the head. It was Hegel once again who described modern history as the secularization of the spiritual. Foucault would agree with the accuracy of this description but not with the positive judgment it implies. In his view secular reason is almost wholly positivistic and barren of content; its triumph over madness was won through denial and constraint. As reason and unreason ceased to confront each other, Foucault's argument suggests, reason was increasingly cut off from one of its chief sources of strength, its dialectical counterpart. Whether one agrees with Foucault's thesis or the tendency of his mind, a point of considerable importance is being made here.

Madness and Civilization shows how madness, bit by bit, lost all its metaphysical and occult powers, how it was demystified. Max Weber was fond of saying that the fate of our times was characterized in Schiller's phrase "the disenchantment of the world" (*die Entzauberung der Welt*). This magisterial epigram owes much of its force to its ambiguity; it fully expresses both the emancipation and the attrition which have accompanied reason's historical transformation of reality. It is not being harshly critical of Foucault to remark that in the present work he responds only to the attrition. Given the difficult nature of his undertaking, it is hard to imagine what other possible attitude he could have taken.

Although I have been dealing with that part of Foucault's analysis which is conducted at a very high level of generality, it should not be concluded that his book is barren of historical substance. On the contrary, it is full of the most valuable kind of specific insights. Here, for example, is a typical instance. "For the nineteenth century, the initial model of madness would be to believe oneself to be God, while for the preceding centuries it had been to deny God." A radical transformation of sensibility is captured in such a remark. And Foucault's work should have a considerable effect on the way the literature of the eighteenth century is conventionally written about and taught. For he demonstrates with abundant clarity that the age's desperate insistence on the values associated with reason was accompanied by an awareness—however muted it may have been—that society itself might also become a madhouse. Nevertheless, Foucault's work is not to be understood within the usual categories of intellectual or social history. At one point he describes his method as "the archeology of knowledge"; and at another he states that he has attempted to write "the archeology of that silence" in which madness has been immured. What he has actually written, however, is a phenomenology of madness and of its historical confrontation with several of the faces of reason. He has attempted exhaustively to describe, and dramatize from within, the appearances ascribed to madness during the last five hundred years. He has not, however, attempted to explain why this all happened or what it all means—if we think of explanation as involving something more than minutely detailed representation and internal analysis.

He has not done so because he does not, in the first place, believe in the validity of such kinds of explanation; and in the second, he does not believe that madness or unreason can be explained. For him it is both a fundamental and ultimate category of human existence, and its utterances reveal ultimate truths. And at this point it seems to me relevant to say that Foucault has written a history of the devil's party, and knows it, and that *Madness and Civilization* is a kind of contemporary version of *The Marriage of Heaven and Hell*. Here is Foucault's Descartes, who in order to be "secured against the dazzlement of the madman" "closes his eyes and plugs up his ears the better to see the true brightness of essential daylight." Whom does this ironically drawn philosopher resemble except Blake's typical modern man who "has closed himself up, till he sees all things thro' narrow chinks of his cavern"? The Christ whom Foucault is interested in was the Christ who honored and sanctified madness, "who chose to be surrounded by lunatics, demoniacs, madmen, the tempted and the possessed," who was a scandal to the world, and whose own madness was his glory. How far is this from the antinomian Jesus of Blake's devil, who states that "no virtue can exist without breaking these ten commandments," and that "Jesus was all virtue; and acted from impulse, not from rules"? Indeed, the interplay of reason and madness in Foucault's history is hardly to be distinguished from the dialectic of Heaven and Hell, Reason and Energy, in Blake. And Foucault's imagery of confinement and sequestration is equally integral to Blake's vision of the modern world.

I have instituted this comparison not so much to demonstrate the astonishing and perennial modernity of Blake as to suggest the direction in which Foucault's thinking moves. He is concerned to articulate the "truth" of madness and direct our attention to "the sovereign enterprise of unreason." It is difficult to determine just what this truth and this enterprise are, if they are anything more than the principal generalities of Nietzschean and existentialist discourse—namely, that existence cannot be ethically justified; that life has no rational meaning, is founded on nothing, suspended over nothing, and passes away into nothing; that it is a mad world we inhabit and create, and that reason in its effort to defecate the world of its madness has if anything made it even madder, turning the earth itself into a universal madhouse. These are among the gravest and most poignant contentions of modern thought, but Foucault implies that madness is something more than the sum of such assertions. In criticizing the modern institution of the asylum he states that it "substituted for the free terror of madness the stifling anguish of responsibility." One can agree with the second part of this assertion without assenting to the first. For Foucault does not simply mean that madness was at one time unchained and unconfined; he means that madness is really a form of freedom. To advance such an unqualified statement, even within the context of the dialectics of Blake and Nietzsche, is to precipitate oneself into a swamp of hopelessly reversible propositions. For if reason is only constraint and madness freedom, then it is equally plausible to affirm without modification that reason is freedom and madness total impotence. (Passion is slavery, said Spinoza; our instinctual drives are conservative, circular, and tyrannical, added Freud.) Moreover, at such points—as when he also speaks of "the serene world of mental illness"

—Foucault is at his most literary and rationalistic, and furthest removed from experience. Thus, although Foucault discusses *King Lear*, he has no way of explaining why Lear should cry, "O! let me not be mad, not mad, sweet heaven: Keep me in temper; I would not be mad!" In the urgencies of his argument, Foucault himself occasionally loses sight of certain existential realities: the anguish of mental affliction, the quiet despair of psychosis, the often unspeakable agonies suffered by those who are the victims of their own imaginations and fears—all of these sometimes appear in his text as chimeras, pure contrivances of consciousness. Inheritor of the great tradition of rationalism and in rebellion against that tradition, Foucault nonetheless regularly reveals its famous indifference to concrete experience.

Still, Foucault is genuinely in favor of freedom; it is more precise to say, perhaps, he is opposed to authority, particularly the authority of physicians and psychiatrists. One cannot take issue with him here. No one who is at all acquainted with the history of the medical profession will be inclined to disagree with the notion that the personal and moral authority attributed to and arrogated by physicians has been and continues to be out of all proportion to their knowledge or their powers; or that the conceit of the profession as a whole is nowhere more clearly revealed than in the history of the treatment of mental afflictions. Foucault's ambivalence to Freud is in part a result of Freud's having been a physician, although, as Foucault himself states, Freud's use of his professional authority was of a new and inspired order.

What Foucault is finally against, however, is the authority of reason. In this connection he is correct to regard Freud as a presiding figure; in his work the great intellectual systems of explanation invented by the nineteenth century reach some kind of culmination. From Hegel and the historians, to Marx and Darwin and on through Freud and Weber and Durkheim, the nineteenth century brought forth a series of vast analytical systems through which history, society, and the individual self were made to appear as complex, coherent wholes. The principle of coherence in these systems was essentially a historical one, the belief that causal and genetic explanations were in some ultimate sense binding. The methods of these systems all finally referred to reason, although their content was almost always the world of unreason. Although he knows and thoroughly understands such systems, Foucault no longer has any use for them or any belief in their authority. They have been around for a long time now; they are no longer fresh or vivid or surprising; there is much that they have failed to explain and much that they have explained inadequately or incorrectly. The great historical systems have themselves become part of the history that they both invented and transformed.

In this Foucault represents an important tendency in advanced contemporary thought. In his despair of the transcendent powers of the rational intellect Foucault embodies one abiding truth of our time—the failure of the nineteenth century to make good on its promises. This is partly why he turns at the end of the mad and half-mad artists and thinkers of the modern age, to Goya and Sade, Hölderlin and Nietzsche, Van Gogh, Nerval, *et al.* Through their utterances the world is arraigned; mediated by their madness, the language of their art dramatizes the culpability of the world and forces it to recognize itself and reorder its consciousness. One cannot in good conscience deny the force and the truth of these observations; they catch a reality of the intellectual situation of the present moment—a moment that is coming to think of itself as post-everything, post-modern, post-history, post-sociology, post-psychology. Yet I should like to enter one reservation, a reservation which Foucault's remarkable work brings continually to mind. Post-everything as we are, we are in the position of having rejected the great nineteenth- and twentieth-century systems of thought without having superseded them, of having outworn them without having transcended them with new truth, or discovered anything of comparable magnitude to take their place. I take this to reveal not so much the desperate situation of intellectual life. For even as we reject the large categories invented by the past, we continue to live on their capital. Those bearded old men left us an inheritance so rich that—short of blowing it all up—we can hardly fritter it away. It is this condition of unprecedented affluence that has permitted Foucault to write a brilliant work about the history of psychology while rejecting psychology itself, and without feeling any compunction to subsume the repudiated categories within some more inclusive and deeper set of analytic ideas. It has also permitted him to write a work about the relation of reason and madness which is consciously and in itself an instance of the phenomenon it is discussing, and which rejects transcendence as a game not worth the effort. This kind of intellectual relaxation, this easy living of the spirit—in which, I might repeat, most of us participate—is only possible in an age which is aware of how much it still has to fall back on.

(1964; 1966)

Awakening from the Nightmare? Notes on the Historical Novel

The impulse to regard genres of literature or kinds of art as if they were living species of the natural world is apparently irresistible. The analogy to biological evolution is self-evidently attractive and convenient. On this explanatory model, types or kinds of literature rise out of variations within other types, go through their own development, adapt to changing circumstances, give rise in turn to further mutated forms, and perish when their species-life or powers of adaptability are exhausted. To no genre of literature has this kind of description been more generally and freely applied than the novel. In its alleged contemporary decline, accordingly, the novel is implicitly compared to one of those species doomed to extinction—the "loose, baggy monster" of Henry James's famous characterizing phrase becomes materialized in detail as a race of metaphorical dinosaurs or cultural mastodons. Furthermore, although the species itself may be on the way out, its individual members probably have no awareness that this is so, and go on about their browsing or novelizing as if it were everlastingly business as usual and time must never have a stop.

If such a statement has some suggestive value in connection with the novel generally, it seems to me to take on increased cogency when we apply it to a specific sub-genre of the novel. I am thinking of the historical novel, a variety of fiction whose own historical development and career can be set forth with relative precision. Despite minor pedantries and cavilings literary historians tend to agree that the historical novel came into existence in 1814 with the publication of *Waverley* by Sir Walter Scott. The sub-genre was from the outset a great popular success, and by the turn of the century literally thousands of historical novels had been published in English alone. The flood has not noticeably slackened, and right up until the present a practically uncountable number of novels, romances, or fictional narratives that call themselves historical continue to be written, published, sold, and even, apparently, read.

In one sense all this concerted activity of production, distribution, and consumption has little to do with whether the historical novel as a kind of literature is still actually alive—whether it remains capable of representing experience in authentic and significant ways, whether the construction of a fictional historical world conveys meaning to the present in a manner that no other form of human expression can. If we look to the past, we can find an instructive parallel. For a period of nearly a century—from the end of the eighteenth century until about 1890—almost nothing of lasting value was written for the English stage. From the lapsing of Sheridan's career as a writer until the appearance of Oscar Wilde and Shaw, the English drama was as good as dead. Nevertheless, although not a single important play for the stage was written throughout that extremely long era, playwrights, producers, directors, actors, and audiences were continually and unremittingly hard at work. Apparently the cultural-economic activity of the world of the theater did not and could not by itself produce dramatic literature of decided significance. At the same time it would be at least misleading to assert that there are no important connections·between an art whose historic origins are popular, whose development has always been affected by the general life of society, and the economic and social life conducted by that society at particular moments in its history. There are connections and causalities, but they are not simple or unmediated. Economic-cultural activity, it may be true, does not by itself bring forth creativity or great works of literature or art; by the same token, however, although art or literature are in some measure autonomous, they are *not* so in the sense of being unrelated to or independent of the contexts out of which they arise.

All the same there has since the very beginning been something especially equivocal about the historical novel. Scott started out by writing an impressive series of novels about the Scottish eighteenth and seventeenth centuries. In 1819, however, he published *Ivanhoe*, the first of his many novels about the English and European Middle Ages and Renaissance. In these works, which became and remained even more popular and influential than those of his novels that were set in the more recent local past, Scott invented the horse opera, or more properly the horse-and-clanking-armor opera. From that time onward, historical romance, historical pageant, historical travelogue were equally entitled to make their claims to novelistic standing. From that time onward, the historical novel, like the novel itself—whose larger developments it generally tends to condense and parody—has evolved along several lines and at several levels of discourse. Along with the serious and enduring historical narratives of, say, Balzac or Dickens or Tolstoy or Flaubert or Faulkner, there has regularly coexisted that steady flow of kitsch, light reading, exotic tales of adventure in historical drag, antiquarian anecdotes accompanied by dialogue, and popular biographies of world-historical figures arranged in narrative form and furnished with appropriate domestic and sexual details—all of these latter in their numerous permutations making up what most people think of when the term historical novel is referred to. On one of their sides they are nothing more than part of the entertainment industry, an oddly venerable part when you come to think of it. Nevertheless, even today, when the literary packaging of junk in velveteen breeches and the recycling of garbage in togas seem proportionately greater than ever before, one does now and then come across serious efforts. William Styron's *The Confessions of Nat Turner* of a few years ago represents such an effort, however adversely one may judge of its success. As in another context, and another sub-variety of the tradition, does Thomas Pynchon's *Gravity's Rainbow*.

If we ask why people read and continue to read historical novels, the answers are likely to be as diverse as the sub-types of the form itself and lead out in all directions. Serious readers turn to novels about the past for the same reasons that they read novels about the world in which they live. Their engagement in the present and their desire to understand in its fullness and texture the world of the present prompt them to turn to contemporary representations of the life of the past. In the words of the Marxist critic George Lukács, they are interested in those fictional and imaginative representations that bring the past to life as the prehistory of the present, as its necessary concrete precondition. Or as the reflex of this interest, they read such novels as *Gravity's Rainbow* because in them the present is itself represented as history. In either sense such readers are expressing the opposite attitude to that affirmed by Dr.

Cornelius, professor of history and protagonist of Thomas Mann's great story "Disorder and Early Sorrow." Dr. Cornelius was drawn to the study of history precisely because for him it was finished and done with, closed off, completed and inert, dead, and dead in its perfection, like a jewel or a scarab or a Grecian urn. Such a determination is only a few steps removed from the impulse of those who seek to learn or read about the past as an escape from the present, as reverie, fantasy, or idle wish-fulfillment. Everything bad that can be said about using art or literature as an escape from the reality of the present has already been said—I should only like to add the following reservations. Strictly speaking, there is no such thing as an escape from the present; there are only diverse modes of present existence. Moreover, those who do attempt to flee may at least become aware that there is something unpleasant that they are trying to get away from; and our responsibility is primarily to examine and determine what it is that brings about such efforts at flight rather than to condemn those who flee.

There are a number of further motives that merit notice. Some people read historical novels for the same reasons that they read serious history—to find constructions and representations of human experience which render that experience coherent and meaningful within certain specified categories and terms. Others by contrast read historical novels *instead* of reading history; such readers often seek to educate themselves painlessly and to acquire information at cut rates. For them, historical novels are more or less to history as Classic Comics are (or were) to literature. Other readers are driven by curiosity about the "otherness" of characters, personages, and groups of people who lived in the past, who spoke and ate and dressed so differently from us, yet who are at the same time our cultural ancestors. This tendency is the obverse side of the attitude held implicitly by many that history is essentially a family affair; as

Aldous Huxley once ironically remarked, "all the more or less picturesque figures of history are our cultural uncles, our cultural aunts." To domesticate or familialize the past is to turn history into something quaint and cozy and comfortable. Such an attitude typically discovers a trifling and reductive "inner secret" or cause in what is traditionally taken as historically momentous: e.g., Napoleon had heartburn and therefore the battle of Waterloo was lost. Or, collaterally: The Thirty Years War was brought to an end by the unrecorded actions of an obscure youth, unknown to history, who . . . etc. Maneuverings of this kind tend to de-historicize historical experience.

Consider, in this regard, the current best seller *Burr*. What Gore Vidal has done is to represent historical experience in the pseudopersonal, meretriciously intimate fashion of the Hollywood gossip column. In this imagination the great personages of history are all transformed into celebrities or mountebanks (or both), while the most petty, squalid, and inconsequential details of personal scandal—of spite, bitchery, and ambition in their meanest forms—are by inference identified as the real stuff of which history is made. The cynicism of this view is no more than simple-minded liberal idealism turned inside out—certainly no improvement on it. It is not to be confused with the Olympian skepticism of Gibbon, who could assert that history was little more than "the register of the crimes, follies, and misfortunes of mankind." For Gibbon also remained responsive to the magnitude of the issues at stake in the historical drama and to the stature of its principal actors. In his hands the historical drama never became show biz. Moreover, his sense that history violates so much in man that protests against injustice never deteriorated into the cheerful nihilism that in Vidal's work is the substitute for historical judgment.

Vidal's kind of nonsense suggests that although history may continue to draw and fascinate us, it also acts to arouse our anxiety. One of the most common defenses against the anxiety created by history (and our sneaking awareness that we do not understand it) is to trivialize or falsely personalize it, just as one of the most common defenses against the anxiety created by the consciousness of real and intractable human cultural differences is to invoke a factitious universal, something on the order, say, of the U.N.'s "family of man."

It is not difficult to understand why this should be so. The inception of the modern sense of history and the rise of the historical novel are inseparable developments. Both are among the results of two of the greatest upheavals that Western civilization has ever undergone—the simultaneous and convergent occurrence of the French and Industrial Revolutions. The modern world was brought to birth in these world-transforming events. One of the distinctive features of this new world was to be found in the uninterrupted persistence in it of rapid large-scale social change. And the modern awareness that history itself is a continuous process that leaves virtually nothing unaltered and no one untouched, that reaches into the life of every individual no matter where or who he is, has its origins at this time as well. The exhilarations and anxieties, the nostalgias and expectations, the insecurities and opportunities that these new conditions of permanent transformation evoked were all brought to expression in this new historical consciousness—or historical sensibility—and in one of its principal by-products, the historical novel. In our own time we have witnessed in this connection one further notable development. At some point near the middle of the twentieth century, the rate and scale of technological and social change underwent a quantum jump. Among the many paradoxical and disconcerting consequences of this alteration in the quality of historical change has been an appreciable tendency toward obliterating the sense of history that rapid large-scale social change had itself originally brought into existence. Or to put it another way, the extraordinary nature of contemporary history has worked to destroy the sense of history. The epic character of social change in contemporary society has outstripped the capacity of historical consciousness to comprehend it. That consciousness in its bewilderment and defeat has in turn taken to dismantling itself.

In America this development has been peculiarly and poignantly visible. To begin with, the sense of the historical past, the awareness of history and of histories, has always led a relatively precarious existence here. The nineteenth- and early twentieth-century genteel snobberies about our American culture desert and historical vacuum had this much point: that the monuments, the detritus, the archives, the material leavings of the past—all the *visibilia* that dot and clot the European landscape—were simply not to be found here and were therefore not part of a world that Americans internalized. With the partial exception of the Old South—where Sir Walter Scott's notions of honor and chivalry were regarded with such piety that Mark Twain once blamed him for causing the Civil War—Americans in general have had to do without the kind of inherited cultural history that many Europeans have enjoyed and that many others have wanted to rid themselves of. This situation has produced any number of anomalies and contradictions. For example, Americans were and are quite capable of devouring historical romances and seeing limitless numbers of historical movies while at the same time believing with Henry Ford that history is the bunk. Or more recently there is the phenomenon known as urban renewal, in which the term "renewal" regularly means destruction. Our cities are a material part of our history; one way in which we preserve that history is by razing it to the ground.

More recently still, certain pertinent developments in education can be observed to have occurred. The changes I am referring to have to do with the history and social

science curricula in both secondary schools and under-
graduate higher education. These changes are being instituted in both Europe and America, though no one, naturally,
has gone so far so quickly as we have. What they amount
to is the final abandonment of the old model of teaching
and conceiving of history. The old model was itself put
together in many versions, but the basic scheme ran essentially as follows. It was founded primarily on the assumption
—itself long since rendered obsolete—of a classical education. History began with the Greeks and Romans (with a
sidelong glance at the Jews and the Bible; but that was
Religion), moved on to the Middle Ages and Reformation,
sailed off on the voyages of discovery and conquest in both
the New World and the East, and returned to the climaxes
of the bourgeois revolutions in England and France, the
consolidation of the great nation-states, and the founding
of the modern world. From there on, specific national or
group histories were fed with varying degrees of consistency
and continuity into the larger scheme.

Such a conception of history has been accused, with
justice, of cultural myopia, of snobbery, of ethnocentrism.
And to be sure there was a touch of the absurd in the idea
of teaching nineteenth-century young Englishmen or Bos-
tonians to take Spartans or Republican Romans as models
for the conduct of personal, moral, and political life. The
absurdity grew more palpable when the young Anglo-
American gentlemen began to be replaced as pupils by the
sons of peasant immigrants from Italy and Russia and the
Balkans, and the sons and grandsons of former slaves. Part
of the absurdity was to be found in the "irrelevance" of the
Greeks or the Romans and the Middle Ages to the present,
to the dynamic, mobile life of modern society. Part of it was
also to be found in the reversed yet related circumstance
that the "history"—such as it was—that was taught was
torn out of its proper contexts and applied ahistorically to
the present. As there was also something patently unreason-

able in the inflation of one particular tradition of historical development into *the* tradition, the single line of advance that superseded and subsumed all others. The absurdities in question are the absurdities of provinciality; their passing need not be mourned. What has as a rule taken their place, however, seems at least as problematical. In numbers of high schools and community colleges what has been substituted for the old required courses in history are assorted projects of study alternatively called social studies or area studies or cultural studies or thematic studies. Students in Scarsdale or Seattle are no longer subjected to the tortures of the Counter-Reformation or the protracted obscurities of the Long Parliament. When they aren't working at the here and now, what thirteen- and fourteen-year-olds are often put to doing is to "study" an entire society and culture: "Chinese Society and Culture," for example, is one currently popular topic good for a semester or even a year's activity.

Now, there is nothing inherently amiss with China and the Chinese—or with the study of them both. Or with Japan and the Japanese, or India and the Indians, for that matter. They are all great historic cultures and make their individually appropriate demands upon an educated consciousness. There is, nevertheless, the question of whether in replacing the old model of historical studies with this newly modernized form we aren't substituting the provinciality of cultural relativism for the provinciality of ethnocentrism and Western cultural imperialism. One says this within the awareness that cultural relativism is itself one of the consequences of the great nineteenth-century age of history and historiography (along with the historical novel). One says it as well within the awareness that we are all cultural relativists, that very few of us today can assert the superiority of Western, rationalized, industrial society and its values over non-industrialized, non-rationality-driven societies and their values with anything resembling the confidence that inspired our cultural ancestors of a hundred years ago. And it is only right that the unthinking certitudes and arrogant assumptions of cultural superiority associated with the era of imperialism should disappear along with the dissolution of the old empires themselves. Nevertheless, although we are all equally favored children of that great cultural relativist in the sky, and although every ethnic group has the right to claim the priority of its own study for itself, this is not the same as saying that all productions of all cultures are equally worthwhile, equally excellent, that there is no way of judging as between some things and other things, or that there are no standards of value that apply between cultures and what they create, let alone within them and what they create.

Another way of regarding some of these changes is to describe them within the contexts of the academic and intellectual worlds. In these spheres of activity as well there has been a shift in both dominant perspectives and in the kind of authority that certain kinds of discourse exercise. In brief, there has been a tendency to replace history with anthropology. We can observe this in the intellectual world at large, in which the structural anthropology of Lévi-Strauss has opposed itself to and won adherents away from the various Marxist and historicist groupings in France and elsewhere. And we can observe it as well in the academic world, in which an increasing number of historians are taking to using the data and adapting the methods of modern anthropology to historical topics and problems. At the same time, there is little if any evidence in this connection of a mutuality of influence.

A corresponding development has occurred within the historical novel itself. Within recent years a sizable number of historical novels have been published that are essentially or largely anthropological in both subject matter and point of view. In some measure they can be thought of as prehistorical novels. Naturally, they come in different forms and exist at different degrees of intelligence and difficulty. I should like briefly to examine three of them, for they concretely dramatize and represent in intimate detail the kinds of changes that I have so far described only generally and abstractly.

The first of these, *The Inheritors* by William Golding, was published about ten years ago. It is a very clever, and sometimes moving, imaginative tour de force. The chief persons of the narrative are a group of eight Neanderthal men, perhaps the last of their kind. The world in which this dwindling microsociety lives is invaded by men who come from a historically and culturally more "advanced" variety of a human group. The meeting of the two results in the abrupt end of the Neanderthal men and their world. Almost the entire book, however, is arranged so that the narration seems to be composed from the point of view of the Neanderthal men as they look out over themselves, their world, and the "others," or "new people" as they call the group that is about to make them extinct. At the very end of the book, after they have been extinguished, the point of view changes to that of the new people, the inheritors of the title, whom we instantly recognize (if we have not long since) as ourselves or, what is next to the same thing, our direct ancestors.

Golding spends most of his time in working up the vanished world of the Neanderthal man. This world, as he constructs it through the language within which he imagines Neanderthal man to have existed, is intensely physical, animistic, unpredictable, and vivid. It is not a world characterized by a high degree of either differentiation or integration. Golding's Neanderthal men find it very difficult to concentrate mentally upon any object and are easily distracted from their short span of attention. They think, or feel, more or less collectively, and are intensely social in a small herdlike way. These harmless and amiable creatures have virtually no sense of causality, or of a connected sequence of events; as a result, their reality is essentially unstable and unmoored: it is continually bewildering and continually too complex for them to grasp; and they have no idea of the future, of the steady extension of the present into a different dimension that is nonetheless continuous with it. Though they have a language, they find it excruciatingly difficult to translate perceptions, images, and memories into articulate speech; and it is almost impossible for them to distinguish between the mental and physical aspects of their experience and thus of the world. Apart from fire they have no technology. They are food gatherers and scavengers, not hunters; they eat the meat they scavenge from predators only out of necessity, preferring fruits and berries which in the Northern Europe of the inter-glacial eras were in very short supply. In short, their abilities to cope with, adapt to, or dominate the circumstances and challenges that chance or nature throw in their way are extremely limited, and they are in fact doomed.

By contrast, the inheritors are well advanced along the evolutionary highway. They are a broken-off part of a hunting tribe, and their totemic social organization and religion represent a degree of complexity that far surpasses the simple collective animism of the Neanderthalers. They have an advanced hunting technology, which includes weapons, poisons, boats and ropes and sails. They wear clothing to protect their hairless, furless skin and to hide the nakedness of which they are already ashamed; at the same time they adorn themselves with bones and stones and other jewelry, and practice the arts of plastic and dramatic representation as religious and magical aids in their hunting. They are aggressive and warlike and cruel; they are also articulate, imaginative, and sexy. They practice blood sacrifice and mutilation as rituals before hunting, and alcohol, drunkenness, and something like orgies as rituals after hunting. They have already invented the ideas of property and money—of things that have a price on them—and are in a continual state of conflict and disputation with one another. This state is generalized and extended to the world at large; when they meet the Neanderthal men they immediately think of them as devils or demons—as anything but members of the same or nearly the same species—and promptly set about to exterminate them. They have already developed individual consciousnesses and a distinctive sense of personal self-hood; they experience the privacy of conscious personal identity—and along with it the loneliness, isolation, and anxiety of a single and unsharable personal existence. They are the future.

What Golding has rather successfully done is to bring into dramatic confrontation two species of the primate genus Homo. He has also juxtaposed two conceptions of culture and of the nature of man. It is almost as if he were staging a meeting between the harmless natural man of Jean-Jacques Rousseau's great second discourse *On the Origins of Inequality* and man in the state of nature as he was earlier depicted by Thomas Hobbes in *Leviathan*. In Hobbes's view the state of nature was a condition of universal war, and life therein solitary, poor, nasty, brutish, and short. When these two models of humanity and its world come into vital contact, the outcome is deadly and never in doubt. Yet part of the point in such an imaginary confrontation is to emphasize still more pointedly the aggressivity, cruelty, and individual isolation of the inheritors, who are ourselves; and to emphasize as well what we have as a species and a group sacrificed in order to develop in the ways we have. In this connection Golding's novel still shares one of the incidental virtues of the traditional historical novel. Frequently the conflict in a historical novel is imagined from or out of a partial identification with the losing side; it is written from a double perspective, and the reader is invited to take part in that perspective. When such an imagination succeeds, the reader is able to achieve a sense of what is lost and has gone under in the historical and evolutionary process—and in the human choices that propel it—as much as what is new, what has been gained, and where the future is taking us. This is part of an explanation of how it is that many of the best historical novels are written by novelists who ambivalently identify with lost causes—such as Scott with his Highlanders and eighteenth-century lairds, or Faulkner (and other Southern novelists) with the Old South, or Royalists, both English and French, in general.

Yet *The Inheritors* is really a pre-historical novel, a kind of archaeological or anthropological (or anthropolitical) science fiction. Golding begins it with an epigraph describing Neanderthal man that is taken from H. G. Wells's *Outline of History*. Wells is of course the great inventive figure in modern science fiction—that kind of fiction which tends to imagine a future that is beyond history, a past that exists before history, as well as other worlds and dimensions that exist outside of history. And the extremely popular *Outline of History* was one of the early important efforts to collapse historical perspective and the historical record into the perspectives of evolution, biology, paleography, anthropology, and technology. That effort is still being carried forward today.

The second novel I want to discuss is the recently published *The Death of Attila* by Cecelia Holland. This work deserves to be placed somewhere near the bottom (or is it the top?) of anyone's list of dreadful books, and I shall try to be mercifully brief about its infirmities. What is interesting about this novel, however, is that although it is so exceedingly feeble, it is animated (insofar as it is animated at all) by a series of conceptions that are remarkably similar to those at work in *The Inheritors*. *The Death of Attila* is set in Pannonia (Austria/Yugoslavia) in about 453 A.D. It is about the climax and the end of the Hun domination of Europe and about the end of Hun society and culture. It attempts to do this through dramatizing the meeting, friendship, and final parting of Dietric, a young German and son of the king of the Gepids—a tribe under the rule of Attila—and Tacs, a semi-crippled Hun horseman and warrior, a gifted linguist and quasi-outcast among his fellows. At the apex of their power, the Huns are at the same time decadents. Unified in conquest by Attila, they are also a dying culture. Attila muses to himself about

> how the Huns had once covered the plains, hordes of warriors, each clan with its own king . . . as numerous then as the Ostrogoths or the Franks now. Since that time something had happened to them. Gradually the Hiung [Huns] were dying. Sickness that left Germans healthy as before killed Hiung, and Hiung women bore children and the children lived a year or two years and died. The young men went on raids and into wars and to join the armies of the Romans and were killed, or they married the women of Germans and their children were Germans, not Hiung.

Once a society of great horsemen, the Huns have forgotten how to hunt, allowing their dependents to feed them. They have let their old tribal religion and its magic lapse. They have lost their mission as a heroic, conquering people. When Attila suddenly dies, there is nothing to hold them together any longer. Their subject Germans flee, and the Huns disperse back into their old disunified existence of intra-tribal feud, bloodshed, and rapine—they are precipitated back into the Hobbesian world out of which they had first arisen, but this time without strength or numbers. At the end they are wiped out by their former bondsmen in a brutal battle in which the Huns have no chance.

Although Cecelia Holland's interest in the Huns is ostensibly anthropological, in the novelistic sense I have been discussing, that interest is expressed in the most naïve and innocent way, and to the most unfortunate effects. She makes no visible effort to disguise or transform her own foreign sensibility and modern consciousness, but leaves them there uninflected and in the open, and indeed unconsciously imposes them on the characters in the novel. Here, for example, is her representation of how a Hun ruminates over whether he can bury a dead companion, and related matters:

> Through the early afternoon he tried to argue himself into it, although the taboos and rituals of their people required three witnesses to bury a warrior . . . he switched to thinking of how he would catch frogs to eat, once he reached the river. The frog was one of his totems, and eating its meat made him agile.

However Huns may have thought, you can bet your last totem and taboo that they. didn't think like this. "Natives" don't walk around spouting anthropology, any more than bourgeois gentlemen walk around speaking prose. The historical sensibility revealed in such a passage is actually pre-Scott and ahistorical; more properly, perhaps, it is post-historical. Or there is this, imputed to the consciousness of the German king as he watches a group of Parthians in a marketplace: "Some people said that the Parthians traded in other than cloth: opium and hashish and other filth, smuggled in between layers of silk." Although there can be no doubt that German kings in the fifth century had plenty to worry about, it is safe to say that the drug trade was not a "problem" for them—or for anyone else at that time anywhere. This witless projection of modern problems back onto the past, this trafficking in the stuff that makes up our daily newspapers, is in fact anti-historical. Many if not most "historical" novels are.

Like *The Inheritors* and like other historical novels of this tendency, *The Death of Attila* is about two disparate and alien cultures at their point of meeting. It is about what can be communicated across cultural barriers and about what cannot. Its very problematic—the notion that there may be ethnic irreconcilabilities—identifies it as a characteristic work of the present period of modern history. Composed from the point of view of cultural relativism, it represents two mutually estranged and antagonistic cultures, neither of which possesses a sense of the culturally relative. It orchestrates that representation by dramatically contrasting the insurmountable differences in values held by the two societies—in particular their religious values. The Huns are tribal pagans and believe in demons and demiurges; as opposed to the Christian Germans and Romans they have no idea of a supreme deity and no notion of a life after death. The central part of the novel is given over to a long series of discussions between a Hun Shaman and a Roman monk, which are there for the purpose of illustrating these differences. It is while reading these parts of the novel that a light began to dawn for me. The Shaman is a clever and mysterious man; he half disbelieves in his own magic, yet is the most successful of all medicine men. He uses tricks to fool his clients, yet he isn't sure that this faking isn't part of being an authentic and real Shaman. At some point along in here it suddenly struck me that all these passages about the Shaman and his art are lifted bodily from Lévi-Strauss' famous essay, "The Sorcerer and His Magic."

Now, there is nothing out of line in a novelist doing his homework or research or pilfering—whichever description one prefers. He has to get what he knows from somewhere; and besides, great writers are often gifted thieves—take Shakespeare, for one. The pertinent questions have to do with what one does to and what one does with what one takes. In the case of *The Death of Attila* the answer is less than nothing. The material borrowed from Lévi-Strauss is not transmuted in the least—except in the sense that it is drastically simplified. Moreover, if one reads Lévi-Strauss' essay with its haunting evocation of the impenetrable mystery and opacity of experience, one is in fact much closer to literature—to what novels do or could once do—than one ever is in *The Death of Attila*. In this work we have a slightly new wrinkle: the novel as kitsch anthropology. The sociologist Leo Lowenthal once pointed out that the writer of popular biographies of great historical personages is the supplier of sociology for mass consumption. In a similar way novels of the kind we have been discussing serve among other things as a kind of anthropology for large-scale consumption.

One further theme that is shared by novels of this kind has been described in a term developed concurrently by the ethnologist Konrad Lorenz and the psychoanalyst Erik Erikson. The term is called pseudo-speciation, and it refers to the fact that in contrast to most other species of animals, the different sub-groups that make up the human species tend regularly to regard each other as members of other species. One of the many consequences of this tendency is that if one group or society thinks of itself as human and of other groups as non-human, infra-human or sub-human there is very little to inhibit it from doing violence of any kind to any group it so regards. The paradox that this circumstance raises is that what makes us so pernicious and devastating as a species is also what makes us so inexhaustibly interesting—and that the vast range of human cultures with their different languages, cosmogonies, religions, mythologies, and arts is also inseparable from this tendency of men to develop in groups that think of themselves as exclusively human or essentially superior to others; humanity's rich cultural and social plurality is itself one of the specific means through which pseudo-speciation develops and operates.

This interest figures substantially as well in the third of the novels I have chosen, Mary Renault's *The Persian Boy*. This is her second volume about the career of Alexander the Great, and it is terribly boring. It is, however, a recognizable novel and registers about midway between the other two on the Marcus scale for fictions that fail to shake the surface of the earth. It is about Alexander's life from the age of twenty-six until his death and is told from the point of view of Bagoas, his Persian slave-boy, eunuch, catamite, courtesan, and lover. The point of view, in other words, is feminized and is that of private life. It is as if Amelia Sedley were to be the narrator of *Vanity Fair*; and the results are as stirring.

In this novel the tragi-comedy of comparative cultures consists primarily of the juxtaposition of the Persian-Eastern ancient world to the new society of the Macedonian-Greek-Western vision. To the Persians, the Macedonians appear to be "barbarians . . . red-haired savages who paint themselves blue." When Bagoas first sees the beardless Alexander among his followers, he is equally perplexed:

"They had no eunuchs. I was the only one. . . . There was discipline, but not the reverence one expects to surround a king. . . . They called him Alexander, without title, like one of themselves; they laughed aloud in his presence, and far from rebuking them he joined in. . . . It amazed me to find [Alexander's bedroom] not much better than a common captain's, with scarcely room for two."

In turn the free, masculine, and non-deferential Greeks find the Persians with their arts and courtiership and elaborate hierarchies and ceremonials laughable when they are not incomprehensible. And the same thing happens again when we set out to follow Alexander on his conquests, a historical-cultural travelogue through antiquity.

As we move about imaginatively in this unpacified world —the essential *mise en scène* of almost all historical novels —we see that Alexander is a charismatic and world-histori-

cal figure who embodies in his person and behavior something significantly new. What is new is an enlarged idea of
humanity, an inclusive and universalistic conception of our
possibilities.

> "I was mistaught as a boy," he said. "I won't insult you
> with what I was told to think about Persians. . . . The
> truth is that all men are God's children. The excellent
> ones, he makes more his own than the rest; but one
> can find them anywhere."

And he longs to make "one kingdom" out of the human
world. He is in other words a proto-Christian on the one
hand and a proto-Roman on the other. And this notion of
an inclusive unity, indeed of a species-unity, seems to me
to be one of the underlying and informing notions of the
historical novel as a genre, and of its anthropologico-histori-
cal offshoot. The dialectical counterpart to this notion is
the abiding interest in the concrete particularities and diver-
sities of culture, which is the paradoxical way in which our
species makes its universality manifest.

As we follow Mary Renault's narrative of Alexander's
exploits in Asia, we see him fighting in endless battles, plun-
dering defeated foes, and founding many cities—most of
which he names after himself and one of which he names
after Bucephalus, his horse. Hegel once remarked that
Alexander, the hero who brings the Greek world to an end,
was the very type of "youthful individuality." To Mary
Renault he unites in one person the virtues of his two ideal
figures—Achilles, the greatest of warriors, and Cyrus, the
greatest of kings. In this novel we see him continually represented as dramatizing in both action and speech certain
heroic ideals. Among these are martial prowess, bravery,
the impulse to strive continually, the impulse to steadfastly
endure pain and discomfort, the desire for fame, the love
of glory, the passion for honor, the wish to excel extremely,

to be the greatest and mightiest of men. Alexander lives by the classical heroic virtues—which are in large part military and aggressive virtues. And here we come upon further difficulties, for it is precisely these qualities and values that have been most radically discredited in our own time. The history and immediate pre-history of the present era have rendered these military and aggressive virtues less credible, less viable, more vulnerable to disbelief than ever before. The terrible history of our times has made it imperative that such a devaluation should have been undertaken.

Yet this discrepancy of values must also figure as part of our sense of why the historical novel in all its forms has come upon bad times. Its bankruptcy is part of the bankruptcy in our culture of the heroic ideal in its older forms. And when people read historical fiction, one of the many things they are doing is exercising their yearning for an older and simpler world, a culture in which these martial notions of courage and honor and a right side and a wrong side still held firm. And when they read historical novels in the anthropological versions I have been talking about, they are disclosing an impulse as well toward an earlier or simpler stage of cultural and social evolution—a stage in which these same aggressive virtues were still respectable possibilities. They are expressing that impulse and, as I have tried to show, are simultaneously acknowledging some critical awareness of its limitations. The historical novel in all its forms and varieties may be currently bankrupt; that does not prevent people in great numbers from continuing to write and read such novels; and it does not prevent them from needing to find some way to express those impulses that the historical novel can no longer satisfy, if indeed it ever could.

(1973)

Literature and Social Theory:
Starting In with George Eliot

1

George Eliot and Dickens represent the two great instances in English fiction of the middle nineteenth century in which consciousness may be observed as realizing itself in the maximum possibilities available to it at that moment in time. These possibilities are realized in different ways and, I believe, toward different ends; it would be both excessive and excessively symmetrical to affirm that they represent polar opposites or antitheses, although it remains nonetheless true that these two writers diverge radically from one another and that their work embodies two extremes, even if it may not be possible to define with adequate precision how the character of those extremities is constituted.

I begin at what, for a literary critic, I take to be a rarefied altitude because it is my sense that the subject requires it. Whether this flight in space will result in anything more than anoxia and the bends will only be determined after we have returned to earth and have tried to put the observations and abstractions arrived at from a distance to close and concrete use. In this preliminary and tentative exploration, I should like to examine certain of the modes, methods, and devices through which George Eliot establishes her account of the human world. These fictional, linguistic, and conceptual arrangements and conventions can be demonstrated, I think, as bearing upon the meaning of her novels, upon the novel in the nineteenth century as a whole, and even perhaps upon the idea of the novel itself.

Let us begin, then, at what seems to be an arbitrary point, namely, with the opening paragraphs of George Eliot's first published work of fiction, and the first of the *Scenes of Clerical Life*, "The Sad Fortunes of the Reverend Amos Barton." This is a justly celebrated passage, and I am encouraged to quote it because of its familiarity and because of the wealth of comment it has elicited. It should contain little to surprise us. It starts as follows: "Shepperton Church was a very different-looking building five-and-twenty years ago. To be sure, its substantial stone tower looks at you through its intelligent eye, the clock, with the friendly expression of former days; but in everything else what changes! Now there is a wide span of slated roof flanking the old steeple. . . ." and she goes on throughout the remainder of this introductory paragraph to enumerate with warmth and irony the changes and improvements that have been worked upon the fabric of the parish church within the imaginary interval of a quarter of a century that is the precondition of her imagining and writing this story and that thus becomes the precondition of our reading it. She mentions the new "tall and symmetrical windows," the outer and inner doors with their respective graining and baize-covering, the walls from which the lichen has been cleaned, the new seating-arrangements downstairs and the "ample galleries . . . supported on iron pillars" above. She concludes this catalogue and paragraph by referring to the church-organ, also a new addition, which is played by "a collector of small rents, differentiated by the force of circumstances into an organist," making in her use of the word "differentiated" what today is thought of as an "in" or "ingroup" reference. She is alluding, of course, rapidly, lightly, ironically to those theories of social change that may be summarized by adducing the names of Auguste Comte and Herbert Spencer. The irony, however, is at once nudged back into place by a counterbalancing and reflexive shift in perspective and attack; in the very next clause the differentiated organist "will accompany the alacrity of your departure after the blessing" with his playing. It is the reader himself who now suddenly discovers that he is being gently but firmly prodded in the ribs, although it is not altogether clear why he should all at once find himself on the wrong end of the stick (there are a considerable number of possibilities of meaning in this sentence, which I cannot pause here to discuss). The effect, however, is momentarily to loosen the reader's grip on the sequence of statements through which he has just worked his way and to cause him to look back, if only for a fraction of an instant, to see if he can ascertain the logical or syntactical course which has led him to this uncertainly dislocated and slightly suspended position. And while he is doing so, George Eliot is writing her second paragraph and he is perforce reading along.

The second paragraph is by way of explanation of and comment upon the first. It reads as follows: "Immense improvement! says the well-regulated mind, which unintermittingly rejoices in the New Police, the Tithe Commutation Act, the penny-post, and all guarantees of human advancement, and has no moments when conservative-reforming intellect takes a nap, while imagination does a little Toryism

by the sly, revelling in regret that dear, old, brown, crum-
bling, picturesque inefficiency is everywhere giving place to
spick-and-span new-painted, new-varnished efficiency, which
will yield endless diagrams, plans, elevations, and sections,
but alas! no picture. Mine, I fear, is not a well-regulated
mind: it has an occasional tenderness for old abuses; it
lingers with a certain fondness over the days of nasal clerks
and top-booted parsons, and has a sigh for the departed
shades of vulgar errors. So it is not surprising that I recall
with a fond sadness Shepperton Church as it was in the old
days, with its outer coat of rough stucco, its . . ." etc., etc.
Even the less than attentive reader will understand that these
paragraphs undertake to do more than, as it used to be said,
"set the scene." And the mass of comment that these passages
have drawn has proceeded according to this impression.

In the first and simplest place, this passage mentally
transports the reader back to pre-Reform England. One of
the many assumptions implicit in this act is that both writer
and audience share a modern sensibility and consciousness,
and that they are engaged in common in reflecting upon the
immediately pre-modern. They share as well an awareness
of social change, and the regard for the present in which
they both exist is affected by the habit or manner of their
regard for what has recently come before. On the writer's
part, however, this habit of consciousness is neither direct
nor uninflected, but is informed with reservations, ambivalences, and ironies, with qualifications that move out along
an undetermined but numerous series of radial lines. If one
should ask what advantages accrue to George Eliot by virtue
of her beginning a story or novel in this manner, a number
of explanations and analogies spring at once to mind. One
can suggest that her attitude in this connection resembles
that of David Strauss on the translation of whose *Life of
Jesus* she had labored faithfully and with suitable agoniz-
ings. No longer able to believe what she had once believed
in in the past, she can at least reconstruct it imaginatively;

by means of the historical imagination she can love and appreciate the cultural as well as her personal past, she can make it live with historical life, and so appropriate it congenially and legitimately for herself and her readers. To be sure, she does a good deal more than this, but the partial analogy with Strauss still seems to me to hold.

Nevertheless, it must also be said that in resorting in her fiction to a historically conscious imagination of reality, George Eliot is on the face of it doing nothing exceptional or out of the way. In the nineteenth century both the novel and history undergo immense and concomitant developments, and the connections between these two organizations of ideas about human experience are both complex and deep-seated. In a sense, the historical narrative is, so to speak, the "natural," as it is the largely unexamined, form for the English and European novel in the nineteenth century. In the instance of George Eliot, however, we can observe that form being put to use with an exclusiveness, an obsessiveness, an intensity, and a consciousness whose combination at a particular moment makes, in my view, for an unusual if not a unique circumstance. It is true to say that she was almost unable to set pen to paper on a work of fiction without invoking or repairing to the historical past. In her work we may discover the historical narrative as existing in hypostatic, not to say reified, form.

Many reasons are at hand which might help to explain why George Eliot found this particular means of distancing necessary to her writing. Some of these are undoubtedly of a personal and psychological character, and any full account of her novels would have to make provision for such explanations. Without overlooking the validity and relevance of considerations of this order, I should like to direct attention to certain general questions which appear to me to attach to this context. This may be particularly useful for us as students of the nineteenth century who are in addition committed to the study of history; many of us work so close to our material for such protracted periods of time that we tend to set aside or forget the assumptions and conventions under which we operate. In the first place, it is pertinent to recall that, strictly speaking, the past is only a mode of the present—to affirm this is not to deny its existence but to describe the conditions under which it exists. Then, we might also remind ourselves that the past as we tend to conceive of it is not a universal phenomenon; certain languages, for example, appear to get along satisfactorily without a past tense. Having remembered that, we remember as well that the idea of the historical past is itself a historical notion; moreover, once that idea establishes itself, it proliferates a number of competing and often incompatible notions of what it is that has been established. When we turn to those structures of behavior that we classify under the terms of art and literature, we come upon similar circumstances. Certain forms of art do not use or require the historical past; or, to put it another way, they constitute themselves out of means to which ideas of the past are irrelevant. And in literature itself, the situation is more loosely circumscribed than one might be led to expect. In lyric poetry and the drama, for example, the past, both as a grammatical organization and as a historical idea is not necessary or necessarily dominating. Even in the novel itself, there are sufficient instances available from both the distant past and the recent present, instances in which the historical narrative structure is either abandoned or tampered with or in which the present or the present perfect is used instead of the past (Joyce, Kafka, Bellow, Beckett, Robbe-Grillet; Sterne, Diderot; epistolary novels, etc.), to recall us to the awareness that the nineteenth-century novel as we commonly tend to know it, immensely impressive and important as it is, is nonetheless a convention. It is a convention of consciousness, and of language; and it is a social convention as well.

Having reminded ourselves of these possibilities, we

may go on to examine certain of the presuppositions which seem to lie behind the use of the historical narrative, and in the instance of George Eliot, behind the use of a historical narrative that is both deliberately remote and conscious of its historicity. A narrative itself sets up in us certain expectations; and in a historical narrative these expectations are raised to a further degree of intensity and certitude. The expectations in question have to do with a temporal series or sequence of events; these units arrange themselves in an intelligible or coherent order, and by an almost irresistible pressure the temporal sequence of events is conflated with a causal sequence—that is to say, a causal (and therefore totally intelligible) structure is made to rise out of a temporal flow that has already been chopped up into distinctive units, almost as if one were to try to demonstrate logically that Venus had to step out of this particular wave rather than the one before or behind it. Furthermore, the historical narrative tends to presuppose a world that has already been constructed, and which, because it seems to have been finished before we make acquaintance with it, gives off its own significance as it is unrolled before us. The fiction or myth on whose terms we accept it is that *this* world, unlike the present in which we live when we are aware of it, is neither contingent, problematical, nor opaque. The world, then, appears itself to be a kind of narrative, a story that can be told, a history that can be recited, and everything that occurs in it is a circumstance with a meaning. Regarded in this light, the historical narrative inclines itself to resemble one of those great nineteenth-century systems of explanation, with this difference: that the conditions under which it is both produced and consumed militate against the acknowledgment that it is an explanatory system. (In fairness to the novelists, I might add that certain of the great nineteenth-century system-makers also tended occasionally to forget that they were creating systems of abstractions and not literal reproductions of reality.)

In sum, reality within this system of consciousness tends to be represented as a recollection; it is remarkably stable, and its laws of both expression and development appear to rise immanently and, once again, "naturally," out of the material it selects as its content rather than out of the consciousness that selects the material. These laws tend in their turn to operate and to be felt as norms; and whatever else the world may be in this form of historically conceived of narrative, it is not, to adapt a phrase of George Orwell's, a raft floating through space. It is secured by its own presuppositions, which it regularly regards not as operations of thought or consciousness but as activities of nature in the classical sense. It offers assurance to its society of readers because the world it represents has already been defined and in some sense closed off; things in it, in other words, *have already happened*.[1] And in this respect one of its central purposes is the purpose of control. By possessing the past we assert our possession of the present as well; by defining the past in a certain way we control the possibilities of the present.

These general tendencies which may be found in almost any conventional novel are to be found, I have implied, in hypertrophied form in the novels of George Eliot. What is more, she is intermittently aware of some such thing. She is intermittently aware of the extraordinary remoteness that she has imposed on her material. For example, one of the things that she does in "The Sad Fortunes of the Reverend Amos Barton" and elsewhere is to introduce a scene by turning to her imaginary reader, addressing him confidentially in the present tense and then turning to describe the scene she is about to dramatize; her opening description of this scene tends also to be in the present tense—although

---

[1] I should like to acknowledge a debt in this part of my argument to the French writer Roland Barthes, in particular to certain passages in *Writing Degree Zero*.

it is supposed to have taken place in the distant past—but as soon as she begins actually to compose the drama she drops back again into the past and remains there. To be sure, this was a hackneyed convention of the fiction of the time, and an awkward one besides, but George Eliot's frequent use of it suggests an awareness on her part that something had to be done at least to appear to overcome some of the distance that was at the same time a precondition of her writing fiction at all. Another moment of such uneasy awareness is to be found in the first scene of this short novel; it occurs after tea has been cleared away and Mr. Hackit makes an allusion to brandy-and-water, which prompts Miss Gibbs to bring in the liquor decanters; upon which George Eliot comments, "for in bucolic society five-and-twenty years ago, the human animal of the male sex was understood to be perpetually athirst, and 'something to drink' was as necessary a 'condition of thought' as Time and Space." This learned, if rather clumsy, irony works in a variety of directions; "Immanuel Kant in the parish," or "Jane Austen and The Critique of Pure Reason" will always be good for a chuckle in certain circles; and the absurdity of the juxtaposition serves as well to emphasize the contrast, the disparity in consciousness, between "us" and "them," "now" and "then." It serves in addition to make a point that George Eliot rarely tired of making: that in the past, as in "other" cultures, people tend to ascribe to nature what is in point of fact the responsibility of an institution of culture—an insight that she applies with considerable ingenuity to others if infrequently to herself. And yet I cannot help but suspect that she is making a quasi-apologetic, and perhaps unconscious, if fleeting, reference to herself and her own practices here, and is implying that the historical time and psychological distance that she senses as necessities of her own are necessary conditions of thought as well. But the Time of Kant is not the time we have been discussing or that George Eliot has been manipulating. It is time as pure and abstract succession and duration. It is a conception of time so terrifying in its lucidity, barrenness, and inner solitude that when another great young writer, Heinrich von Kleist, first read about it and absorbed its implications, he wrote that he felt as if the world had become unhinged, that the ground had given way beneath his feet, and that there was literally nothing left for him to cling to or to place any confidence in. If I am correct in my interpretation of this buried association, then George Eliot is leaning momentarily on Immanuel Kant for support he is unable to give.

A third, and much simpler, illustration of George Eliot's slight but discernible apprehensiveness about the fictitious historical distance she has created is to be found in the time-scheme of the story itself. Although the narrative is at first apparently set "five-and-twenty years ago," that is, in about 1831, by the time we are halfway through it, we discover ourselves at the end of 1837 or the beginning of 1838; for we learn there that *Pickwick Papers* had been "recently completed." I think we should take this lapse as we have learned to take other lapses of an unconscious nature; in my view it suggests George Eliot's uncertainty about the optimum imaginary interval that she required to assure both authority over her material and yet for that material to remain alive and current.

Finally, there is one other instance in which I am unable to determine the degree to which George Eliot is conscious of what she is doing. It occurs in the second paragraph of the short novel, which I quoted earlier but did not discuss. The reader will recall that after enumerating the contrasts between Shepperton Church today and what it was like twenty-five years before, George Eliot pauses to apostrophize the modern "well-regulated mind," and then mentions several of the new advances of rationality and efficiency, such as the New Police, the penny-post, and the Tithe Commutation Act. In contrast to this, to "conservative-reforming intellect," she places "imagination," which she represents as a sly Tory, regretting the past, with its "picturesque inefficiency" and "old abuses," and sighing "for the shades of vulgar errors." The past, she remarks, yields to her mind a "picture," while the present with its "new-painted, new-varnished efficiency" yields only "endless diagrams, plans, elevations, and sections." At a certain pitch of discourse, one has no trouble in following what George Eliot is saying; she is, to be very brief, taking a page out of *Hard Times*, with all that is implied in such a choice. But if one takes either one step forward or one step back, one suddenly observes what I can only with the best will in the world call an intellectual confidence trick being performed before our eyes. For George Eliot is also asserting that the past is not regulated, not constructed, not selected, not clear in its outlines—but that it is full with the concrete fullness of a picture (as if a picture were not equally a construction and selection). The present, on the other side, is all intellect, efficiency, and regulation—it yields nothing but abstractions, diagrams, and plans. The confidence trick involves a simple reversal of terms. For it is the present in the sense of immediate existence with all its opacity and impenetrable density that is not well regulated; and it is the past that our minds incessantly and automatically convert the present into that is the theater of operations for regulating and diagramming and abstracting. Nevertheless, that George Eliot should have felt it necessary to formulate such a series of assertions suggests, I believe, something of the urgency with which the matters we have been discussing—and with what these matters set off and imply—beset her. Statements and instances of this character supply further substance to Henry James's penetrating critical remark that although the material and the figures in George Eliot's novels "are deeply studied and massively supported . . . they are not *seen*, in the irresponsible plastic way."

I have taken the liberty of pressing with this austerity on certain passages in George Eliot in part because of the magnitude of the claim she makes upon us and in lesser part because of the magnitude of the claims that have been made in her behalf. But I have also felt justified in this procedure because at the time she began to write her fiction, the conventional, historical mode of consciousness in fiction had already, as it were, become problematical. In 1852 Dickens had embarked upon what, to my mind, was the most audacious and significant act of the novelistic imagination in England in the nineteenth century. In *Bleak House* he took a novel and broke it in half; the narrator of one half of this novel is an impersonal voice who exists nowhere and everywhere; his narration is given, it exists, totally in the present. Sometimes he speaks in the simple present, sometimes in the present progressive; and sometimes he speaks in fragments of sentences, without verbs at all, so that the syntax remains unclosed, so that the statements hover before us in both immediate and interminable duration. This tremendous voice sends forth its utterances out of the viscous and impenetrable fog that reality was becoming for Dickens. It is true that it is also at this moment that his obsession with the past can be observed suddenly to intensify, but the character of this obsession, I believe, can be demonstrated to be very different from the disposition that exists in George Eliot. For Dickens the past had become an arcanum, a darkness, a problematical mental region to which one is driven only because the present is even more problematical, mysterious, oppressive, and contingent. Thus Dickens may be regarded as becoming obsessed with the historical past at the very moment that the norm of historical consciousness is breaking down in him. And it may even be that George Eliot's unwavering affirmation of it afterwards is, among other things, a sign of her intuition of how precarious a norm or convention it was in the course of becoming.

These linguistic, narrative, and conceptual transactions with the past and with the idea of the historical past serve

George Eliot as means of control. The question then arises: What is there that is being controlled, or that needs all these controls? We shall have to defer answering this question for a short space.

2

The second important fictional device that I should like to discuss is to be found in the opening scene of "The Sad Fortunes of the Reverend Amos Barton." This is the first scene in George Eliot's fiction, and one of the striking things about it is that in it she discovers a mode of dramatized discourse that she will use with frequency and consistency throughout her entire career as a novelist, and that is, I believe, central to her way of conceiving the human world. The scene is a tea party at Mrs. Patten's and what takes place in this scene is an extended and elaborate conversation about someone who is not there. This person is the central figure in the story, the Reverend Amos Barton, and thus we are introduced to him through the conversation, or gossip, about him that is occurring in the community. And what holds true here, holds true throughout George Eliot's fiction; we see a great deal of her characters not only in themselves, and occasionally not even primarily or fundamentally in themselves, but in the talk about them that circulates through the society they inhabit—in "The Sad Fortunes of the Reverend Amos Barton," in fact, this talk is the central principle of structure in the narrative.

This device is as well known to students of George Eliot as her use of the historical past, and so when we inquire into its meanings we are in the comfortable situation of dealing, at least in the first instance, with material that has become familiar to us since it has been handled so often.[2] The first possibility that such a fictional method

[2] Most notably in Quentin Anderson, "George Eliot in *Middlemarch*," in *From Dickens to Hardy*, ed. Boris Ford (Penguin, 1958), pp. 274–293.

offers is that it enables us to regard the characters that are being created from a number of different points of view. And what is being quite simply implied as these points of view accumulate is something about the relativity or relativism of human reality. But something else is happening as well, and this, too, has drawn a certain amount of attention from a number of commentators. Such scenes as they recur dramatize the conception that we do not exist simply or merely in ourselves as over against the outside world. We exist in addition in the lives of others, and this existence is also part of ourselves. We exist, in other words, in a society or a community, and this other existence of ours is not to be altogether separated (however odd, inaccurate, or malicious the talk or opinions about us may be) from our personal and intimate sense of existence. We are, in short, social beings, and our identities are to a considerable extent made up of our sustained existence in the eyes and minds of others—to put the same idea in another form, they constitute part of ourselves. As a result, this medium of gossip is in a considerable measure constitutive both of ourselves and others, and it demonstrates in addition how society exists: it exists in and through these transactions and interactions among persons. Moreover, it is through this kind of community and these kinds of communal activities that we are upheld and sustained.

This view of life or social existence is, among other things, plainly and emphatically normative in its conception. But it is much more than this; it intimates a coherent theoretical vision of experience and the social world. And at this point I think it might be useful to move back and offer a summary, in abstract terms, of that theoretical and quasi-systematic view. I resort to this strategy not only because of the requirements of time and space—real time and space, I might add—and not only because to demonstrate the existence of this theoretical structure bit by bit would be an extraordinarily tedious procedure (tedious to inflict upon the reader I mean; I ask him to believe or to assume that I have already done this), but because, in my opinion, George Eliot demands it. Parenthetically, one of the more interesting things about dealing with important novelists is that they compel us to improvise new critical procedures if we are to deal with them closely and on their own terms. The summary is drawn from her early novels, where the theory or quasi-system is represented in its least elaborate forms; in her later novels she modifies and complicates her notions to take in possibilities that are not envisaged in the earlier works, but it is my belief that even in the later novels one can still make out the workings of the theory as one can also make out the persistence of a strongly systematic sensibility. Finally, it should be kept in mind that I am presenting a summary.

In George Eliot's novels society and individual persons are conceived of as being related in determinate ways. Society, in these novels, is represented as a living whole, composed or articulated of differentiated members, each of which fulfills or possesses a special function. As a consequence, the individual person is not separable from the human whole; and in turn the social whole is equally dependent on each individual person, since each contributes to the common life. Society and individual persons, then, are not separable or distinct phenomena, but are in reality the collective and distributive aspects of the same circumstance or thing; one expresses the group as a whole, the other the members that compose it. (To this it must be added, however, that when society is regarded, macroscopically, as a systematic structure or organization of the whole, processes come into view which are invisible in the parts alone; and conversely the same would theoretically hold true of a microscopic examination of the parts.) Because of this inseparability, it is both a logical error and an existential impossibility to conceive or to speak of an opposition between the (or an) individual person and society—one can legitimately only speak of one individual opposing one or several or many other individual persons.

Groups or societies, then, are "living wholes" in which various processes of organization are at work. One result of this circumstance is that freedom, such freedom as we may have, is exercised largely if not exclusively through cooperation with others; to join a social group—a team, a club, a university, a church—increases one's freedom, since it allows one to express himself more fully, to realize himself; that is to say, it permits further articulation and differentiation. This is what freedom is because human life, social life is a whole, and each individual person is a *member* and not a *fragment*. (Strictly speaking, there are no fragments —and so much for Jeremy Bentham.)

By the same token, our particular minds and wills are members of a slowly changing, growing, and evolving whole, and they are at any given moment limited in range and defined in scope by the state of the whole, in particular by the state of those parts of it with which we are in most active, intimate, and regular contact or communication. Therefore, we are, as it were, enveloped by the larger sentiments, attitudes, and habits of the collective world in which we live; and we are in addition and for the largest part unaware of them as different, as really different, from the sentiments, attitudes, and habits of others. They constitute the norm for us. This is principally why so many people find it difficult to understand or to communicate with people from outside their groups or societies. And this is why our manners and customs seem to us as if they were creations of nature and not conventions of culture. (I might say, in passing, that in such connections George Eliot seems to me the best theoretical French mind that ever wrote in English.)

One of the consequences of all this is the insight that the human mind is to a large degree social; and the corollary of this notion is that society is then to a similar degree mental; and both are different aspects of the same whole. Society, therefore, largely consists in *communications* among individuals, and speech or conversation may be understood as the principal mode or means of socialization. The mind is observed to live in a state of perpetual or unending conversation—with itself and with others; when it converses with itself it assumes for itself the mode of an other. Conscious or complex thought, therefore, is invariably a kind of imaginary conversation, and thought is in reality the equivalent of communication. Without expression, active expression, thought cannot exist or endure, and so communication is necessary to self-preservation. (That George Eliot took this notion literally can be demonstrated if we merely think of the fate of Hetty Sorrel in *Adam Bede*; or of Janet Dempster.) Thus thought and personal intercourse or communication are themselves aspects of the same thing; and mind and sociability are equally inseparable. As for the others, the other individual persons, they—or to be more precise their images—live in my mind and form the society in which I exist. Society, as a consequence, may be described as a system of relations between or among personal ideas; actual persons come together to form or make up a society, but they do so as embodied ideas in the minds of all the members. And it is here in these minds that the essential contact of persons takes place. Society exists in my mind as the interanimation and reciprocal influencing of certain ideas named "I," "mother," "father." When D. H. Lawrence wrote: "It was George Eliot who started it all. It was she who started putting all the action inside," he did not quite have this in mind, but his statement is certainly compatible with this view.

It follows, then, that the imaginations that persons have of one another are the substantial and material facts of society, and to observe, study, and understand them is the great object not only of the novel but of all the human or social sciences. The object of study is the imagination of men, that is, what they think of one another. To this it must be added that an individual person's reality is established only if he exists as real in the minds of others, as well as in his own mind. Furthermore, self and other, as they are commonly understood, do not exist in opposition either; when they do seem to be opposed, their opposition is not in a separateness, a distinctiveness, or an alienation such as may be postulated of two material objects or bodies; on the contrary, they are opposed on the ground of community, and hostility or enmity between one's self and another must always be described as hostile or negative sympathy.

Sympathy is exclusively a social sentiment. It is the power of entering into and sharing the minds of other persons; it is the power of sharing mental states that can be communicated. (It does not, as George Eliot applies it, necessarily mean what we ordinarily mean when we use it today—it does not necessarily imply pity, although it may). Sympathy, in short, is the power of communion itself; and it is not merely a social sentiment, it is *the enabling* social sentiment, it is the sentiment beyond all others of unification and solidarity. A view or conception of the world or of society which founds itself on this sentiment will tend quite candidly to be conservative in the sense that it will be sensitive to those circumstances that bind men together, that they possess in common and that make for community among them. It will be a normative view as well, since it will take as a norm those common ideas and feelings that any group of people share and that connects them within that system of agreements, assumptions, forbearances, and authorizations which are the substance of communal existence.

At this juncture I propose to break off this abstract account. What I have presented is, as I remarked earlier, an organized summary of what I take to be a quasi- or virtual-systematic social theory existing immanently and on occasion explicitly in the early novels of George Eliot. The materials of the theory are dispersed throughout the individual works, but the dispersal acts, in my view, to make the theory even more pervasive and in the long run no less systematic in its intention. All I have done is to bring certain bits together, make a number of abstractions, terminological translations, and arrange them in a roughly logical sequence. But what I have also been setting down at the same time is an abstract summary of the first two-thirds, the theoretical sections, of a book called *Human Nature and the Social Order*. The author of this book is the late nineteenth and early twentieth century American sociologist and social psychologist Charles Horton Cooley. Since I have made some remarks earlier in this essay about intellectual confidence tricks and since the circumstances that have led me to say what I have just said make up one of the oddest episodes in my intellectual experience, it may be of some use if I explain myself.

I had gotten just to the point at which my abstract synopsis breaks off, namely, to the discussion of the meaning and function of sympathy in George Eliot, when it struck me that actually I didn't know what I was talking about. I had read George Eliot often and closely enough to believe that I understood what she meant by it; and I had read enough of the comment on her to understand what her commentators understood her to mean by it, but what in fact was sympathy itself? Since Immanuel Kant was fresh in my mind, the impossibility of answering *that* question when it was put in such a form speedily followed the question itself. The next best thing, perhaps, was to try to determine what the early sociologists or social philosophers of her own time, or maybe slightly later, meant when they used the term. I began to go through a number of likely-seeming books from the period, and in due time I came across this work by Cooley. In the index there were several page references under the entry "sympathy." I turned to the appropriate places and found a number of passages that began more or less like this: "Sympathy, as George Eliot says. . . ." To find the dog catching up with his tail is not an uncommon experience in the pursuit of literary studies; I must confess, however, that I felt a twinge of *Schadenfreude* when I discovered an instance of it in the social sciences—it's rather encouraging to feel now and then that we're all together in the same leaky intellectual boat. Since the index also contained a number of stray references to Spencer and G. H. Lewes, I thought it might be worthwhile in a general way to read through the book. I began to do so, and after about twenty-five pages the appalling suspicion began to dawn on me that I was reading an expanded version of the abstract précis that I had just put together. And this is indeed what happened. The theoretical account I have just presented is in point of fact the draft that I had composed before I read Cooley's work, with these alterations: three or four clauses in it were added after I read Cooley and are close paraphrases of his; in addition, I added or changed about eight or ten odd words; and in two places I inverted the order of sentences. Apart from this, the logical précis that I had abstracted from George Eliot's novels simply and literally reproduced the structure of argument along with the substance of *Human Nature and the Social Order*.

How is one to account for this decidedly curious occurrence? Setting aside the possibility of some supernatural, extrasensory, or paranormal intervention, I first thought that my unconscious mind might be playing a common enough trick on me, and that I had read Cooley's work some time in the past, had forgotten this, but then on the appropriate occasion had summoned up what I had read without recalling that I had read it. After what I think was adequate self-examination on this subject, I had to abandon this explanation; and indeed I should add that I had hardly ever heard of Cooley before I came across the work I have been referring to. (There is, of course, still another explanation: it may simply be that I have one of the better American minds of the late nineteenth century; that would solve a number of problems, but I leave this possibility for others to explore.) There is, I believe, a more ordinary and sensible explanation for this coincidence. For now that I have done further reading in this particular discipline, I believe that I could find connected passages in Herbert Spencer, in Comte, and certainly in the writings of Emile Durkheim that would follow similar lines of argumentative development and that could be applied or juxtaposed to certain tendencies in the fiction of George Eliot without doing excessive violence to what fiction as fiction is undertaking to do. To say this is only to affirm what has been suggested by others: that George Eliot really does belong to a tradition of thinking and theorizing about society. And if the coincidence that I have just described demonstrates anything at all (and if the abstract summary that I have composed is not an excessive distortion of both actualities and tendencies in her work), it demonstrates the reality of a tradition of systematic thought and the depth to which it can penetrate and inform a mind and a sensibility that are predisposed to it.

What, then, are some of the implications of this theoretical view of society? It certainly seems to tend by virtue of the ways in which it defines itself to minimize the part played by conflict in human and social affairs. Since individual persons cannot be opposed to their societies, since all societies are living wholes or totalities, and since everyone is a member and no one can be a fragment, the place of conflict in such a structure can hardly be a central or organic one. (For a novelist, whose stock in trade is bound to be human conflict, this makes for an extremely awkward situation; and indeed, I believe that this awkwardness is often apparent in George Eliot's novels.) Similarly, it tends to overlook the possibilities of the kinds of experience that are described by the idea of alienation—a term that I use here in the sense put to it by Hegel and the early Marx. And it disregards as well the possibilities of both experience and knowledge that are suggested by the notion of radical negativity; in this scheme of ideas radical negativity appears as nihilistic or self-destructive activity, a revolt against the very conditions of existence and not against something which men have created but over which they appear to have lost command. Society, however errant and unfair some of its arrangements may be, is never a scandal in this way of conceiving of things. To say so would be tantamount to saying that human existence itself is a scandal. Since this scheme further de-emphasizes the importance of conflict in its notion of society as a slowly growing or evolving whole, society in this view is, if I may use Spencer's tantalizing phrase, "a moving equilibrium"—a notion, I will be so bold to add, out of which a number of modern American social scientists have made themselves a considerable fortune. The stress in practice seems regularly to fall on the equilibrium and not on the movement. And since society in this scheme seems to evolve not through the forces generated by large conflicts, but by a process of slowly complicating and clarifying ideas, by changes in thought, and since society is also to a considerable degree a mental phenomenon, this view seems to be thoroughly and systematically opposed to the kind of view of society represented by a figure such as Marx. Finally, in the importance it attributes to sympathy as a binding social power it reciprocally diminishes the importance of interest, for interest always carries with it the latent possibility of conflicts of interest. Moreover, in the centrality of the sentiment of sympathy, the sentiment of unification and solidarity, of communion and community, society itself appears to be re-sacralized. Society, or social relations, are revealed, if we may refer to the terms used by Durkheim, as the sacred, and the realm of the profane is somewhere else again. There is, one must admit, even in the religion of humanity an element of remystification.[3]

[3] For a full, critical examination of these questions, see Gertrud Lenzer, *Auguste Comte and Positivism* (New York, 1975).

The direction in which all these conclusions seem to point should be fairly evident by now. They point once again toward some means of control, and what there is to be controlled, what has to be controlled, seems fairly clear as well.

3

The third large structural mode in George Eliot's fiction that I should like to discuss is what for want of a more modest term I should have to call her epistemology or theory of knowledge. It is not possible here to develop a discussion of this theory with anything that approaches adequacy, so it will have to be enough for the moment if I say that this theory is skeptical and relativistic, that it places great weight for both good and ill on blind faith, human ignorance, and inadequate ideas and knowledge, and that it regards human thought as existing along a continuum, with unreflecting acceptance of the world and religious ignorance and bigotry at one end and with something like scientific rationality enriched with historical and humane fullness of understanding at the other, but without any final qualitative difference between the two. The difference is one of degree and of relative increasing clarity and adequacy. This theory is applied with considerable rigor, I believe, and with one exception. The exception is that George Eliot on important occasions does not apply it to herself. It is a bad critical practice to chide writers for what they have failed to do, and I disapprove of this habit in others. I cannot help wondering, however, what George Eliot's fiction would have been like had she applied this theory to herself with greater consistency. Her novels would, I believe, have been even more extraordinary than they are now. Nevertheless, the tendency or effect of this theory of knowledge is to reinforce or support the fictional and intellectual kind of operations that the two other large fictional modes that I have already discussed stimulate and further. It, too, works in the service of control and as a means of control.

What we have, then, if this analysis of certain modes that are to be found in George Eliot's early fiction is reasonable, is, to employ the terminology of psychoanalysis, a complex system of defenses. These defenses, like all (unconscious) defenses, function in two directions and in two different intra-psychic systems or institutions at the same time. On their internal face, so to speak, they act to regulate, divert, and displace certain impulses, ideas, wants, desires, or images that are not acceptable in unmodified form to one's conscious mind. On the side that is directed toward external reality, they function in an adaptive capacity; that is to say, a successful defense employs the unconscious instinctual energies at its disposal to make adaptations in the real world, to the problems it confronts us with, as well as to the demands we make upon it for our own needs and gratifications. An unsuccessful defense, on the other side, will ordinarily issue in a symptom—that is, a defense that entails a failure of function. And sometimes, in greatly gifted persons, when defensive structures break down, there is radical regression. For the most part, if not entirely, George Eliot's defenses did not convert themselves into symptoms; they helped her to adapt to the world, and part of that adaptation is visible in these elaborated quasi-systematic notions in which she represented or interpreted the human world to herself and her contemporaries. Moreover, since she was a very talented person, these unconscious formations have more than a personal or idiosyncratic meaning to them; they have at the same time a historical meaning—in them we can observe how the unconscious mind, at a certain historical moment, finds means of expressing itself that reveal in themselves historical significance.

If we regard the early work of George Eliot and ask what these defenses have been constructed to control, we find three principal subjects, themes, or focuses of interest. These are: passion, in particular sexual passion; large and violent conflict, in particular social conflict that has a class character; and third, at a more elevated degree of discourse (though its orgins are, I believe, quite primitive), the possibility of a world without sense, meaning, or intelligibility. At such a moment of junction, we can observe how problems which are in origin of a personal nature intersect and resonate with problems that have a specific cultural and historical density. In *Scenes of Clerical Life* we see represented the destructive effects of passion, passion which is unmediated, timeless, absolutely direct and peremptory; of sexual passion in Caterina and Mr. Gilfil, for example; in the passions of jealous rage and uncontrollable anger in Caterina and Dempster, and even of religious passion in Mr. Tryan. In *Adam Bede* we see once again the consequences of sexual passion, or passionate egoism (they seem to George Eliot at certain moments the same thing), in the fates of Arthur and Hetty; but even more in that relation and in Arthur's relation to Adam we see the setting up of a situation of incipient and violent class conflict, which George Eliot then devotes all her energies to diverting and transforming. Indeed, it may be suggested that the entire structure of the novel is devoted to finding a way of getting rid of the two centers of conflict, Arthur and Hetty, sexual passion and class advantage, so that the stage can be left to Adam and Dinah, who between them will establish a kind of miniature, ideal Victorian England, founded on work, faith, family, and fellowship. In *The Mill on the Floss*, which represents a large step forward, she does try to deal directly with a conflict of a sexual nature; but the results, as everyone has long since recognized, are disastrous; the only way she can deal with it at the end is by killing off its agents.

These are, however, only scattered examples and not methodical demonstrations. In the short time that remains to us, let us look a bit more closely at one of the stories, the one I have discussed most here, "The Sad Fortunes of the Reverend Amos Barton." This is by common consent the best of the stories, though it is difficult to say why it is so good a work of fiction; indeed, this story succeeds in obscuring its meaning with extraordinary skill—and perhaps I carry something of a grudge against George Eliot for having forced me to read this story so many times before I could discover what it was about. The reader will recall that almost half of this story consists of scenes of gossip; the objects of this gossip, which is carried on in various circles, are the Reverend Amos Barton, his wife, and their relation with the Countess Czerlaski. And the gossip consists almost entirely in a series of innuendos of a sexual nature which in the end graduates into outright slander. It begins in the very first scene when Mr. Pilgrim makes a neutral-sounding remark about Barton being "rather a low-bred fellow." The remark remains neutral, but Mrs. Hackit soon follows it up with the statement that Barton is "not overburthen'd i' th' upper storey," a remark which she immediately supplements with the knowing observation that although his wife is "a delicate creature," she's pregnant again, "six children, and another a-coming." And a bit later the ladies of the parish complain that "Mr. Barton did not more uninterruptedly exhibit a superiority to the things of the flesh." Then there is the gossip about the Countess and her brother Mr. Bridmain. No one believes he is her brother, and everyone, apparently, except those innocents the Bartons, is convinced that she is his kept mistress. It is, naturally, not true, and when the Countess moves in with the Bartons after having left her brother—ironically enough, because he has decided to marry the Countess' maid; she found them kissing and walked out in disgust—the gossip gets into high gear. Now Barton is supposed to have a pregnant wife and a mistress under one roof, and everyone speculates on the wonder of it. What could make the Countess go after such a creature as him, muses Mrs. Hackit. "Mr. Barton may have attractions we don't know of," Mr. Pilgrim answers with pointed insinuation. Mrs. Hackit answers, referring to poor Mrs.

Barton, "What she must have to go through!"—a remark which has about five different meanings in this context. Mr. Pilgrim replies by quoting Mrs. Farquhar, who said, "I think Mrs. Barton a v-e-r-y w-e-a-k w-o-m-a-n," a statement which is also ambiguous and may have several different meanings, all of them nasty in a sexual way. And Miss Gibbs caps it all by saying "if I was a wife, nothing should induce me to bear what Mrs. Barton does"—simply another dirty joke. When the local clergy get together, the same procedure is gone through, and Mr. Fellowes has to remark that "Barton is certainly either the greatest gull in existence, or he has some cunning secret—some philtre or other to make himself charming in the eyes of a fair lady. It isn't all of us that can make conquests when our ugliness is past its bloom."

The point, of course, is that none of this is true. Barton, George Eliot keeps protesting, is a terribly ordinary, an even less than ordinary, man. He has an unprepossessing appearance, "a narrow face of no particular complexion," although that complexion has been pitted by smallpox; his features are "of no particular shape," his eyes "of no particular expression." He is forty, bald, most of his teeth have fallen out and those that remain are "few in number, and very much the worse for wear." He is a man without charm, he cannot spell properly, he has passed through the mysteries of a university education and remained puzzled, he is an uninspired and tactless clergyman, he is self-opinionated in a small way, and, remarks George Eliot, laying it on with a trowel, "it was not in his nature to be superlative in anything; unless, indeed, he was superlatively middling, the quintessential extract of mediocrity."

But there is a kind of mystery about Amos Barton, and that has to do with his wife, Milly. She is the first of what I think of as George Eliot's big beauties, "large, fair, gentle Madonna," full-figured, flowing lines, elegant, a "tall graceful, substantial presence . . . imposing in its mildness," full of love and loving, an altogether desirable wife and mother. The question must then arise: how and why did she marry Barton? We are told that she has "shortsighted eyes," by which I take George Eliot to mean myopia and something more; but even if she cannot see her husband clearly in both a physical and an intellectual or spiritual sense, this has in no way interfered with her happiness with him, for clearly she is exceptionally happy. George Eliot senses that all is not right here, and then goes into a long hoo-hah in which she tries to explain why she thinks these beautiful, superior women ought to marry "poor devil[s]" and second-raters, but this is pretty clearly a smoke screen. Something is not getting said.

The story, as the reader knows, continues smoothly; the Countess is gotten rid of, Milly has her seventh child, which soon dies, and so does she. The gossip of the community turns to sympathy when all this suffering becomes evident, but it does not prevent another blow falling; Barton loses his curacy and is forced to move with his orphaned children to a manufacturing town. This affecting story ends, as it were, floating about in inconclusive space.

And so it seemed to me, until I discovered the lapse or hitch in the time sequence of the story that I mentioned earlier, and read it through again with further attentiveness in this regard. What I discovered in it was yet another sequence of dates which I had overlooked before but which led, for me, to understanding what this story was so mutedly trying to say. It begins in February, there is "a freezing February bitterness outside," we are told, and during the first scene Mrs. Hackit makes the remark about Milly Barton being a delicate creature, and that she is pregnant with her seventh child. That is, I think it is clear, that in February she is *visibly* pregnant. Time moves along, spring passes, the month of May is mentioned, the Countess moves in, and stays, "the summer and harvest had fled," we keep on counting, we are now in November, Mrs. Hackit mentions yet again that Mrs. Barton has another child "comin' on," the Countess finally leaves, and about six weeks after her departure, the baby is born—that is, in the middle of December. This birth, we then read, "came prematurely," and what was born was a "seven months baby." At this moment I was prepared to give up the belief that George Eliot was a woman, but in actuality I had overlooked, or misread, a moment in the middle of the story. Sometime in the spring, "when the last snow had melted, when the purple and yellow crocuses were coming up in the garden," sometime, that is, between mid-March and April, Milly "had an illness which made her lips look pale," as a consequence of which she must rest and drink some wine. Since she has been represented from the beginning of the story as radiant yet delicate, and since other things are at the moment going on, one is inclined to pass by this detail. But what has in fact happened, what could only have happened, is that she has had a miscarriage. She is up and about again "as the days brightened," but Mrs. Hackit, watching her, remarks that "she won't stan' hain' many more children." But now we know that she is pregnant once again by mid-May, and that she dies after giving birth to the premature seventh child and as a result of it. At this moment the meaning of the story rapidly begins to clarify itself.

As she is dying, her last words to her husband are "You —have—made me—very—happy." And so the gossips, that monstrous collective consciousness, though they were wrong, were also in a way right. For what they sensed was the presence of some extraordinary sexual rapport between Barton and his wife. It is not simply that she is exceptionally fertile, for George Eliot makes the point quite clearly (or as clearly as anything is made in this dimness) that she feels and is fulfilled as a wife as well as a mother, and that Barton was "an affectionate husband," a mid-nineteenth-century circumlocution that was understood to hold worlds of meaning. Mrs. Barton dies, then, as a result of her love and her passion; the sexual rapport that has been the foundation of their happiness is what kills her; one can say that she is destroyed by her passionate happiness. Her death is a consequence of a passionately happy marriage.

What are we up against here? Are we back in that Victorian swamp in which the state of medical science was used as an excuse for pronouncements about existential terrors?[4] In part we are, but only in part. For George Eliot also makes us feel that we are in the presence here of some mystery. There is the mystery of sexual happiness itself, there is the mystery of an ordinary and less than ordinary man like Barton being able to fulfill an extraordinary woman (there is, besides mystery, a lot of fantasy going on here, I need hardly add), and there is the mystery of sexual passion itself, which both terrifies and fascinates George Eliot. Yet behind all this there is another mystery or question: what does this all mean? what's the *reason* for all this? why did she die? At this point we come up against facts, the absolute facts of human destiny, and George Eliot takes us up to this point, looks over the edge, and then departs. She describes the orphaned children gathering around the grave of their mother, and then writes the following sentence: "They had not learned to decipher that terrible handwriting

---

[4] How much so has only recently been disclosed by a graduate student of mine, Lennard Davis. Mr. Davis has discovered a detail—or a missing detail—in *Daniel Deronda* that throws the whole central plot of the novel out of kilter. Deronda's identity is a mystery to himself and has always been. It is only when he is a grown man, having been to Eton and Cambridge, that he discovers that he is a Jew. What this has to mean—given the conventions of medical practice at the time— is that he never looked down. In order for the plot of Daniel Deronda to work, Deronda's circumcised penis must be invisible, or nonexistent—which is one more demonstration in detail of why the plot does not in fact work. Yet this peculiarity of circumstance—which, I think it should be remarked, has never been noticed before—is, I have been arguing, characteristic in several senses of both George Eliot and the culture she was representing.

of human destiny, illness and death." This sentence can be read in two ways. It can mean that the children had not yet learned about the absolute unavoidability and universality of death, that they were too young to understand this most ordinary of facts which is at the same time absolute and universal, terrible and exalted. But in its ambiguity the sentence can also be read as if there was something there to decipher, as if it could be deciphered, as if human illness and death were a code to which a meaning could be attached, and that someone is in possession of the cipher. It is in such an ambiguity that we may observe the defensive structures coming into play again, as we have observed them at work throughout the emergence of the obscured theme of the story. It is in some such way, I suggest, that George Eliot's novels have to be read, if we are to determine their meanings more fully and adequately than we have. That last sentence, like the elaborated theme of the story, balances precariously between two possibilities: it may promise a profound exploration of human and social life, or it may be a gigantic swindle. The future career of George Eliot as a novelist, I believe, demonstrates the shifting proportions between these two extremes.

(1974)

Language into Structure:
Pickwick Papers

Mysteries in real life exist in order to be solved, and literary mysteries exist in order to be consulted. As one who has already tried his hand in picking at the greatest of Dickens' mysteries—*Pickwick Papers*—I feel no need to apologize for frequenting these grounds again, nor for consulting the mystery in the hope that this time it will prove still more receptive and less resistant to critical interrogation. For the mystery has been and remains essentially a critical one: Where is the critical handle for such a work of genius to be found?

Let us begin, then, at the beginning. And, as it is only appropriate in such a perplexing context, we discover the beginning before the beginning and after the ending. I am referring to the advertisement that was published before the first number of *Pickwick Papers* appeared and to the prefaces that Dickens wrote after he had completed the novel. The advertisement begins as follows: "On the 31st of March will be published, to be continued Monthly, price One Shilling, the First Number of *The Posthumous Papers of the Pickwick Club*; containing a faithful record of the perambulations, perils, travels, adventures, and sporting transactions of the corresponding members. Edited by 'Boz.' And each Monthly Part embellished with Four Illustrations by Seymour." It is all thoroughly inauspicious and conventional. Amid these conventionalities, however, and indeed as part of them, three things persist in attracting the attention of the modern reader. First, the papers are "posthumous"—but to what? To the club itself, presumably. But what does this mean, and why? It is not alive, it is not there, it is dead or has disappeared. It exists in a negative state or as a negation, in a condition of almost pure otherness. But the papers themselves may be posthumous as well in the sense that they are dead before they have ever come alive; they are being produced as a piece of hack work and will be or are dead as literature before they are even written.

Second, these papers are not "written" but "edited." This, too, was a convention of popular fiction and other writing, although Carlyle had recently made considerable creative play with it in *Sartor Resartus*. But it implies a statement similar to that contained in "posthumous." The agent behind this publication is as it were not yet the novelist; he exists again in a kind of negative or not-yet-appeared or absent state. He is not writing the work; he does not create it or own or possess it. Somehow it is written through him. But at the same time, once more there is a sense of some slight distance and disavowal present and being communicated. And third, the editor is Boz, not Dickens. Boz who did "sketches," not Dickens who wrote novels. Moreover, we are to learn in the future that Boz was not even in the first place Dickens' pseudonym for himself. It was a nickname that he had given to a younger brother, so that his using it for himself is on one of its sides another form of a complex, inexplicit disavowal, though on another side it is a characteristic gesture of aggrandizement. Boz contains the suggestion—retrospectively to be sure—that Dickens so to speak is not yet here, that he has not yet been created, as he will eventually be. And thus the novel announces itself beforehand in a cluster of negations, of othernesses and circumstances which are not there, or are not yet there.

If we turn next to the preface to the first edition, we come across a number of equally arresting phrases and formulations. This was written some year and a half later, at the conclusion of the work, and with that work figuratively present in its entirety before the writer. We all know what had happened to *Pickwick Papers* in that interval; and we know in addition that an occurrence of similar magnitude had taken place in the young writer, that he had undergone a transformation and become Charles Dickens. It is to be supposed, therefore, that he would undertake to communicate some part of this momentousness in his prefatory leavetaking. But he does nothing of the kind. The first sentence of that preface begins as follows: "The author's object in this work was to place before the reader a constant succession of characters and incidents." We should note in passing that although he has become "the author," he has continued speaking in the distant and distancing convention of the authorial or editorial third person rather than the first person, which he subsequently adopted on such occasions. What stops us, however, is his formulation of his "object"—"a constant succession." There is some notion here of endless movement, of incessant motion, an idea that is elaborated along one line later on when he tells us that the only sport at which he was really good (the word he uses is "great") was "all kinds of locomotion." But that is only one line of development, and we shall return to this conception in due course.

He then goes on to describe the conditions of the imaginative inception of the work. "Deferring to the judgement of others in the outset of the undertaking," he writes, "he [Dickens] adopted the machinery of the club, which was suggested as that best adapted to his purpose." It is always interesting to find an occasion on which Dickens refers in public to some act of deference on his part; and it is not surprising that he should do so with a touch of ill-nature—the supererogatory double emphasis and quasi-circularity of phrasing make his annoyance sufficiently clear. He did not, he is saying, want this "machinery" there at the beginning; and, he continues, finding as he wrote "that it tended rather to his embarrassment than otherwise, he gradually abandoned it, considering it a matter of very little importance to the work." The implication seems virtually to be that he wanted no machinery at all; that had he had his own way he would have begun without any machinery— that is to say, he would have begun in some other and almost entirely unimaginable way. He cannot of course tell us what that way would have been, but he does remark that the form or "general design" of the work, owing to its mode of publication, had to be as "simple" as possible. And the linking between the separate events and numbers, if they were to "form one tolerably harmonious whole," had to follow "a gentle and not-unnatural progress of adventure." After having misspent a certain number of years contemplating this utterance, I find that my response to it is to say— "meaning what?" A progress in what "not-unnatural" sense? A progress that is pure succession? The one thing that is indisputably clear about this assertion is that Dickens was in no position to understand discursively what it was that he had done—which may in point of creative fact have been exactly the most advantageous position for him to have occupied.

These observations are supported by what follows shortly, a description in one sentence by Dickens of his manner of writing *Pickwick Papers.* "The following pages," he states, "have been written from time to time, almost as the periodical occasion arose." Again it is the subdued uncertainty and unintended ambiguity that draw the attention of the reader. On the one hand Dickens seems to be describing an activity that occurred spontaneously, and almost at random; on the other he tends to represent himself as writing by order for the occasion, or as the occasion "arose," which introduces an uncertainty of another kind. The point about this ambiguity is that it happens to correspond to an actuality. The parts were written by the yard, to prearranged mechanical specifications; at the same time they were composed spontaneously. It was not only Dickens who stood in puzzlement over this circumstance.

Ten years later the occasion arose again, and Dickens took the opportunity of the publication of the First Cheap Edition of his works to write a new preface in which he described more fully the circumstances of the inception of the now legendary novel. He recalls how William Hall came to his rooms in Furnivall's Inn to propose "a something that should be published in shilling numbers." This something soon becomes a "monthly something," both of the ironic phrases suggesting Dickens' growing awareness of the extraordinarily unformed and unconscious character of what it was that—ten years before—was then about to happen to him and unfold out of him. He next describes how it was proposed to him that his writing should be the "vehicle" for Seymour's plates, how he objected to this view of the project and proposed successfully to reverse it. "My views being deferred to," he states, "I thought of Mr. Pickwick and wrote the first number." The deference of the preface to the first edition is now on the other foot. As for the famous statement about Mr. Pickwick, I have discussed its deceptive complexities elsewhere and there is no need to rehearse them here. But the second half of this sentence introduces still further difficulties, for after remarking that he "wrote the first number," Dickens goes on to add "from the proof-sheets of which, Mr. Seymour made his drawing of the club and that happy portrait of its founder, by which he is always recognized and which may be said to have made him a reality." Which may be said by whom? and in what sense? and for Dickens as well as for others? The confusion, however, was to be still worse confounded, for twenty years later Dickens revised the preface once again, took out the second half of that sentence, and substituted this: "from the proof-sheets of which, Mr. Seymour made his drawing of the Club, and his happy portrait of its founder:—the latter on Mr. Edward Chapman's description of the dress and bearing of a real personage whom he had often seen." This revision had its origin in assertions that were made on Seymour's behalf, that had to do with the part he played in the primary imagination of the novel, and that cannot be discussed here. Dickens' "clarification," however, serves primarily to divert and distract one's attention. The sentence is still running in two directions—Seymour making his drawing now from both the proof sheets and Chapman's description of "a real personage" no less. Once more Dickens cannot withstand the impulse to introduce some such word as "real" or "reality." And each time that he does make such an introduction our sense of his permanent uncertainty about what it was that had happened to him is augmented. This observation holds for the well-known following paragraph about Mr. Pickwick's changing character as the novel develops, in which Dickens speaks about him as if he were a real and independent being from the very beginning and a complete invention at the same time.

What we are left with, then, after these extended prefatory marchings and countermarchings is a distinct conviction of how mysterious almost everything about *Pickwick Papers* remained to Dickens himself. We are therefore rather

better off than we were when we began; we are still in darkness, but at least we have been joined there by the man who
"may be said to have made [it] a reality." And if we can rely
no further upon the teller, we have to turn to the tale, which
begins thus:

The Pickwickians

The first ray of light which illumines the gloom, and
converts into a dazzling brilliancy that obscurity in
which the earlier history of the public career of the
immortal Pickwick would appear to be involved, is derived from the perusal of the following entry in the
Transactions of the Pickwick Club, which the editor of
these papers feels the highest pleasure in laying before
his readers, as a proof of the careful attention, inde-
fatigable assiduity, and nice discrimination, with which
his search among the multifarious documents confided
to him has been conducted.

It opens with a title followed by a single epic sentence, a
paragraph long, that closes in a dying fall. It is a parody,
which later on and at length we learn is in part not a parody.
It begins at the beginning, with the "creation" itself, with
the Logos appearing out of "obscurity"—that is, the "earlier
history . . . of the immortal Pickwick"—and into the light
of creation. But it also dramatizes the fundamental activity
of the Logos; it dramatizes the notion of cosmic creation
as a word—which is how God, as the Logos, created the
world: *fiat lux*, said God, when he was speaking Latin, and
so it was. And here too, in this novel, we begin the creation
with a word, with language; with Dickens' language on the
one hand and the word "Pickwickians" on the other. Mr.
Pickwick and Dickens are each of them the Logos as well,
emerging brightly out of their immanence and creating. And
each of them is in his separate, distinctive way the Word
made flesh—as are those documents and papers mentioned

by the "editor," which do not exist, or do not exist just yet, but will become another incarnation of language, a novel, a printed book. Thus we begin with a comic, cosmic creation in the form of the Logos, the word.[1]

There follows the second sentence of the novel, which is the first sentence of the mythical papers, enclosed in quotation marks. "May 12, 1827. Joseph Smiggers, Esq., P.V.P.M.P.C.* presiding." The work is set in the past. And although the date is not 4004 B.C., there appears to be something equally accidental and gratuitous about May 12, 1827; in addition, readers of *Pickwick Papers*, like readers of the Bible, have encountered certain difficulties in keeping its chronology straight or consistent. But that date is not in actuality gratuitous, although we have to go outside of the book to find its significance: May, 1827, was the date at which the fifteen-year-old Charles Dickens first went to work as a clerk in the law firm of Ellis and Blackmore. In the popular idiom of the time, it was the moment at which he "began the world." Then there are those funny letters that follow Smiggers' name. At the risk of appearing absurd, we may ask why they are there; and if we put to one side the simple comic intention and effect of the long set of initials (and the extravagant title to which they refer), we may observe that letters arranged in such a novel and quasi-arbitrary way sometimes form words, or suggest a code that is different from, though related to, the codes by which we ordinarily communicate. They are almost a kind of doodling, which may be a first clue for us to hold on to. (What I am suggesting is that in this instance the letters P.V.P.M.P.C. are more important than the words to which they refer. It

---

[1] It was Freud, of course, who preeminently taught us to distinguish between thoughts and behavior, disclosing how in the unconscious, intentions or verbal expressions are taken as the equivalent of deliberate actions. Yet it was also Freud who wrote to Thomas Mann that "an author's words are deeds," transfusing that commonplace with new kinds of meaning.

is the letters themselves that make one laugh at first; the humor in the footnoted explanation of their reference and of the inflation in the title is certainly there, but it is secondary.)

There follows an account of the meeting of the club, which first records that Mr. Pickwick had read his celebrated paper entitled "Speculations on the Source of the Hampstead Ponds, with some Observations on the Theory of Tittlebats." Whatever the theory of tittlebats may be, the term itself is of interest. It is, the *Oxford English Dictionary* records, a variant form of stickleback; it comes into use in about 1820, and has its origin in "childish" pronunciation of the fish's name.[2] Once again, as the novel feels about for its beginning, it presses itself and the reader back into words themselves, into matters connected with learning words and with some kind of fundamental or primitive relation to the language.

As for the meeting as a whole, it is conceived of at the outset as the mildest of burlesques upon the transactions of some scientific or scholarly association. It is that, but it is also a parody of a scene in heaven, a fanciful rendering of an unwritten episode of *Paradise Lost*. These comic-epic, immortally foolish creatures are going to visit the earth and report in their correspondence on what they see. And if Mr. Pickwick is the blandest of parodic imaginations of a traveler, explorer, observer, scientist, and scholar, he is just as much a parodic refraction of a god visiting his creation. There follows immediately upon the reading of the resolu-

---

[2] The *Oxford English Dictionary* misses out on an earlier appearance of the word in a variant form. In *An Island in the Moon* (1784), there occurs the following: "Here ladies and gentlemen said he I'll show you a louse [climing] or a flea or a butterfly or a cock chafer the blade bone of a tittle back no no heres a bottle of wind that I took up in the bog house." David V. Erdman, ed., *The Poetry and Prose of William Blake* (New York, 1965), p. 452.

tions that assign their work of traveling and reporting to Mr. Pickwick and his companions a first description of this deity: "A casual observer, adds the secretary, . . . might possibly have remarked nothing extraordinary in the bald head, and circular spectacles, which were intently turned towards his (the secretary's) face, during the reading of the above resolutions: to those who knew that the gigantic brain of Pickwick was working beneath that forehead, and that the beaming eyes of Pickwick were twinkling behind those glasses, the sight was indeed an interesting one." The image of Pickwick's face is itself almost like a doodle: a number of blank circles to be filled in later—even the solid dots and lines of his "beaming eyes" are not there yet and have to be imagined.

Mr. Pickwick stands on a Windsor chair. His coattails, tights, and gaiters are mentioned; Tupman, Snodgrass, and Winkle are cursorily sketched, while Dickens readies himself to do what comes next. What comes next is that Mr. Pickwick begins to speak; or more precisely, the secretary begins to transcribe in the third person the speech of Mr. Pickwick. At once we see that a travesty parliamentary speech is in the course of being composed, and the best parliamentary reporter of his time is spitballing away in a Homeric doodle, letting the language improvisationally, incontinently, and inconsequentially run on. For example: "The praise of mankind was his [Mr. Pickwick's] Swing; philanthropy was his insurance office. (Vehement cheering). . . . Still he could not but feel that they had selected him for a service of great honour, and of some danger. Travelling was in a troubled state, and the minds of coachmen were unsettled. Let them look abroad and contemplate the scenes which were enacting around them. Stage coaches were upsetting in all directions, horses were bolting, boats were overturning, and boilers were bursting. (Cheers—a voice 'No.') No! (Cheers.)" It runs on until Blotton makes his objection, the altercation between him and Mr. Pickwick breaks out, he calls Pickwick a "humbug"[3]—"Immense confusion, and loud cries of 'Chair,' and 'Order' "—and a compromise settlement is reached when Blotton asserts that he had used that word or expression "in its Pickwickian sense." At this point, of course, Dickens—and his readers—have hit upon something.

What is the Pickwickian sense? If we recall that the chapter begins with the Logos and with the word Pickwickians, we can begin by suggesting that it is a sense in which the word is seized creatively in the first instance almost as a kind of doodle, as a play of the pen, as a kind of verbal scribble or game. It is the word—or verbal expression— actively regarded not primarily as conscious imitation of either nature or pre-existent models, but rather as largely unconscious invention, whose meaning is created essentially as it is spontaneously uttered or written down. It is the world, language, writing, as these exist in each other, as a complex process that is self-generating—so that beginning, so to say, either with the name Pickwick, or the word or title Pickwickian, the world, the language, and the writing implicit in or unfolded by such words appears to generate itself. It is language with the shackles removed from certain of its deeper creative powers, which henceforth becomes capable of a constant, rapid, and virtually limitless multiplication of its own effects and forms in new inventions and combinations and configurations. *Mutatis mutandis* it is the timely equivalent in written novelistic prose of the takeoff into self-sustained growth. In *Pickwick Papers* the English novel becomes, as it were, airborne.[4]

What we have, in short, is something rather new and

[3] Humbug, an expression to which Dickens would give memorable life on a later occasion, is another word whose etymological origin is cloaked in obscurity.

[4] The analogy being drawn with terms taken from the language of economic historians is only partly fanciful, although this is not the place to work out the mediations that would provide it with substance. I annex the figure of being airborne from E. J. Hobsbawm.

spectacular. Such a breakthrough in literature would in the nature of the case have to be largely unconscious; it could not at first have been understood by the person who was the bearer of such a force. For Dickens has committed him-self at the outset of *Pickwick Papers* to something like pure writing, to language itself. No novelist had, I believe, ever quite done this in such a measure before—certainly not Sterne. In addition, the commitment was paradoxically en-sured and enforced by the circumstance of compelled spon-taneity in which Dickens wrote, by the necessity he accepted of turning it out every month, of being regularly spontaneous and self-generatingly creative on demand. Dickens was, if it may be said, undertaking to let the writing write the book. There are several other ways of stating this notion and several explanatory means that may be applied to its elabo-ration—out of which I shall choose one. Dickens was able to abandon himself or give expression to what Freud called the primary process in a degree that was unprecedented in English fictional prose; he was able to let the fundamental and primitive mental processes of condensation, displace-ment, and equivalence or substitution find their way into consciousness with a minimum of inhibition, impedence, or resistance. These processes correspond to and are con-stituents of the deep non-logical, the metaphoric and meto-nymic, processes of language—and it was these processes that Dickens allowed to have their run. It may be asked why such a development, in anything like a similar degree, had not occurred before in the English novel. Poets have, after all, often written in just such a way. Was it too frightening a prospect for novelists? Such a question inevitably involves historical circumstances of enormous complexity, and only a partial and provisional answer is possible here. In a sense the possibilities opened up by such an experience were too unnerving for most novelists. The novel had been built primarily on the secondary, logical processes, processes that develop ontogenetically at a later state of mental existence and form the essential structures of consciousness. The regression implied by this manner of composition, the threat of an ego overwhelmed by such regression and loss or abdication of control, must have appeared too alarming to English novelists hitherto. Or we can put it another way and state that before Dickens no English novelist had appeared with an ego of such imperial powers and with a sense of reality so secure that he could temporarily abandon those powers without fear of being overwhelmed or of their permanent loss. At the same time, such an abandonment, successfully carried through, marks the opening up of a new dimension of freedom for the English novel, if not for the human mind in general. Thus at the outset of *Pickwick Papers*, Dickens has allowed the language to go into motion within him, and it is to the motion of that language, to its movement in writing, that we must first attend.

Chapter 2 opens with Mr. Pickwick about to begin experiencing the world, which is as yet unformed, undifferentiated, and uncreated, as he is himself. He has had almost no experience, but as we quickly learn, the experience that he has not had is essentially linguistic experience. As his encounter with the cab man demonstrates at once:

> "How old is that horse, my friend?" inquired Mr. Pickwick, rubbing his nose with the shilling he had reserved for the fare.
>
> "Forty-two," replied the driver, eyeing him askant.
>
> "What!" ejaculated Mr. Pickwick, laying his hand upon his notebook. The driver reiterated his former statement . . .
>
> "And how long do you keep him out at a time?" inquired Mr. Pickwick, searching for further information.
>
> "Two or three weeks," replied the man.

"Weeks!" said Mr. Pickwick in astonishment—and out came the notebook again.

"He lives at Pentonwil when he's at home," observed the driver, coolly, "but we seldom takes him home, on account of his veakness."

"On account of his weakness!" reiterated the perplexed Mr. Pickwick.

"He always falls down when he's took out o' the cab," continued the driver, "but when he's in it, we bears him up werry tight, and takes him in werry short, so as he can't werry well fall down; and we've got a pair o' precious large wheels on, so ven he *does* move, they run after him, and he must go on—he can't help it."

What we learn from this meeting of minds is that the cab man is using language in the Pickwickian sense, but Mr. Pickwick is not. Mr. Pickwick's use of the language is literal, abstractly symbolic, and almost entirely denotative and normative, and as the novel continues, this characteristic of his becomes increasingly pronounced. He does not yet understand language, and his innocence is primarily a linguistic innocence. And yet we recall that he is supposed to be the Logos as well, whose principal creation is language, the means of which comprise all other creation, including those utterances that are his self-creation. In this reversal and paradox, Dickens has erected for himself a problem whose multiple workings-out will occupy considerable space throughout the novel.

But Dickens is not yet ready for that, and the affray between the Pickwickians and the cab man is brought to an end by the entrance of Jingle, who delivers them from the embraces of the crowd that surrounds them and into the equally vigorous embrace of volubility and verbiage with which he succeeds to envelop them:

"Heads, heads—take care of your heads!" cried the loquacious stranger as they came out under the low archway, which in those days formed the entrance to the coach-yard. "Terrible place—dangerous work—other day—five children—mother—tall lady, eating sandwiches —forgot the arch—crash—knock—children look round —mother's head off—sandwich in her hand—no mouth to put it in—head of a family off—shocking, shocking! Looking at Whitehall, sir?—fine place—little window— somebody else's head off there, eh, sir?—he didn't keep a sharp look-out enough either—eh, sir, eh?"

At this point, it may be said, *Pickwick Papers* is off and running; it has really begun to find itself. Jingle is an approximation of uninflected linguistic energy. He seems incoherent but he is not; his speech proceeds rapidly and by associations; his syntactical mode is abbreviatory and contracted; his logic is elliptical, abstractly minimal, and apropositional. He brings us into closer touch with the primary process. He is, moreover, the first expression of the "constant succession" that Dickens mentions in his preface to the first edition; but the constant succession, as it first appears here and will persist throughout the novel, is the constant succession of writing, of characters rising up to speak in print in unending torrents of words, of language in incessant motion, of writing apparently and extraordinarily writing itself—through the no less extraordinary means of Dickens. It is almost as if in Jingle, Dickens had hit upon or invented a way of dramatizing or embodying this unconscious apprehension or conception that somehow language itself is spontaneously creating this novel—and it is that conception that provides the dramatic substructure of rather more than half the novel.

But Jingle's speech is something more than this. At a slightly later point Dickens refers to it as a "system of stenography," and here we arrive on closer grounds. For

Dickens had of course been a stenographer, a writer of shorthand, the very best shorthand writer of his time. He started to learn it soon after he went to work as a clerk at Ellis and Blackmore's, before he was sixteen years old; he had written in it for years in his work in Doctors' Commons and other courts and as a parliamentary reporter; and he was never to forget it, as he reminded his audience in a memorable speech made in his later life.[5] For a number of important formative years he had worked as a kind of written recording device for the human voice, for speech, for the English language. He had been a writing instrument for others, their language flowing through his writing. In one sense those written voices were all inside of him, wonderfully and instantaneously recorded on the most remarkable of all electronic tapes, and now were about to be played back and expressed—although the mechanical and electronic analogy is, I should forcibly state, far from being an adequate approximation to what it was that went on inside him. In another sense Dickens was acting as the stenographer of his characters and of the language itself as well as of its written form; he was transcribing writing, writing down what that particular mode of the language said to him and through him. And yet these notions of stenographic memory and transcription, however useful and suggestive they may

[5] "I have never forgotten the fascination of that old pursuit. The pleasure that I used to feel in the rapidity and dexterity of its exercise has never faded out of my breast. Whatever little cunning of hand or head I took to it, or acquired in it, I have so retained as that I fully believe I could resume it tomorrow, very little the worse from long disuse. To this present year of my life, when I sit in this hall, or where not, hearing a dull speech—the phenomenon does occur—I sometimes beguile the tedium of the moment by mentally following the speaker in the old way; and sometimes, if you can believe me, I even find my hand going on the table cloth, taking an imaginary note of it all." Speech to the Newspaper Press Fund, May 20, 1865, in K. J. Fielding, ed., *The Speeches of Charles Dickens* (Oxford, 1960), pp. 347–348.

be, are surely insufficient, for nothing is less unmistakable about the writing of *Pickwick Papers* than its qualities of free inventiveness, of active, spontaneous creativity, of its movement in a higher imaginative order than that which is circumscribed by storage, memory, or recoverable transcriptions alone.

There is, however, another side to this experience that is relevant to our argument. Dickens describes what it was like to learn shorthand in a famous passage in *David Copperfield* (Chapter 38). He had laid out the sum of half a guinea on "an approved scheme of the noble art and mystery of stenography"—it was Gurney's textbook, *Brachygraphy, or an Easy and Compendious System of Shorthand*—

> and plunged into a sea of perplexity that brought me, in a few weeks, to the confines of distraction. The changes that were rung upon dots, which in such a position meant such a thing, and in another position something else, entirely different; the wonderful vagaries that were played by circles; the unaccountable consequences that resulted from marks like flies' legs; the tremendous effects of a curve in a wrong place; not only troubled my waking hours, but reappeared before me in my sleep. When I had groped my way, blindly, through these difficulties, and had mastered the alphabet, which was an Egyptian Temple in itself, there then appeared a procession of new horrors, called arbitrary characters; the most despotic characters I have ever known; who insisted, for instance, that a thing like the beginning of a cobweb, meant expectation, and that a pen-and-ink sky-rocket stood for disadvantageous. When I had fixed these wretches in my mind, I found that they had driven everything else out of it; then, beginning again, I forgot them; while I was picking them up, I dropped the other fragments of the system.

He goes on to describe how after three or four months, when he first made an attempt to take down a speech at Doctors' Commons, the "speaker walked off from me before I began, and left my imbecile pencil staggering about the paper as if it were in a fit!" He turns to practicing at night with Traddles, who reads out speeches to him from "Enfield's Speaker or a volume of parliamentary orations," which the aspiring young writer faithfully takes down. "But, as to reading them after I had got them, I might as well have copied the Chinese inscription on an immense collection of tea-chests, or the golden characters on all the great red and green bottles in the chemists' shops!" In short, he concludes, he spent this period "making the most desperate efforts to know these elusive characters by sight whenever I met them."[6] I should like to suggest that Dickens' prolonged experience as a shorthand writer had a significant effect on what for a writer must be the most important of relations, the relation between speech and writing. The brachygraphic characters, as he describes them in recollection, were themselves doodles—apparently random plays of the pen, out of which figures or partial figures would emerge and to which meaning could be ascribed. It was almost as if the nascent novelist had providentially been given or discovered another way of structurally relating himself to the language. Speech could now be rendered not only in the abstract forms of cursive or printed letters and units; it could be

---

[6] It should be noted that in these passages, Dickens is deliberately fusing and conflating the sense of "characters" as written, conventional marks or pieces of code with the sense of "characters" as actual persons or representations of them in written literature. Once again the playful, paradoxical, and reflexive series of interchanges between the actual process or the behavioral representation of the act of writing in language and the objects which that representation refers to and re-presents are emphatically, and delightfully, brought to the forefront of our awareness.

represented *graphically* as well—the two other forms of written transcription that he refers to are Egyptian hieroglyphics and Chinese ideograms (along with the written code of science, chemistry). What I am suggesting is that this experience of an alternative, quasi-graphic way of representing speech had among other things the effect upon Dickens of loosening up the rigid relations between speech and writing that prevail in our linguistic and cultural system. By providing him with an experience of something that closely resembled a hieroglyphic means of preserving speech, it allowed the spoken language to enter into his writing with a parity it had never enjoyed before in English fictional prose. Speech here was not the traditional subordinate of its written representation; it could appear now in writing with a freedom and spontaneity that made it virtually, if momentarily, writing's equal. And yet whenever a development of this magnitude takes place in writing, in literature, the capacities and possibilities of that written art are themselves suddenly multiplied and enhanced.[7]

This kind of free, wild, inventive doodling language tends to break out in character after character in *Pickwick Papers*, even the most minor ones. The instances are almost limitless, and one more will have to stand for all the rest. After the Dingley Dell–Muggleton cricket match (at which, by the way, Jingle makes another sensational appearance with an account of his own epic match with Sir Thomas Blazo in the West Indies), little Mr. Staple arises to address the assembled company:

> But, sir, while we remember that Muggleton has given birth to a Dumkins and a Podder, let us never forget

[7] In this section I have been adapting a number of analytical and speculative theses put forward separately and in concert by the psychoanalyst Ernst Kris and the art historian E. H. Gombrich. See *Psychoanalytic Explorations of Art* (New York, 1952), pp. 173–216; *Art and Illusion* (Princeton, 1961), pp. 330–358.

that Dingley Dell can boast a Luffey and a Struggles. . . .
Every gentleman who hears me, is probably acquainted
with the reply made by an individual, who—to use an
ordinary figure of speech—"hung out" in a tub, to the
emperor Alexander:—"If I were not Diogenes," said he,
"I would be Alexander." I can well imagine these gentlemen to say, "If I were not Dumkins I would be Luffey;
if I were not Podder I would be Struggles." (Enthu-
siasm.) But . . . is it in cricket alone that your fellow-
townsmen stand preeminent? Have you never heard of
Dumkins and determination? Have you never been
taught to associate Podder with prosperity? (Great
applause.)

But this kind of language in which the primary process is
having a field day (which does not mean that it is pure
fantasy without reference to realities of every description,
external as well as internal and linguistic) gets into Dickens'
authorial prose as well. It is to be found particularly in his
metaphoric figures. Here are two examples: "The evening
grew more dull every moment, and a melancholy wind
sounded through the deserted fields, like a distant giant
whistling for his house-dog" (Chapter 2). Or there is this
from Dingley Dell and the courtship of Tupman and Miss
Wardle. "It was evening . . . the buxom servants were loung-
ing at the side-door, enjoying the pleasantness of the hour,
and the delights of a flirtation, on first principles, with certain unwieldy animals attached to the farm; and there sat
the interesting pair, uncared for by all, caring for none, and
dreaming only of themselves; there they sat, in short, like a
pair of carefully-folded kid gloves—bound up in each other"
(Chapter 8).

As the novel advances, Dickens becomes increasingly preoccupied with what it is he is doing in this connection, and
at a crucial juncture in its early development this preoccupation surfaces and begins consciously to inform the entire

substance of an episode. I am referring to the stone and "Bill Stumps, his mark." Mr. Pickwick discovers the stone and its "fragment of an inscription," but although he can make out the markings and letters, he cannot decipher their meaning. Writing and language remain a secret, a puzzle, an arcanum to him. What he finds is a species of writing, a hieroglyphic, that for him does not reduce to ordinary sense. He thereupon writes a pamphlet ninety-six pages long that contains "twenty-seven different readings of the inscription," and achieves great renown among the learned societies of the civilized world. At this point the vicious Blotton turns up again with another of his poisonous accusations. He denies "the antiquity of the inscription," accuses Pickwick of being a mystifier or a fool, and produces the evidence of the man who sold the stone to Mr. Pickwick. Yet if Blotton is correct, what has he found except writing that is precisely a kind of doodling. It was written or inscribed "in an idle mood," that is to say at random; it is writing apparently for the sake of writing alone. Moreover, it contains still another paradox within itself, since what is supposed to have been written down is the traditional formula that is used when an illiterate man makes his mark. Hence this is the utterly confounding riddle of writing by a man who appears to be *illiterate,* and so perhaps Mr. Pickwick is right after all. In any case, right or wrong, Pickwick or Blotton, what we are confronted with here is writing in the Pickwickian sense once more. And so at this juncture, too, the book reveals itself as being at some deep structural level about the act of its own coming into existence. It is writing about writing, and writing itself—as is "BILL STUMPS, HIS MARK." As a result, Dickens remarks, the stone is "an illegible monument" to Mr. Pickwick, something written but mysteriously unreadable, as in a sense is Dickens in *Pickwick Papers.*

The importance I attribute to this episode is supported by what comes immediately after it. In the very next chapter the novel takes its first really large swerve of development, which is in fact a double swerve. Mr. Pickwick does two things. He sends for Sam Weller, the great master of language and invention, who by virtue of that mastery is going to protect Mr. Pickwick from the world. But while he is doing so he gets into trouble with Mrs. Bardell precisely by being betrayed by the language, which, Pickwick will never be quite able to learn, has an ambiguous social life all its own. The sexual and linguistic plays and implications of the scene need only be touched upon. While Mr. Pickwick is begetting his only begotten son—it is one of the few truly immaculate conceptions in world history—he is having a conversation with Mrs. Bardell that is full of sexual double entendres, none of which are apparent or intelligible to him. Although he has not committed criminal conversation with Mrs. Bardell, he is going to be found guilty of a linguistic offense at law, for which he will be punished, namely breach of promise. His bafflement by language, by the inescapable form in which the experience of this novel (and he himself) is created, is going to lead to his suffering. This eventuality is, however, postponed to a later part of the book, for at this moment, with the active entry of Sam Weller, the novel's proportions are altered again, and it has at last settled into its full course. From now on, Mr. Pickwick will be explicitly represented as employing the language in an essentially innocent or single-minded sense, and out of this his moral innocence and goodness will inexorably grow. At the same time, in Sam, Dickens has invented a virtuoso of language, of both the primary and secondary processes; he is a master hand at managing means and ends, of actively engaging reality through rational, symbolic language as well as appreciating it and playing with it through the other kind. He is unmistakeably Dickens' principal surrogate in the novel itself, the novelist-poet within the novel, and becomes from the moment of his effective entry its dominant creative center.

Hereafter the novel becomes even more clearly a "continuous succession" of language or writing in constant motion, moving itself. We pass directly on to Eatanswill, where we have the language or diction of politics, generating its own obfuscation. Along with this there is Mr. Pott and his journalistic writings and style—in relation to which Mr. Pickwick remains the linguistic innocent. Pott asks Mr. Pickwick to read with him some of his leaders, upon which Dickens comments: "We have every reason to believe that he was perfectly enraptured with the vigour and freshness of the style; indeed . . . his eyes were closed, as if with excess of pleasure, during the whole time of their perusal" (Chapter 13). And indeed one of the most charming moments in the entire novel is when Mr. Pickwick forgets how to speak altogether. Soon, however, everything is breaking into speech, including the furniture, as the chair does in "The Bagman's Tale" of Tom Smart. There naturally follows Mrs. Leo Hunter and her literary breakfasts—the subject of which is literature and writing, and we find again that the writing, the novel, takes itself for its subject in the very act of its creation. Pope gets into it under false pretenses—"feasts of reason, sir, and flows of soul," quotes Mr. Leo Hunter, who then adds "as somebody who wrote a sonnet to Mrs. Leo Hunter on her breakfasts, feelingly and originally observed"—as do language and writing in almost innumerable forms, some of them indescribable. Even foreigners are dragged into the act, as in the passages about Count Smorltork and his pursuit of English under difficulties, passages which Dickens was going to use again but to other effects almost thirty years later in *Our Mutual Friend.*

By this time it seems evident that Dickens was intermittently and fleetingly close to being aware of the extraordinary thing that was happening to him or that he was doing—it is never quite clear which. There are any number of instances that indicate such an oblique and partial awareness, out of which mass I shall choose but one. It occurs at the beginning of Chapter 17, with Mr. Pickwick in bed with an attack of rheumatism brought on by his night spent out-doors in the damp. The bulk of the chapter consists of the tale of "The Parish Clerk," which Mr. Pickwick produces, "with sundry blushes . . . as having been 'edited' by himself, during his recent indisposition, from his notes of Mr. Wel-ler's unsophisticated recital." This is a wonderful bit of play, and what we have is as follows: at this moment Pickwick is to Sam as Dickens is to Mr. Pickwick. Yet we know as well that Sam is in some closely intimate sense also Dickens. So Pickwick is to Dickens as Dickens is to Pickwick—that is, for an instant Pickwick is editing Dickens, or in other words, writing his own book. Once again writing seems to be re-flexively writing itself. Another embodiment of this circum-stance begins to take shape with the increasing presence in the novel of the law, which is another kind of language and another kind of writing. Mr. Pickwick first becomes aware of its ominous presence when he receives a letter from Dodson and Fogg informing him "that a writ has been issued against you in this suit in the Court of Common Pleas" (Chapter 18). The novel thus proceeds to make itself by this continuous succession of kinds of writing spontane-ously introduced—and that for the most part is what con-stitutes its structure. It is a structure that is, like the events themselves, "a gross violation of all established rules and precedents," which may, for all I know, be what Dickens meant when he referred to "a gentle and not-unnatural progress of adventure."[8] For it constitutes itself in the main by Dickens' repeatedly rising up in the form of one charac-ter after another and bursting irrepressibly "into an ani-mated torrent of words" (Chapter 20).

But that is by no means all *Pickwick Papers* is. There are, for example, those notorious interpolated tales. On this

---

[8] The characterizing "gross violation" and so forth is made by the gamekeeper as a heartfelt protest "against the introduction into a shooting party, of a gentleman in a barrow" (Chapter 19).

reading—as on others—they dramatically represent the obverse principle to that which informs the body of the novel. In them motion and movement of both language and event come to a dead halt. In almost every one of them, even the funny ones, someone is paralyzed, immobilized, or locked up and imprisoned in something. Their language is not the free, wild, astonishingly creative language of the balance of the novel. It tends almost uniformly to be obsessed, imprisoned, anal, caught in various immobile, repetitive modes— to be for the largest part unmastered. One passage will remind us adequately of the effect of the whole. It comes from the most important of those tales, "The Old Man's Tale about the Queer Client."

> That night, in the silence and desolation of his miserable room, the wretched man knelt down by the dead body of his wife, and called on God to witness a terrible oath, that from that hour, he devoted himself to revenge her death and that of his child; that thenceforth to the last moment of his life, his whole energies should be directed to this *one object*; that his revenge should be protracted and terrible; that his hatred should be undying and inextinguishable; and should hunt its *object* through the world [my italics] (Chapter 21).

The object in question is the antithesis of that "constant succession" which Dickens asserted to be his overarching creative intention. The language in which that object is represented is itself as yet utterly unfree; and the tales of that language are accordingly encapsulated, stuck, encysted, and imbedded in the movement of the novel which moves about and around them.

As that movement proceeds, it takes a still wilder turn with the introduction of Tony Weller. Tony is in some measure a representation in language of the energies and workings of the primary process itself; he is Sam without the rationality, the logic, the instrumental relation to the world. Much of him may be caught from this one interchange with Mr. Pickwick, on the nature of the "Wery queer life" led by turnpike keepers.

> "They's all on 'em men as has met vith some disappointment in life," said Mr. Weller senior.
>
> "Ay, ay?" said Mr. Pickwick.
>
> "Yes. Consequence of vich, they retires from the world, and shuts themselves up in pikes; partly vith the view of being solitary, and partly to rewenge themselves on mankind, by takin' tolls."
>
> "Dear me," said Mr. Pickwick, "I never knew that before."
>
> "Fact, sir," said Mr. Weller; "if they was gen'l'm'n you'd call them misanthropes, but as it is, they only takes to pike-keepin' " (Chapter 22).

And Dickens proceeds to remark that Tony's conversation had "the inestimable charm" and virtue of "blending amusement with instruction," thus implying that he is, in short, literature itself. With Sam and Tony entering upon dialogue the novel finds its most creative moments, many of which are about its own mysterious nature, about the activity whereby it continues to bring itself into being. The *locus classicus*, of course, is Chapter 33, which is about Sam's writing a valentine, and Mr. Weller "the elder" delivering "some Critical Sentiments respecting Literary Composition." Detail after detail is brought lightly to bear upon this fundamental preoccupation. There is, for example, the boy who comes looking for Sam with a message from Tony—"young brockiley sprout" Sam calls him—who having delivered his message "walked away, awakening all the echoes in George Yard as he did so, with several chaste and extremely correct imitations of a drover's whistle, delivered in a tone of peculiar richness and volume." Then there is Sam, looking in a stationer's window and seeing a valentine, which Dickens thereupon describes:

> The particular picture on which Sam Weller's eyes were fixed . . . was a highly coloured representation of a couple of human hearts skewered together with an arrow cooking before a cheerful fire, while a male and female cannibal in modern attire: the gentleman being clad in a blue coat and white trousers, and the lady in a deep red pelisse with a parasol of the same: were approaching the meal with hungry eyes, up a serpentine gravel path leading thereunto. A decidedly indelicate young gentleman, in a pair of wings and nothing else, was depicted as superintending the cooking; a representation of the spire of the church in Langham Place, London, appeared in the distance; and the whole formed a "valentine," of which, as a written inscription in the window testified, there was a large assortment within, which the shopkeeper pledged himself to dispose of, to his countrymen generally, at the reduced rate of one and sixpence each.

Sam then walks on toward Leadenhall Market in search of the Blue Boar, whence his father's summons had emanated. "Looking round him, he there beheld a sign-board on which the painter's art had delineated something remotely resembling a cerulean elephant with an aquiline nose in lieu of a trunk. Rightly conjecturing that this was the Blue Boar himself," he steps inside and begins to compose his valentine while waiting for his father. In due time Tony arrives and the immortal conversation about "literary composition" takes place. "Lovely creetur," begins Sam's valentine.

"Tain't in poetry, is it?" interposed his father.

"No, no," replied Sam.

"Werry glad to hear it," said Mr. Weller. "Poetry's un-nat'ral; no man ever talked poetry 'cept a beadle on boxin' day, or Warren's blackin', or Rowland's oil, or some o' them low fellows; never you let yourself down to talk poetry, my boy. Begin agin, Sammy."

And he goes on in the course of this conversation to make similar magisterial observations about words, style, metaphor, and writing in general.

In this chapter the young Dickens is writing at the very top of his inventive bent, and what he is implicitly and covertly asserting is that there is nothing he cannot capture and represent in his writing. He can gratuitously bring to life the sound of a drover's whistle, or even an extremely correct imitation of that sound, if that is what is wanted. He can turn pictures into writing which is more vivid, more graphic, more representational than the pictures themselves —as he does with the valentine. He can represent things more accurately and graphically than graphic art, as he does with the sign of the Blue Boar. His writing is superior even to poetry, both because it is more "natural" and because it can include all poetry, its agents and its objects, within its limitless range. It can even include Warren's blacking, and when we take note of this inclusion we understand that what Dickens is unconsciously asserting is that there is at this moment nothing he cannot overcome, there is nothing he cannot transcend, by writing about it, or through *writing it*. He genuinely feels free, for he is writing in freedom. He is perhaps the first novelist ever to have done so in such a degree.

It is very much to the point that it is at just this moment that Dickens chooses to emphasize that Sam, great poet and impresario of the language that he is, can hardly write. Dickens is the writer and Sam is what he is writing—that is, one brilliantly split off, deflected, and reorganized segment of himself. It was part of Dickens' genius as a writer to write Sam, or to tap that untapped resource of language in the near-illiterate, and to get that speech, and *its* genius into writing, into his writing. It was his genius, in other words, to be able *to write that as yet unwritten language.* It is at such a juncture that society and social change on the one hand and language and writing on the other all come richly together.

Correlative with this development, Dickens and Sam both become increasingly conscious of the meaning and value of Pickwick. At one point, it is asserted that Pickwick is a "magic word," and in a subsequent episode the cat is let entirely out of the bag. They are waiting in the travelers' room of the White Horse Cellar, when Sam emphatically draws his master's attention to a coach that is standing outside, and to what is written on its door: "and there, sure enough, in gilt letters of a goodly size, was the magic name of PICKWICK!" (Chapter 35). At this moment both the magic and the reality that in collaboration go into the formation of creative originality are brought into active conjunction. For the name of Pickwick was clearly taken by Dickens from the actual man who ran the Bath coach. Moreover, as Sam does not fail indignantly to inform us, his first name was Moses. And at this point it becomes our turn to recall that "Boz" is a shortened version of Moses—and to realize again and in another way what we already know differently, that Boz and Pickwick are of course one. Even more, however, the real Pickwick was a coachman—and thus we realize once again that Mr. Pickwick and Tony are also in reality one, as in point of fact they were, both of them imaginative refractions and idealizations of John Dickens. It is Sam who voices Dickens' final comment on this nexus, saying something for once that is beyond his own enlarged understanding. To put the name Moses before Pickwick, he says, is what "I call addin' insult to injury, as the parrot said ven they not only took him from his native land, but made him talk the English langwidge arterwards" (Chapter 35). The whole secret is in learning the English language; the secret lies in that primordial mystery that seems spontaneously to be creating out of itself, out of its own inherent resources, this marvelous work.

Finally there is the trial, which is a veritable mania of language in almost all the forms that have appeared before. There is the language, or languages, of the law itself; there is more court reporting on Dickens' part and more shorthand writing in an ideally transcribed form. There is the rhetoric of Buzfuz, and his masterful dealing with writing, with Mrs. Bardell's "written placard"—"I intreat the attention of the jury to the wording of this document. 'Apartments furnished for a single gentleman'!"—as well as with Mr. Pickwick's fatally compromising letters. There is the presiding judge, Mr. Justice Stareleigh, who wakening from the slumber in which he conducts almost all of the trial "immediately wrote down something with a pen without any ink in it," and whose questioning of Winkle follows a similar intelligible line.

"What's your Christian name, sir?" angrily inquired the little judge.

"Nathaniel, sir."

"Daniel,—any other name?"

"Nathaniel, sir—my Lord, I mean."

"Nathaniel Daniel, or Daniel Nathaniel?"

"No, my Lord, only Nathaniel; not Daniel at all."

"What did you tell me it was Daniel for, then, sir?" inquired the judge.

"I didn't, my Lord," replied Mr. Winkle.

"You did, sir," replied the judge, with a severe frown. "How could I have got Daniel on my notes, unless you told me so, sir?"

This argument was, of course, unanswerable.

Exactly. As are those arguments and circumstances through which Mr. Pickwick at length finds himself in prison, at which point, as everyone knows, the novel makes its final, momentous turn of development. Mr. Pickwick has in effect let himself be put in prison by the law, by its licentious abuse and misuse of language. And as he is thus confined within the world or precincts of the law, Dickens' writing, too, becomes imprisoned and immobile, preoccupied again as it was in the tales with intensities and obsessions and closeness and deprivation and filth, bound in by the law, by cases, by the past, by the accumulated weight of mold and dirt and misery that the prison and the law represent. But the writing in these crucial passages is not exactly the same as the writing in the interpolated tales; it is harder and has a greater bite to it. That writing, which before was free, has become like Mr. Pickwick himself engaged and involved, and engaged and involved with society. For in the person of the law Pickwick and Dickens have run into something which though it may seem at first to be an unalloyed linguistic universe is in fact much more than a world of words. It is and it represents society and its structures, in particular those structures known as property and money, both of them extralinguistic phenomena. Property and money are more than words, and words cannot make you free of them. It is a matter of the very largest moment for Dickens' development as a writer—and a testimony to his exceptional inner integrity—that he should, in the midst of his greatest celebration of his freedom and transcendence as a genius of language, engage himself imaginatively in those very conditions which were calculated most powerfully to nullify that freedom. His entire future development is contained by anticipation in that nullification.

In one of his later utterances, Hegel undertook to settle a long-outstanding score between himself and Rousseau. As for the Rousseauian idea of some original state of freedom, he declared bluntly, it simply makes no sense. Hegel was a great genius, but he was an old man when he made this remark and had long since forgotten his childhood and youth, let alone his youthful writings. Dickens was also a great genius, who wrote *Pickwick Papers* in the flush of his young manhood, as a celebration of the positive sides of the childhood and youth that he yet remembered and as an exercise of what may be the highest kind of freedom that an individual person can enjoy: the freedom that consists in the exercise of one's native powers and that has as its consequence the creation out of one's self of an object that is of lasting value and that is at the same time an activity of self-creation. What Hegel goes on next to say, however, is of larger pertinence. It is true, he declares, that we are all unfree, that we all suffer from a pervasive sense of limitation, confinement, and constraint; yet that very constraint, he states, "is part of the process through which is first produced the consciouness of and the desire for freedom in its true, that is, its rational and ideal form." Indeed, he continues, every terrible limitation upon impulse, desire, and passion that we feel is itself "the very condition leading to liberation; and society and the state are the very conditions in which freedom is realized." What Hegel in his prodigious austerity is saying is that freedom can only come about, can only be realized, in and through its negation. A truly human freedom, that freedom which is the one goal worthy of being the "destination" of men as the human species, can only be achieved through the most profound historical experience of negativity. It is, it seems to me, no accident that Dickens installed that negativity at the dramatic center of his first and freest novel, at the very moment when he was sustaining himself with a freedom that was virtually unexampled in the history of the novel. The consequences that such a creative act of courage had are known to us all— they are nothing less than Dickens' long and arduous subsequent development, a development that as the later novels make increasingly clear is in fact a search for a wider, a more general, and a truly human freedom.

(1972)

Freud and Dora: Story, History, Case History

1

It is generally agreed that Freud's case histories are unique. Today more than half a century after they were written they are still widely read. Even more, they are still widely used for instruction and training in psychoanalytic institutes. One of the inferences that such a vigorous condition of survival prompts is that these writings have not yet been superseded. Like other masterpieces of literature or the arts, these works seem to possess certain transhistorical qualities—although it may by no means be easy to specify what those qualities are. The implacable "march of science" has not—or has not yet—consigned them to "mere" history. Their singular and mysterious complexity, density, and richness have thus far prevented such a transformation and demotion.

This state of affairs has received less attention than it merits. Freud's case histories—and his works in general— are unique as pieces or kinds of writing, and it may be useful to regard them from the standpoint that this statement implies. I shall undertake, then, to examine one of Freud's case histories from the point of view of literary criticism, to analyze it as a piece of writing, and to determine whether this method of proceeding may yield results that other means have not. The assumption with which I begin, as well as the end that I hope to demonstrate, is that Freud is a great writer and that one of his major case histories is a great work of literature—that is to say, it is both an outstanding creative and imaginative performance and an intellectual and cognitive achievement of the highest order. And yet, as we shall see, this triumphant greatness is in part connected with the circumstance that it is about a kind of failure, and that part of the failure remains in fact unacknowledged and unconscious.[1]

"Fragment of an Analysis of a Case of Hysteria," better known to future readers as the case of Dora, is Freud's first great case history—oddly enough, he was to write only four others. It may be helpful for the reader if at the outset I refresh his memory by briefly reviewing some of the external facts of the case. In the autumn of 1900 Dora, an eighteen-year-old young woman, began treatment with Freud. She did so reluctantly and against her will, and, Freud writes, "it was only her father's authority which induced her to come to me at all." (22)[2] Neither Dora nor her

---

[1] The empirical rule that literary criticism generally follows is to trust the tale and not the teller; indeed, it was the empirical rule pursued by Freud himself.

[2] All quotations have been drawn from *The Standard Edition of the Complete Psychological Works of Sigmund Freud*, VII, 3–122. Num-

father was a stranger to Freud. He had made separate acquaintance with both of them in the past, during certain episodes of illness that characterized their lives if not the life of the family as a whole. (Freud knew other members of the family as well.) Dora's father was a man "of rather unusual activity and talents, a large manufacturer in very comfortable circumstances." (18) In 1888 he had fallen ill with tuberculosis, which had made it necessary for the family to move to small town with a good climate in some southern part of Austria; for the next ten years or so that remained their chief place of residence. In 1892 he suffered a detached retina which led to a permanent impairment of his vision. Two years later he fell gravely ill—it was "a confusional attack, followed by symptoms of paralysis and slight mental disturbances." (19) He was persuaded by a friend to come to Vienna and consult with Freud, who was then a rising young neurologist and psychiatrist. Freud settled upon the diagnosis of "diffuse vascular affection," a meningeal disturbance associated with the tertiary stage of syphilis; and since the patient admitted to having had a "specific infection" of syphilis before he married, Freud prescribed "an energetic course of anti-luetic treatment, as a result of which all the remaining disturbances passed off." (19) By 1899 his constitution had sufficiently recovered from the tuberculosis to justify the family's leaving the health resort and moving to "the town in which his factory was situated"; and in 1900 they moved again and settled permanently in Vienna.

Despite this long and protracted history of illness—he also at one time had apparently been infected with gonorrhea, which he may have passed on to his wife—Dora's

---

bers in parentheses represent pages from which quotations have been taken. The Strachey translation has been checked against the text in *Gesammelte Werke*, V, 163–286. In a few places the translation has been corrected.

father was clearly a dominating figure: vigorous, active, energetic, enterprising, and intelligent. Nothing of the sort could be said of Dora's mother, who from the accounts received of her by Freud appeared to his imagination as

> an uncultivated woman and above all as a foolish one, who had concentrated all her interests upon domestic affairs, especially since her husband's illness and the estrangement to which it led. She presented the picture, in fact, of what might be called the "housewife's psychosis." She had no understanding of her children's more active interests, and was occupied all day long in cleaning the house with its furniture and in keeping them clean—to such an extent as to make it almost impossible to use or enjoy them. (20)

The immediate family circle was completed by a brother, a year and a half older than Dora, who hardly figures in the account rendered by Freud and who seems to have escaped from his childhood and family experiences without severe disablements. In adult life he became a leading figure in Socialist politics and apparently led an active, successful, and distinguished career up to his death many years later.

As for Dora herself, her afflictions, both mental and physical, had begun in early childhood and had persisted and flourished with variations and fluctuating intensities until she was presented to Freud for therapy. Among the symptoms from which she suffered were to be found dyspnea, migraine, and periodic attacks of nervous coughing often accompanied by complete loss of voice during part of the episode. Dora had in fact first been brought by her father to Freud two years earlier, when she was sixteen and suffering from a cough and hoarseness; he had then "proposed giving her psychological treatment," but this suggestion was not adopted, since "the attack in question, like the others, passed off spontaneously." (22) In the course of his treat-

ment of Dora, Freud also learned of further hysterical—or
hysterically connected—productions on her part, such as a
feverish attack that mimicked appendicitis, a periodic limp,
and a vaginal catarrh or discharge. Moreover, during the
two-year interval between Dora's first visit and the occasion on which her father brought her to Freud a second
time, and "handed her over to me for psychotherapeutic
treatment" (19), "Dora had grown unmistakeably neurotic"
in what today we would recognize as more familiar mani-
festations of emotional distress. Dora was now "in the first
bloom of youth—a girl of intelligent and engaging looks."
(23) Her character had, however, undergone an alteration.
She had become chronically depressed and was generally
dissatisfied with both herself and her family. She had become unfriendly toward the father, whom she had hitherto
loved, idealized, and identified with. She was "on very bad
terms" with her mother, for whom she felt a good deal of
scorn. "She tried to avoid social intercourse, and employed
herself—so far as she was allowed to by the fatigue and
lack of concentration of which she complained—with attending lectures for women and with carrying on more or less
serious studies."[3] (23) Two further events precipitated the
crisis which led to her being delivered to Freud. Her parents
found a written note in which she declared her intention
to commit suicide because "as she said, she could no longer
endure her life." Following this there occurred one day "a
slight passage of words" between Dora and her father,
which ended with Dora suddenly losing consciousness—the
attack, Freud believed, was "accompanied by convulsions
and delirious states," although it was lost to amnesia and
never came up in the analysis.

Having outlined this array of affections, Freud dryly
remarks that such a case "does not upon the whole seem

---

[3] It is worth noting that Freud tells us nothing more about these
activities.

worth recording. It is merely a case of *'petite hystérie'* with the commonest of all somatic and mental symptoms. . . . More interesting cases of hysteria have no doubt been published . . . for nothing will be found in the following pages on the subject of stigmata of cutaneous sensibility, limitation of the visual field, or similar matters." (24) This disavowal of anything sensational to come is of course a bit of shrewd disingenuousness on Freud's part, for what follows at once is his assertion that he is going to elucidate the meaning, origin, and function of every one of these symptoms by means of the events and experiences of Dora's life. He is going, in other words, to discover the "psychological determinants" that will account for Dora's illnesses; among these determinants he lists three principal conditions: "a psychical trauma, a conflict of affects, and . . . a disturbance in the sphere of sexuality." (24) And so Freud begins the treatment by asking Dora to talk about her experiences. What emerges is the substance of the case history, a substance which takes all of Freud's immense analytic, expository, and narrative talents to bring into order. I will again very roughly and briefly summarize some of this material.

Sometime after 1888, when the family had moved to B—— (the health resort where the father's tuberculosis had sent them), an intimate and enduring friendship sprang up between them and a couple named K. Dora's father was deeply unhappy in his marriage and apparently made no bones about it. The K.'s too were unhappily married, as it later turned out. Frau K. took to nursing Dora's father during these years of his illness. She also befriended Dora, and they behaved toward one another in the most familiar way and talked together about the most intimate subjects. Herr K., her husband, also made himself a close friend of Dora's —going regularly for walks with her and giving her presents. Dora in her turn befriended the K.'s two small children, "and had been almost a mother to them." What begins to be slowly if unmistakably disclosed is that Dora's father and Frau K. had established a sexual liaison and that this relation had by the time of Dora's entering into treatment endured for many years. At the same time Dora's father and Frau K. had tacitly connived at turning Dora over to Herr K., just as years later her father "handed her over to me [Freud] for psychotherapeutic treatment." And Dora had herself, at least at first, behaved toward Frau K.'s children in much the same way that Frau K. had behaved toward her. Up to a certain point, then, the characters in this embroilment were virtually behaving as if they were walking in their sleep. In some sense everyone was conspiring to conceal what was going on; and in some yet further sense everyone was conspiring to deny that anything was going on at all. What we have here, on one of its sides, is a classical Victorian domestic drama, that is at the same time a sexual and emotional can of worms.

Matters were brought to a crisis by two events that occurred to Dora at two different periods of her adolescence. When she was fourteen Herr K. contrived one day to be alone with her in his place of business; in a state of sexual excitement, he "suddenly clasped the girl to him and pressed a kiss on her lips." (28) Dora responded with a "violent feeling of disgust," and hurried away. This experience, like those referred to in the foregoing paragraph, was never discussed with or mentioned to anyone, and relations continued as before. The second scene took place two years later in the summer when Dora was sixteen (it was just after she had seen Freud for the first time). She and Herr K. were taking a walk by a lake in the Alps. In Dora's words, as they come filtered to us through Freud, Herr K. "had the audacity to make her a proposal." Apparently he had begun to declare his love for this girl whom he had known so well for so long. "No sooner had she grasped Herr K.'s intention than, without letting him finish what he had to say, she had given him a slap in the face and hurried away." (46). The episode as a whole will lead Freud quite plausibly to ask:

"If Dora loved Herr K., what was the reason for her refusing him in the scene by the lake? Or at any rate, why did her refusal take such a brutal form, as though she were embittered against him? And how could a girl who was in love feel insulted by a proposal which was made in a manner neither tactless nor offensive?" (38) It may occur to us to wonder whether in the extended context of this case that slap in the face was a "brutal form" of refusal; but as for the other questions posed by Freud, they are without question rhetorical in character.

On this second occasion Dora did not remain silent. Her father was preparing to depart from the Alpine lake, and she declared her determination to leave at once with him. Two weeks later she told the story of the scene by the lake to her mother, who relayed it—as Dora had clearly intended—to her father. In due course Herr K. was "called to account" on this score, but he

> denied in the most emphatic terms having on his side made any advances which could have been open to such a construction. He had then proceeded to throw suspicion upon the girl, saying that he had heard from Frau K. that she used to read Mantegazza's *Physiology of Love* and books of that sort in their house on the lake. It was most likely, he had added, that she had been over-excited by such reading and had merely "fancied" the whole scene she had described. (26)

Dora's father "believed" the story concocted by Herr—and Frau—K., and it is from this moment, more than two years before she came to Freud for treatment, that the change in Dora's character can be dated. Her love for the K.'s turned into hatred, and she became obsessed with the idea of getting her father to break off relations with them. She saw through the rationalizations and denials of her father and Frau K., and had "no doubt that what bound her father to this young and beautiful woman was a common love-affair. Nothing that could help to confirm this view had escaped her perception, which in this connection was pitilessly sharp. . . ." (32) Indeed, "the sharp-sighted Dora" was an excellent detective when it came to uncovering her father's clandestine sexual activities, and her withering criticisms of her father's character—that he was "insincere . . . had a strain of baseness in his character . . . only thought of his own enjoyment . . . had a gift for seeing things in the light which suited him best" (34)—were in general concurred in by Freud. As he also agreed that there was something in her embittered if exaggerated contention that "she had been handed over to Herr K. as the price of his tolerating the relations between her father and his wife."[4] (34) Nevertheless, the cause of her greatest embitterment seems to have been her father's "readiness to consider the scene by the lake as a product of her imagination. She was almost beside herself at the idea of its being supposed that she had merely fancied something on that occasion." (46) And although Freud was in his customary way skeptical about such impassioned protestations and repudiations—and surmised that something in the way of an opposite series of thoughts or self-reproaches lay behind them—he was forced to come to "the conclusion that Dora's story must correspond to the facts in every respect." (46) If we try to put ourselves in the place of this girl between her sixteenth and eighteenth years, we can at once recognize that her situation was a desperate one. The three adults to whom she was closest, whom she loved the most in the world, were apparently conspiring—separately, in tandem, or in concert—to

---

[4] Later on, Freud adds to this judgment by affirming that "Dora's father was never entirely straightforward. He had given his support to the treatment so long as he could hope that I should 'talk' Dora out of her belief that there was something more than a friendship between him and Frau K. His interest faded when he observed that it was not my intention to bring about that result." (109)

deny her the reality of her experience. They were conspiring to deny Dora her reality and reality itself. This betrayal touched upon matters that might easily unhinge the mind of a young person; for the three adults were not betraying Dora's love and trust alone, they were betraying the structure of the actual world. And indeed, when Dora's father handed her over to Freud with the parting injunction "Please try and bring her to reason" (26), there were no two ways of taking what he meant. Naturally, he had no idea of the mind and character of the physician to whom he had dealt this leading remark.

Two other persons round out the cast of characters of this late-Victorian romance. And it seems only appropriate that they should come directly from the common stock of Victorian literature and culture, both of them being governesses. The first of these was Dora's own governess, "an unmarried woman, no longer young, who was well read and of advanced views." (36) This woman "used to read every book on sexual life and similar subjects, and talked to the girl about them," at the same time enjoining Dora to secrecy about such conversations. She had long since divined the goings-on between Dora's father and Frau K. and had in the past tried in vain to turn Dora against both Frau K. and her father. Although she had turned a blind eye to this side of things, Dora very quickly penetrated into the governess' real secret: she, too, was in love with Dora's father. And when Dora realized that this governess was actually indifferent to her—Dora's—welfare, she "dropped her." At the same time Dora had to dimly realize that there was an analogy between the governess' behavior in Dora's family and Dora's behavior in relation to the children of the K.'s and Herr K. The second governess made her appearance during Dora's last analytic hour; the appearance was brilliantly elicited by Freud, who remarked that Dora's decision to leave him, arrived at, she said, a fortnight beforehand, " 'sounds just like a maid servant or governess—a fortnight's

warning.'" (105) This second governess was a young girl
employed by the K.'s at the time of Dora's fateful visit to
them at the Alpine lake some two years before. She was a
silent young person, who seemed totally to ignore the existence of Herr K. Yet a day or two before the scene at the
lake she took Dora aside and told her that Herr K. had
approached her sexually, had pleaded his unhappy cause
with her, had in fact seduced her, but had quickly ceased
to care for her. He had, in short, done to her what in a day
or two he was going to try to do again with Dora. The girl
said she now hated Herr K., yet she did not go away at
once, but waited there hoping that Herr K.'s affections
would turn again in her direction. Dora's response at the
lake and afterward was in part a social one—anger at being
treated by Herr K. as if she were a servant or governess;
but it was also in part a response by identification, since
she, too, did not tell the story at once but waited perhaps
for something further from Herr K. And when, after the
two-week interval, she did tell the story, Herr K. did not
renew "his proposals but . . . replied instead with denials
and slanders" (108) in which he was aided and abetted by
Dora's father and Frau K. Dora's cup of bitterness was full
to overflowing, as the following two years of deep unhappi-
ness and deepening illness undeniably suggest.

2

Dora began treatment with Freud sometime in October,
1900, for on the fourteenth of that month Freud writes Fliess
that "I have a new patient, a girl of eighteen; the case has
opened smoothly to my collection of picklocks." According
to this statement the analysis was proceeding well, but it
was also not proceeding well. The material produced was
very rich, but Dora was there more or less against her will.
Moreover, she was more than usually amnesic about events
in her remote past and about her inner and mental life—a
past and a life toward which Freud was continually pressing

her—and met many or even most of his interpretations with statements such as "I don't know," and with a variety of denials, resistances, and grudging silences. The analysis found its focus and climax in two dreams. The first of these was the production by Dora of a dream that in the past she had dreamed recurrently.[5] Among the many messages concealed by it, Freud made out one that he conveyed to his patient: " 'you have decided to give up the treatment,' " he told her, adding, " 'to which, after all, it is only your father who makes you come.' " (70). It was a self-fulfilling interpretation. A few weeks after the first dream, the second dream occurred. Freud spent two hours elucidating it, and at the beginning of the third, which took place on December 31, 1900, Dora informed him that she was there for the last time. Freud pressed on during this hour and presented Dora with a series of stunning and outrageously intelligent interpretations. The analysis ended as follows: "Dora had listened to me without any of her usual contradictions. She seemed to be moved; she said good-bye to me very warmly, with the heartiest wishes for the New Year, and—came no more." (109) Dora's father subsequently called on Freud two or three times to reassure him that Dora was returning, but Freud knew better than to take him at his word. Fifteen months later, in April, 1902, Dora returned for a single visit; what she had to tell Freud on that occasion was of some interest, but he knew that she was done with him, as indeed she was.

Dora was actuated by many impulses in breaking off the treatment; prominent among these partial motives was

[5] Since this dream will be referred to frequently in what is to come, it may be helpful to the reader if I reproduce its wording: "A house was on fire. My father was standing beside my bed and woke me up. I dressed quickly. Mother wanted to stop and save her jewel-case; but Father said: 'I refuse to let myself and my two children be burnt for the sake of your jewel-case.' We hurried downstairs, and as soon as I was outside I woke up." (64)

revenge—upon men in general and at that moment Freud in particular, who was standing for those other men in her life who had betrayed and injured her. He writes rather ruefully of Dora's "breaking off so unexpectedly, just when my hopes of a successful termination of the treatment were at their highest, and her thus bringing those hopes to nothing—this was an unmistakeable act of vengeance on her part." And although Dora's "purpose of self-injury" was also served by this action, Freud goes on clearly to imply that he felt hurt and wounded by her behavior. Yet it could not have been so unexpected as all that, since as early as the first dream, Freud both understood and had communicated this understanding to Dora that she had already decided to give up the treatment.[6] What is suggested by this logical hiatus is that although Dora had done with Freud, Freud had not done with Dora. And this supposition is supported by what immediately followed. As soon as Dora left him, Freud began writing up her case history—a proceeding that, as far as I have been able to ascertain, was not in point of immediacy a usual response for him. He interrupted the composition of the *Psychopathology of Everyday Life* on which he was then engaged and wrote what is substantially the case of Dora during the first three weeks of January, 1901. On January 25 he wrote to Fliess that he had finished the work the day before and added, with that terrifying self-confidence of judgment that he frequently revealed, "Anyhow, it is the most subtle thing I have yet written and will produce an even more horrifying effect than usual." (4) The title he had at first given the new work—"Dreams and Hysteria"— suggests the magnitude of ambition that was at play in him. This specific case history, "in which the explanations are

[6] It is also permissible to question why Freud's hopes for a successful termination were at that moment at their highest—whether they were in fact so, and what in point of fact his entire statement means. We shall return to this passage later.

grouped round two dreams . . . is in fact a continuation of the dream book. It further contains solutions of hysterical symptoms and considerations on the sexual-organic basis of the whole condition." As the provisional title and these further remarks reveal, it was to be nothing less than a concentrated synthesis of Freud's first two major works, *Studies on Hysteria* (1895) and *The Interpretation of Dreams* (1900), to which there had been added the new dimension of the "sexual-organic basis," that is, the psycho-sexual developmental stages that he was going to represent in fuller detail in the *Three Essays on the Theory of Sexuality* (1905). It was thus a summation, a new synthesis, a crossing point and a great leap forward all at once. Dora had taken her revenge on Freud, who in turn chose not to behave in kind. At the same time, however, Freud's settling of his account with Dora took on the proportions of a heroic inner and intellectual enterprise.

Yet that account was still by no means settled, as the obscure subsequent history of this work dramatically demonstrates. In the letter of January 25, 1901, Freud had written to Fliess that the paper had already been accepted by Ziehen, joint editor of the *Monatsschrift für Psychiatrie und Neurologie*, by which he must mean that the acceptance did not include a reading of the piece, which had only been "finished" the day before. On the fifteenth of February, in another letter to Fliess, he remarks that he is now finishing up *The Psychopathology of Everyday Life*, and that when he has done so, he will correct it and the case history—by which he apparently means that he will go through one last revision of the mss. and then "send them off, etc." That "etc." is covering considerable acreage. About two months later, in March, 1901, according to Ernest Jones, Freud showed "his notes of the case"—whatever *that* may mean—to his close friend Oscar Rie. The reception Rie gave to them was such, reports Freud, that "I thereupon determined to make no further effort to break down my state of isolation."[7] That determination was less than unshakable, and on May 8, 1901, Freud wrote to Fliess that he had not yet "made up his mind" to send off the work. One month later he made up his mind and sent it off, announcing to Fliess that "it will meet the gaze of an astonished public in the autumn." (4) But nothing of the sort was to occur, and what happened next was, according to Jones, "entirely mysterious" and remains so. Freud either sent it off to Ziehen, the editor who had already accepted it, and then having sent it, asked for it back. Or he sent it off to another magazine altogether, the *Journal für Psychologie und Neurologie*, whose editor, one Brodmann, refused to publish it, basing his outright rejection, it has been surmised, on the grounds of the improprieties and indiscretions that would be perpetrated by such a publication. (Jones, II, 255f.) The upshot of all those circlings and countercirclings was that Freud returned the manuscript to a drawer for four more years. And when he did at last send it into print, it was in the journal that had accepted it in the first place.

But we are not out of the darkness and perplexities yet, for when Freud finally decided in 1905 to publish the case, he revised the work once again. As James Strachey remarks, "there is no means of deciding the extent" of these revisions, meaning no certain, external, or physical means. Strachey nonetheless maintains that "all the internal evidence suggests . . . that he changed it very little." According to my reading, Strachey is incorrect, and there is considerable internal evidence that intimates much change. But this is no place to argue such matters, and anyway, who can say precisely what Strachey means by "little" or what I mean by

[7] Ernest Jones, *The Life and Work of Sigmund Freud*, 3 vols. (New York, 1953–1957), I, 362. Oscar Rie was a pediatrician who had earlier worked as Freud's assistant at Kassowitz's Institute for Children's Diseases; he became a member of Freud's intimate circle, was a partner at the Saturday night tarok games, and was at the time the Freud family physician.

"much"? There is one further touch of puzzlements to top it all off. Freud got the date of his case wrong. When he wrote or rewrote it, either in January, 1901, or in 1905, he assigned the case to the autumn of 1899 instead of 1900. And he continued to date it incorrectly, repeating the error in 1914 in the "History of the Psychoanalytic Movement" and again in 1923 when he added a number of new footnotes to the essay on the occasion of its publication in the eighth volume of his *Gesammelte Schriften*. Among the many things suggested by this recurrent error is that in some sense he had still not done with Dora, as indeed I think we shall see he had not. The modern reader may be inclined to remark that all this hemming and hawing about dates and obscurities of composition, questions of revision, problems of textual status, and authorial uncertainties of attitude would be more suitable to the discussion of a literary text—a poem, play, or novel—than to a work of "science." If this is so, one has to reply to this hypothetical reader that he is barking up the wrong discourse, and that his conception of the nature of scientific discourse—particularly the modes of discourse that are exercised in those disciplines which are not preponderantly or uniformly mathematical or quantitative —has to undergo a radical revision.

The final form into which Freud casts all this material is as original as it is deceptively straightforward. It is divided into five parts. It opens with a short but extremely dense and condensed series of "Prefatory Remarks." There follows the longest section of the work, called "The Clinical Picture" (*Der Krankheitszustand*). In this part Freud describes the history of Dora's family and of how he got to know them, presents an account of Dora's symptoms and how they seemed to have been acquired, and informs the reader of the process by which she was brought to him for treatment. He also represents some of the progress they had made in the first weeks of the treatment. Throughout he intersperses his account of Dora's illness and treatment with excursions and digressions of varying lengths on an assortment of theoretical topics that the material of the case brought into relevant prominence. The third part of the essay, "The First Dream," consists of the reproduction in part of the analysis of Dora's recurrent dream. Part of it is cast in dramatic dialogue, part in indirect discourse, part in a shifting diversity of narrative and expository modes, each of which is summoned up by Freud with effortless mastery. The entire material of the case up to now is reviewed and re-enacted once more: new material ranging from Dora's early childhood through her early adolescence and down to the moment of the analysis is unearthed and discussed, again from a series of analytic perspectives and explanatory levels that shift about so rapidly that one is inclined to call them rotatory. The fourth part, "The Second Dream," is about the final three sessions of the treatment, and Freud invents yet another series of original compositional devices to present the fluid mingling of dramatic, expository, narrative, and analytic materials that were concentrated in the three hours. The final part of the essay, "Postscript," written indeed after the case was officially "closed" but at an utterly indeterminate set of dates, is true to its title. It is not a conclusion in the traditional sense of neatly rounding off through a final summary and group of generalizations the material dealt with in the body of the work—although it does do some of that. It is rather a group of added remarks, whose effect is to introduce still further considerations, and the work is brought to its proper end by opening up new and indeterminate avenues of exploration; it closes by giving us a glimpse of unexplored mental vistas in whose light presumably the entire case that has gone before would be transfigured yet again.

The general form, then, of what Freud has written bears certain suggestive resemblances to a modern experimental novel. Its narrative and expository course, for example, is neither linear nor rectilinear; instead, its organization is plastic, involuted, and heterogeneous, and follows spontaneously an inner logic that seems frequently to be at odds with itself; it often loops back around itself and is multidimensional in its representation of both its material and itself. Its continuous innovations in formal structure seem unavoidably to be dictated by its substance, by the dangerous, audacious, disreputable, and problematical character of the experiences being represented and dealt with, and by the equally scandalous intentions of the author and the outrageous character of the role he has had the presumption to assume. In content, however, what Freud has written is in parts rather like a play by Ibsen, or more precisely, like a series of Ibsen's plays. And as one reads through the case of Dora, scenes and characters from such works as *Pillars of Society*, *A Doll's House*, *Ghosts*, *An Enemy of the People*, *The Wild Duck*, and *Rosmersholm* rise up and flit through the mind. There is, however, this difference. In this Ibsen-like drama, Freud is not only Ibsen, the creator and playwright; he is also and directly one of the characters in the action, and in the end suffers in a way that is comparable to the suffering of the others.

What I have been reiterating at excessive length is that the case of Dora is first and last an extraordinary piece of writing, and it is to this circumstance in several of its most striking aspects that we should direct our attention. For it is a case history, a kind or genre of writing—a particular way of conceiving and constructing human experience in written language—which in Freud's hands became something that it never was before.

---

8 Freud's chief precursors in this, as in so much else, are the great poets and novelists. There are a number of works of literature that anticipate in both form and substance the kind of thing that Freud was to do. I shall mention only one. Wordsworth's small masterpiece "Ruth" can in my judgment be most thoroughly understood as a kind of proto-case history, as a case history, so to speak, before the fact.

3

The ambiguities and difficulties begin with the very title of the work, "Fragment of an Analysis of a Case of Hysteria." In what sense or senses is this piece of writing that the author describes as "a detailed report of the history of a case" a fragment? (7) Freud himself supplies us with a superabundant wealth of detail on this count. It is a fragment in the sense that its "results" are "incomplete." The treatment was "broken off at the patient's own wish," at a time when certain problems "had not been attacked and others had only been imperfectly elucidated." It follows that the analysis itself is "only a fragment," as are "the following pages" of writing which present it. (12) To which the modern reader, flushed with the superior powers of his educated irony, is tempted to reply: how is it that this fragment is also a whole, an achieved totality, an integral piece of writing called a case history? And how is it, furthermore, that this "fragment" is fuller, richer, and more complete than the most "complete" case histories of anyone else? But there is no more point in asking such questions of Freud—particularly at this preliminary stage of proceedings —than there would be in posing similar "theoretical" questions to Joyce or Proust. And indeed Freud has barely begun.

The work is also fragmentary, he continues, warming to his subject, because of the very method he has chosen to pursue; on this plan, that of non-directional free association, "everything that has to do with the clearing-up of a particular symptom emerges piecemeal, woven into various contexts, and distributed over widely separate periods of time." Freud's technique itself is therefore fragmentary; his way of penetrating to the micro-structure—the "finer structure," as he calls it—of a neurosis is to allow the material to emerge piecemeal. At the same time these fragments only *appear* to be incoherent and disparate; in actuality they eventually will be understood as members of a whole. Still, in the present instance the results were more than usually unfinished and partial, and to explain what in the face of such difficulties he has done, he resorts to one of his favorite metaphorical figures:

> I had no choice but to follow the example of those dis-coverers whose good fortune it is to bring to the light of day after their long burial the priceless though muti-lated relics of antiquity. I have restored what is missing, taking the best models known to me from other anal-yses; but, like a conscientious archaeologist, I have not omitted to mention in each case where the authentic facts end and my constructions begin. (12)[9]

Here the matter has complicated itself one degree further. The mutilated relics or fragments of the past also remain fragments; what Freud has done is to restore, construct, and reconstruct what is missing—an activity and a group of conceptions that introduce an entirely new range of contingencies. And there is more of this in the offing as well.

Furthermore, Freud goes on, there is still another "kind of incompleteness" to be found in this work, and this time it has been "intentionally introduced." He has deliberately chosen not to reproduce "the process of interpretation to

[9] From almost the outset of his career, images drawn from archaeol-ogy worked strongly in Freud's conception of his own creative activ-ity. In *Studies on Hysteria*, Freud remarks that the procedure he fol-lowed with Fräulein Elisabeth von R. was one "of clearing away the pathogenic psychical material layer by layer, and we liked to com-pare it with the technique of excavating a buried city." In a closely related context, he observes that he and Breuer "had often compared the symptomatology of hysteria with a pictographic script which has become intelligible after the discovery of a few bilingual inscriptions." And his way of representing the "highly involved trains of thought" that were determinants in certain of the hysterical attacks of Frau Cäcilie was to compare them to "a series of pictures with explanatory texts." (*SE*, II, 139, 129, 177).

which the patient's associations and communications had
to be subjected, but only the results of that process." That
is to say, what we have before us is not a transcription in
print of a tape recording of eleven weeks of analysis but
something that is abridged, edited, synthesized, and constructed from the very outset. And as if this were not
enough, Freud introduces yet another context in which the
work has to be regarded as fragmentary and incomplete. It
is obvious, he argues, "that a single case history, even if it
were complete and open to no doubt, cannot provide an
answer to all questions arising out of the problem of hysteria." One case of hysteria, in short, cannot exhaust the
structure of all the others. And so in this sense too the work
is a particle or component of a larger entity or whole. It
nevertheless remains at the same time a whole in itself and
has to stand by itself in its own idiosyncratic way—which is
to be simultaneously fragmentary and complete. Thus, like
a modernist writer—which in part he is—Freud begins by
elaborately announcing the problematical status of his
undertaking and the dubious character of his achievement.

Even more, like some familiar "unreliable narrator" in
modernist fiction, Freud pauses at regular intervals to remind the reader of this case history that "my insight into
the complex of events composing it [has] remained fragmentary," that his understanding of it remains in some
essential sense permanently occluded. This darkness and
constraint are the result of a number of converging circumstances, some of which have already been touched on and
include the shortness of the analysis and its having been
broken off by Dora at a crucial point. But it also includes
the circumstance that the analysis—any analysis—must proceed by fragmentary methods, by analyzing thoughts and
events bit by discontinuous bit. Indeed, at the end of one
virtuoso passage in which Freud demonstrates through a
series of referential leaps and juxtapositions the occurrence
in Dora's past of childhood masturbation, he acknowledges

that this is the essence of his procedure. "Part of this material," he writes, "I was able to obtain directly from the analysis, but the rest required supplementing. And, indeed, the method by which the occurrence of masturbation in Dora's case has been verified has shown us that material belonging to a single subject can only be collected piece by piece at various times and in different connections." (80) The method is hence a fragmentary construction and reconstruction which in the end amount to a whole that simultaneously retains its disjointed character—in sum it resembles "reality" itself, a word that, as writers today like to remind us, should always be surrounded by quotation marks.

At the same time, however, Freud protests too much in the opposite direction, as when he remarks that "it is only because the analysis was prematurely broken off that we have been obliged in Dora's case to resort to framing conjectures and filling in deficiencies." (85) At an earlier moment he had asserted that "if the work had been continued, we should no doubt have obtained the fullest possible enlightenment upon every particular of the case." (19) We shall return later to these and other similar remarks, but in the present connection what they serve to underscore is Freud's effort to persuade us, and himself, of how much more he could have done—an effort which, by this point in the writing, the reader is no longer able to take literally.[10] And this tendency to regard such assertions with a certain degree of skepticism is further reinforced when at the end of the essay—after over one hundred pages of dazzling originality, of creative genius performing with a compactness, complexity, daring, and splendor that seem close to incomparable in their order—he returns to this theme, which was,

---

[10] In later years, and after much further experience, Freud was no longer able to make such statements. In *Inhibitions, Symptoms and Anxiety* (1926) he writes: "Even the most exhaustive analysis has gaps in its data and is insufficiently documented." (*SE*, XXI, 107)

we should recall, set going by *the very first word* of his title. He begins the "Postscript" with a statement whose modesty is by now comically outrageous. "It is true," he writes, "that I have introduced this paper as a fragment of an analysis; but the reader will have discovered that it is incomplete to a far greater degree than its title might have led him to expect." (112) This disclaimer is followed by still another rehearsal of what has been left out. In particular, he writes, he has "in this paper entirely left out of account the technique," and, he adds, "I found it quite impracticable . . . to deal simultaneously with the technique of analysis and with the internal structure of a case of hysteria." In any event, he concludes, "I could scarcely have accomplished such a task, and if I had, the result would have been almost unreadable." (112) And if the reader is not grateful for these small mercies, Freud goes on a few pages later to speak of this essay as a "case of whose history and treatment I have published a fragment in these pages." In short, this fragment is itself only a fragment of a fragment. If this is so—and there is every reason to believe that Freud is seriously bandying about with words—then we are compelled to conclude that in view of the extreme complexity of this fragment of a fragment, the conception of the whole that Freud has in mind is virtually unimaginable and inconceivable.

We are then obliged to ask—and Freud himself more than anyone else has taught us most about this obligation—*what else* are all these protestations of fragmentariness and incompleteness about? Apart from their slight but continuous unsettling effect upon the reader, and their alerting him to the circumstances that there is an author and a series of contingencies behind the solid mass of printed matter that he is poring over, plowing through, and browsing in, as if it were a piece of nature and not a created artifact—apart from this, what else do these protestations refer to? They refer in some measure, as Freud himself indicates in the postscript, to a central inadequacy and determining incompleteness that he discovered only after it was too late—the "great defect" (118) of the case was to be located in the undeveloped, misdeveloped, and equivocal character of the "transference," of the relation between patient and physician in which so much was focused. Something went wrong in the relation between Freud and Dora or—if there are any analysts still reading—in the relation between Dora and Freud. But the protestations refer, I believe, to something else as well, something of which Freud was not entirely conscious. For the work is also fragmentary or incomplete in the sense of Freud's self-knowledge, both at the time of the actual case and at the time of his writing it. And he communicates in this piece of writing a less than complete understanding of himself, though like any great writer, he provides us with the material for understanding some things that have escaped his own understanding, for filling in some gaps, for restoring certain fragments into wholes.

How else can we finally explain the fact that Freud chose to write up this particular history in such extensive detail? The reasons that he offers in both the "Prefatory Remarks" and the "Postscript" aren't entirely convincing— which doesn't of course deny them a real if fractional validity. Why should he have chosen so problematic a case, when presumably others of a more complete yet equally brief kind were available? I think this can be understood in part through Freud's own unsettled and ambiguous role in the case; that he had not yet, so to speak, "gotten rid" of it; that he had to write it out, in some measure, as an effort of self-understanding—an effort, I think we shall see, that remained heroically unfinished, a failure that nonetheless brought lasting credit with it.

4

If we turn now to the "Prefatory Remarks," it may be illuminating to regard them as a kind of novelistic framing action, as in these few opening pages Freud rehearses his motives, reasons, and intentions and begins at the same time to work his insidious devices upon the reader. First, exactly like a novelist, he remarks that what he is about to let us in on is positively scandalous, for "the complete elucidation of a case of hysteria is bound to involve the revelation of intimacies and the betrayal of . . . secrets." (8) Second, again like a writer of fiction, he has deliberately chosen persons, places, and circumstances that will remain obscure; the scene is laid not in metropolitan Vienna but "in a remote provincial town." He has from the beginning kept the circumstance that Dora was his patient such a close secret that only one other physician—"in whose discretion I have complete confidence"—knows about it. He has "postponed publication" of this essay for "four whole years," also in the cause of discretion, and in the same cause has "allowed no name to stand which could put a non-medical reader on the scent." (8) Finally, he has buried the case even deeper by publishing it "in a purely scientific and technical periodical" in order to secure yet another "guarantee against unauthorized readers." He has, in short, made his own mystery within a mystery, and one of the effects of such obscure preliminary goings-on is to create a kind of Nabokovian frame—what we have here is a history framed by an explanation which is itself slightly out of focus.[11]

[11] One is in a position now to understand rather better the quasi-meretricious fits of detestation that overtake Nabokov whenever Freud's name is mentioned. That "elderly gentleman from Vienna" whom Nabokov has accused of "inflicting his dreams upon me" was in fact a past master at all the tricks, ruses, and sleights-of-hand that Nabokov has devoted his entire career to. The difference is this: that in Freud such devices are merely a minor item in the immense store of his literary resources.

Nabokov's revenge has been such cuties as "Dr. Sig Heiler," "Sigismund Lejoyeux," and one "Dr. Froit of Signy-Mondieu-Mondieu." At an entirely different level an analogous relation existed between Charlie Chaplin and W. C. Fields. The latter often tried to get his own back on the comic genius by calling him "that god-damned juggler" along with similar phrases of endearment.

Third, he roundly declares, this case history is science and not literature: "I am aware that—in this city, at least—there are many physicians who (revolting though it may seem) choose to read a case history of this kind not as a contribution to the psychopathology of neuroses, but as a *roman à clef* designed for their private delectation." (9) This may indeed be true; but it is equally true that nothing is more literary—and more modern—than the disavowal of all literary intentions. And when Freud does this again later on toward the end of "The Clinical Picture," the situation becomes even less credible. The passage merits quotation at length.

> I must now turn to consider a further complication to which I should certainly give no space if I were a man of letters engaged upon the creation of a mental state like this for a short story, instead of being a medical man engaged upon its dissection. The element to which I must now allude can only serve to obscure and efface the outlines of the fine poetic conflict which we have been able to ascribe to Dora. This element would rightly fall a sacrifice to the censorship of a writer, for he, after all, simplifies and abstracts when he appears in the character of a psychologist. But in the world of reality, which I am trying to depict here, a complication of motives, an accumulation and conjunction of mental activities—in a word, overdetermination—is the rule (59f.)

In this context it is next to impossible to tell whether Freud is up to another of his crafty maneuverings with the reader or whether he is actually simply unconscious of how much of a modern and modernist writer he is. For when he takes to describing the difference between himself and some hypothetical man of letters and writer of short stories he is in fact embarked upon an eloborate obfuscation. That hypothetical writer is nothing but a straw man; and when Freud in apparent contrast represents himself and his own activities, he is truly representing how a genuine creative writer writes. And this passage, we must also recall, came from the same pen that only a little more than a year earlier had written passages about Oedipus and Hamlet that changed for good the ways in which the civilized world would henceforth think about literature and writers.[12] What might be thought of as this sly unliterariness of Freud's turns up in other contexts as well.

If we return to the point in the "Prefatory Remarks" from which we have momentarily digressed, we find that Freud then goes on to describe other difficulties, constraints, and problematical circumstances attaching to the situation in which he finds himself. Among them is the problem of "how to record for publication" (10) even such a short case —the long ones are as yet altogether impossible. We shall

[12] Some years earlier Freud had been more candid and more innocent about the relation of his writing to literature. In *Studies on Hysteria* he introduces his discussion of the case of Fräulein Elisabeth von R. with the following disarming admission:

I have not always been a psychotherapist. Like other neuropathologists, I was trained to employ local diagnosis and electro-prognosis, and it still strikes me myself as strange that the case histories I write should read like short stories and that, as one might say, they lack the serious stamp of science. I must console myself with the reflection that the nature of the subject is evidently responsible for this, rather than any preference of my own. The fact is that local diagnosis and electrical reactions lead nowhere in the study of hysteria, whereas a detailed description of mental processes such as we are accustomed to find in the works of imaginative writers enables me, with the use of a few psychological formulas, to obtain at least some kind of insight into the course of that affection. Case histories of this kind are intended to be judged like psychiatric ones; they have, however, one advantage over the latter, namely, an intimate connection between the story of the patient's sufferings and the symptoms of his illness—a connection for which we still search in vain in the biographies of other psychoses. (*SE*, II, 160f.)

presently return to this central passage. Moreover, since the material that critically illuminated this case was grouped about two dreams, their analysis formed a secure point of departure for the writing. (Freud is of course at home with dreams, being the unchallenged master in the reading of them.) Yet this tactical solution pushes the *entire problematic* back only another step further, since Freud at once goes on to his additional presupposition, that only those who are already familiar with "the interpretation of dreams" —that is, *The Interpretation of Dreams* (1900), whose readership in 1901 must have amounted to a little platoon indeed —are likely to be satisfied at all with the present account. Any other reader "will find only bewilderment in these pages." (11) As much as it is like anything else, this is like Borges—as well as Nabokov. In these opening pages Freud actively and purposefully refuses to give the reader a settled point of attachment, and instead works at undercutting and undermining his stability by such slight manipulations as this: i.e., in order to read the case of Dora which the reader presumably has right in front of him, he must also first have read the huge, abstruse, and almost entirely unread dream book of the year before. This off-putting and disconcerting quality, it should go without saying, is characteristically modern; the writer succumbs to no impulse to make it easy for the reader; on the contrary, he is by preference rather forbidding and does not extend a cordial welcome. But Freud has not yet finished piling Pelion upon Ossa, and he goes on to add for good measure that the reader really ought to have read *Studies on Hysteria* as well, if only to be confounded by the differences between this case and those discussed at such briefer length there. With this and with a number of further remarks about the unsatisfactory satisfactory character of what he has done and what is to come, Freud closes this frame of "Prefatory Remarks," leaving what audience he still has left in a bemused, uncertain, and dislocated state of mind. The reader has been, as it were, "softened up" by his first encounter with this unique expository and narrative authority; he is thoroughly off balance and is as a consequence ready to be "educated," by Freud. By the same token, however, if he has followed these opening few pages carefully, he is certainly no longer as prepared as he was to assert the primacy and priority of his own critical sense of things. He is precisely where Freud —and any writer—wants him to be.

At the opening of Part I, "The Clinical Picture," Freud tells us that he begins his "treatment, indeed, by asking the patient to give me the whole story of his life and illness," and immediately adds that "the information I receive is never enough to let me see my way about the case." (16) This inadequacy and unsatisfactoriness in the stories his patients tell is in distinct contrast to what Freud has read in the accounts rendered by his psychiatric contemporaries, and he continues by remarking that "I cannot help wondering how it is that the authorities can produce such smooth and exact histories in cases of hysteria. As a matter of fact the patients are incapable of giving such reports about themselves." There is an immense amount beginning to go on here. In the first place, there is the key assumption that everyone—that every life, every existence—has a story, to which there is appended a corollary that most of us probably tell that story poorly. There follows at once Freud's statement of flat disbelief in the "smooth and exact" histories published by his colleagues who study hysteria. The implications that are latent in this negation are at least twofold: a) these authorities are incompetent and may in some sense be "making up" the histories they publish; b) real case histories are neither "smooth" nor "exact," and the reader cannot expect to find such qualities here in the "real" thing. Furthermore, the relations at this point in Freud's prose between the words "story," "history," and "report" are unspecified, undifferentiated, and unanalyzed and in the nature of the case contain and conceal a wealth of material.

Freud proceeds to specify what it is that is wrong with the stories his patients tell him. The difficulties are in the first instance formal shortcomings of *narrative*: the connections, "even the ostensible ones—are for the most part incoherent," obscured and unclear; "and the sequence of different events is uncertain." In short, these narratives are disorganized, and the patients are unable to tell a coherent story of their lives. What is more, he states, "the patients' inability to give an ordered history of their life in so far as it coincides with the history of their illness is not merely characteristic of the neurosis. It also possesses great theoretical significance." (16) Part of this significance comes into view when we regard this conjecture from its obverse side, which Freud does at once in a footnote.

Another physician once sent his sister to me for psychotherapeutic treatment, telling me that she had for years been treated without success for hysteria (pains and defective gait). The short account which he gave me seemed quite consistent with the diagnosis. In my first hour with the patient I got her to tell me her history herself. When the story came out perfectly clearly and connectedly in spite of the remarkable events it dealt with, I told myself that the case could not be one of hysteria, and immediately instituted a careful physical examination. This led to the diagnosis of a not very advanced stage of tabes, which was later on treated with Hg injections . . . with markedly beneficial results. (16f.)

What we are led at this juncture to conclude is that Freud is implying that a coherent story is in some manner connected with mental health (at the very least, with the absence of hysteria), and this in turn implies assumptions of the broadest and deepest kind about both the nature of coherence and the form and structure of human life. On this reading, human life is, ideally, a connected and coherent story, with all the details in explanatory place, and with everything (or as close to everything as is practically possible) accounted for, in its proper causal or other sequence. And inversely, illness amounts at least in part to suffering from an incoherent story or an inadequate narrative account of oneself.

Freud then describes in technical detail the various types and orders of narrative insufficiency that he commonly finds; they range from disingenuousness both conscious and unconscious to amnesias and paramnesias of several kinds and various other means of severing connections and altering chronologies. In addition, he maintains, this discomposed memory applies with particular force and virulence to "the history of the illness" for which the patient has come for treatment. In the course of a successful treatment, this incoherence, incompleteness, and fragmentariness are progressively transmuted, as facts, events, and memories are brought forward into the forefront of the patient's mind.

> The paramnesias prove untenable, and the gaps in his memory are filled in. It is only towards the end of the treatment that we have before us an intelligible, consistent, and unbroken case history. Whereas the practical aim of the treatment is to remove all possible symptoms and to replace them by conscious thoughts, we may regard it as a second and theoretical aim to repair all the damages to the patient's memory. (18)

And he adds as a conclusion that these two aims "are coincident"—they are reached simultaneously and by the same path.[13] Some of the consequences that can be derived from these tremendous remarks are as follows. The history of any patient's illness is itself only a sub-story (or a sub-plot), although it is at the same time a vital part of a larger structure. Furthermore, in the course of psychoanalytic treatment, nothing less than "reality" itself is made, constructed, or reconstructed. A complete story—"intelligible, consistent, and unbroken"—is the theoretical, created end story. It is a story, or a fiction, not only because it has a narrative structure but also because the narrative account has been rendered in language, in conscious speech, and no longer exists in the deformed language of symptoms, the untranslated speech of the body. At the end—at the successful end—one has come into possession of one's own story. It is a final act of self-appropriation, the appropriation by oneself of one's own history. This is in part so because one's own story is in so large a measure a phenomenon of language, as psychoanalysis is in turn a demonstration of the degree to which language can go in the reading of all our experience. What we end with, then, is a fictional construction which is at the same time satisfactory to us in the form of the truth, and as the form of the truth.

No larger tribute has ever been paid to a culture in which the various narrative and fictional forms had exerted for centuries both moral and philosophical authority and which had produced as one of its chief climaxes the great bourgeois novels of the nineteenth century. Indeed, we must

---

[13] There is a parodic analogue to this passage of some contemporary significance. It is taken from the relatively esoteric but influential field of general systems theory, one of whose important practitioners suffered from severe disturbances of memory. Indeed, he could hardly remember anything. He nonetheless insisted that there was nothing wrong with his memory; in fact, he went on to argue, he had a perfect memory—it was only his retrieval system that wasn't working. In the light of such a comment, it is at least open to others to wonder whether other things as well weren't working.

see Freud's writings—and method—as themselves part of this culmination, and at the same moment, along with the great modernist novels of the first half of the twentieth century, as the beginning of the end of that tradition and its authority. Certainly the passages we have just dealt with contain heroic notions and offer an extension of heroic capabilities if not to all men then to most, at least as a possibility. Yet we cannot leave this matter so relatively unexamined, and must ask ourselves how it is that this "story" is not merely a "history" but a "case history" as well. We must ask ourselves how these associated terms are more intimately related in the nexus that is about to be wound and unwound before us. To begin to understand such questions, we have to turn back to a central passage in the "Prefatory Remarks." Freud undertakes therein "to describe the way in which I have overcome the *technical* difficulties of drawing up the report of this case history." (9) Apparently "the report" and the "case history" referred to in this statement are two discriminable if not altogether discrete entities. If they are, then we can further presume that, ideally at any rate, Dora (or any patient) is as much in possession of the "case history" as Freud himself. And this notion is in some part supported by what comes next. Freud mentions certain other difficulties, such as the fact that he "cannot make notes during the actual session . . . for fear of shaking the patient's confidence and of disturbing his own view of the material under observation." (9) In the case of Dora, however, this obstacle was partly overcome because so much of the material was grouped about two dreams, and "the wording of these dreams was recorded immediately after the session" so that "they thus afforded a secure point of attachment for the chain of interpretations and recollections which proceeded from there." Freud then writes as follows:

The case history itself was only committed to writing

from memory after the treatment was at an end, but
while my recollection of the case was still fresh and
was heightened by my interest in its publication. Thus
the record is not absolutely—phonographically—exact,
but it can claim to possess a high degree of trustworthi-
ness. Nothing of any importance has been altered in it
except in some places the order in which the explanations are given; and this has been done for the sake of
presenting the case in a more connected form. (10)

Such a passage raises more questions than it resolves.
The first sentence is a kind of conundrum in which case
history, writing, and memory dance about in a series of
logical entwinements, of possible alternate combinations,
equivalences, and semi-equivalences. These are followed by
further equivocations about "the record," "phonographic"
exactitude, and so forth—the ambiguities of which jump
out at one as soon as the terms begin to be seriously examined. For example, is "the report" the same thing as "the
record"; and if "the record" were "phonographically" exact,
would it be a "report"? Like the prodigious narrative historian that he is, Freud is enmeshed in an irreducible paradox of history: that the term itself refers to both the activity
of the historian—the writing of history—and to the objects
of his undertaking, what history is "about." I do not think,
therefore, that we can conclude that Freud has created this
thick context of historical contingency and ambiguity out
of what he once referred to as Viennese *schlamperei*.
   The historical difficulties are further compounded by
several other sequential networks that are mentioned at the
outset and that figure discernibly throughout the writing.
First, there is the virtual Proustian complexity of Freud's
interweaving of the various strands of time in the actual
account; or, to change the figure, his geological fusing of
various time strata—strata which are themselves at once

fluid and shifting. We observe this most strikingly in the palimpsest-like quality of the writing itself; which refers back to *Studies on Hysteria* of 1895; which records a treatment that took place at the end of 1900 (although it mistakes the date by a year); which then was written up in first form during the early weeks of 1901; which was then exhumed in 1905 and was revised and rewritten to an indeterminable extent before publication in that year; and to which additional critical comments in the form of footnotes were finally appended in 1923. All of these are of course held together in vital connection and interanimation by nothing else than Freud's consciousness. But we. must take notice as well of the co-presence of still further different time sequences in Freud's presentation—this co-presence being itself a historical or novelistic circumstance of some magnitude. There is first the connection established by the periodically varied rehearsal throughout the account of Freud's own theory and theoretical notions as they had developed up to that point; this practice provides a kind of running applied history of psychoanalytic theory as its development is refracted through the embroiled medium of this particular case. Then there are the different time strata of Dora's own history, which Freud handles with confident and loving exactitude. Indeed, he is never more of a historical virtuoso than when he reveals himself to us as moving with compelling ease back and forth between the complex group of sequential histories and narrative accounts with divergent sets of diction and at different levels of explanation that constitute the extraordinary fabric of this work. He does this most conspicuously in his analytic dealings with Dora's dreams, for every dream, he reminds us, sets up a connection between two "factors," an "event during childhood" and an "event of the present day—and it endeavors to reshape the present on the model of the remote past." (71) The existence or re-creation of the past in the present is in fact "history" in more than one of its manifold senses. And such a passage is also one of Freud's many analogies to the following equally celebrated utterance.

> Men make their own history, but they do not make it just as they please; they do not make it under circumstances chosen by themselves, but under circumstances directly encountered, given and transmitted from the past. The tradition of all the dead generations weighs like a nightmare on the brain of the living. And just when they seem engaged in revolutionising themselves and things, in creating something that has never yet existed, precisely in such periods of revolutionary crisis they anxiously conjure up the spirits of the past to their service and borrow from them names, battle cries, and costumes in order to present the new scene of world history in this time-honored disguise and this borrowed language.[14]

And just as Marx regards the history-makers of the past as sleepwalkers, "who required recollections of past world history in order to drug themselves concerning their own content," so Freud similarly regards the conditions of dream-formation, of neurosis itself, and even of the cure of neurosis, namely, the analytic experience of transference. They are all of them species of living past history in the present. If the last of these works out satisfactorily, then a case history is at the end transfigured. It becomes an inseparable part of an integral life history. Freud is of course the master historian of those transfigurations.[15]

---

[14] K. Marx, *The Eighteenth Brumaire of Louis Bonaparte*, part I.

[15] Erik H. Erikson has waggishly observed that a case history is an account of how someone fell apart, while a life history is an account of how someone held together.

5

We cannot in prudence follow Freud's written analysis of the case in anything like adequate detail. What we can do is try to trace out the persistence and development of certain themes. And we can try as well to keep track of the role—or some of the roles—played by Freud in the remainder of this case out of whose failure this triumph of mind and of literature emerged. At the very beginning, after he had listened to the father's account of "Dora's impossible behavior," Freud abstained from comment, for, he remarks, "I had resolved from the first to suspend my judgement of the true state of affairs till I had heard the other side as well." (26) Such a suspension inevitably recalls an earlier revolutionary project. In describing the originating plan of *Lyrical Ballads*, Coleridge writes that it "was agreed that my endeavours should be directed to persons and characters supernatural, or at least romantic; yet so as to transfer from our inward nature a human interest and a semblance of truth sufficient to procure for these shadows of imagination that willing suspension of disbelief for the moment, which constitutes poetic faith."[16] We know very well that Freud had a more than ordinary capacity in this direction, and that one of the most dramatic moments in the pre-history of psychoanalysis had to do precisely with his taking on faith facts that turned out to be fantasies. Yet Freud is not only the reader suspending judgment and disbelief until he has heard the other side of the story; and he is not only the poet or writer who must induce a similar process in himself if he is to elicit it in his audience. He is also concomitantly a principal, an actor, a living character in the drama that he is unfolding in print before us. Moreover, that suspension of disbelief is in no sense incompatible with a large body of assumptions, many of them definite, a number of them positively alarming. I think that before

[16] *Biographia Literaria*, Chapter 14.

we pursue any further Freud's spectacular gyrations as a writer, we had better confront the chief of these presuppositions.

They have to do largely with sexuality and in particular with female sexuality. They are brought to a focus in the central scene of Dora's life (and case), a scene that Freud "orchestrates" with inimitable richness and to which he recurs thematically at a number of junctures with the tact and sense of form that one associates with a classical composer of music (or with Proust, Mann, or Joyce). Dora told this episode to Freud toward the beginning of their relation, after "the first difficulties of the treatment had been overcome." It is the scene between her and Herr K. which took place when she was fourteen years old—that is, four years before the present tense of the case—and that acted, Freud said, as a "sexual trauma." The reader will recall that on this occasion Herr K. contrived to get Dora alone "at his place of business" in the town of B——, and then without warning or preparation "suddenly clasped the girl to him and pressed a kiss upon her lips." Freud then asserts that "this was *surely* just the situation to call up a *distinct* feeling of sexual excitement in a *girl* of *fourteen* who had *never before* been approached. But Dora had at that moment a violent feeling of disgust, tore herself free from the man, and hurried past him to the staircase and from there to the street door." [all italics are mine] (28). She avoided seeing the K.'s for a few days after this, but then relations returned to "normal"—if such a term survives with any permissible sense in the present context. She continued to meet Herr K., and neither of them ever mentioned "the little scene." Moreover, Freud adds, "according to her account Dora kept it a secret till her confession during the treatment," and he pretty clearly implies that he believes this.

This episode preceded by two years the scene at the lake that acted as the precipitating agent for the severe stage of Dora's illness; and it was this later episode and the entire structure that she and others had elaborated about it that she had first presented to Freud, who continues thus:

> In this scene—second in order of mention, but first in order of time—the behavior of this child of fourteen was already entirely and completely hysterical. I should without question consider a person hysterical in whom an occasion for sexual excitement elicited feelings that were preponderantly or exclusively unpleasurable; and I should do so whether or no the person were capable of producing somatic symptoms. (28)

As if this were not enough, he proceeds to produce another rabbit out of his hat. In Dora's feeling of disgust an obscure psychical mechanism called the "reversal of affect" was brought into play; but so was another process, and here Freud introduces—casually and almost as a throwaway—one more of his grand theoretical-clinical formulations, namely, the idea of the *"displacement* of sensation," or, as it has more commonly come to be referred to, the "displacement upwards." "Instead of the genital sensation which would certainly have been felt by a healthy girl in such circumstances, Dora was overcome by the unpleasurable feeling which is proper to the tract of mucous membrane at the entrance to the alimentary canal—that is by disgust." Although the disgust did not persist as a permanent symptom but remained behind residually and potentially in a general distaste for food and poor appetite, a second displacement upward was the resultant of this scene "in the shape of a sensory hallucination which occurred from time to time and even made its appearance while she was telling me her story. She declared that she could still feel upon the upper part of her body the pressure of Herr K.'s embrace." Dipping into the hat once again, and taking into account certain other of Dora's "inexplicable"—and hitherto un-mentioned—"peculiarities" (such as her phobic reluctance

to walk past any man she saw engaged in animated conversation with a woman), Freud "formed in my own mind
the following reconstruction of the scene. I believe that during the man's passionate embrace she felt not merely his
kiss upon her lips but also his erect member against her
body. The perception was revolting to her; it was dismissed
from her memory, repressed, and replaced by the innocent
sensation of pressure upon her thorax, which in turn derived
an excessive intensity from its repressed source." (30) This
repressed source was located in the erotogenic oral zone,
which in Dora's case had undergone a developmental defor-
mation from the period of infancy. And thus, Freud concludes, "the pressure of the erect member probably led to
an analogous change in the corresponding female organ, the
clitoris; and the excitation of this second erotogenic zone
was referred by a process of displacement to the simultaneous pressure against the thorax and became fixed there."
(30)

This passage of unquestionable genius contains at the
same time something questionable and askew. In it Freud
is at once dogmatically certain and very uncertain. He is
dogmatically certain of what the normative sexual response
in young and other females is, and asserts himself to that
effect. At the same time he is, in my judgment, utterly uncertain about where Dora is, or was, developmentally. At
one moment in the passage he calls her a "girl," at another
a "child"—but in point of fact he treats her throughout as if
this fourteen-, sixteen-, and eighteen-year-old adolescent had
the capacities for sexual response of a grown woman—indeed, at a later point he conjectures again that Dora either
responded, or should have responded, to the embrace with
specific genital heat and moisture. Too many determinations
converge at this locus for us to do much more than single
out a few of the more obvious influencing circumstances. In
the first instance, there was Freud's own state of knowledge
about such matters at the time, which was better than any-

one else's but still relatively crude and undifferentiated. Second, we may be in the presence of what can only be accounted for by assuming that a genuine historical-cultural change has taken place between then and now. It may be that Freud was expressing a legitimate partial assumption of his time and culture when he ascribes to a fourteen-year-old adolescent—whom he calls a "child"—the normative responses that are ascribed today to a fully developed and mature woman.[17] This supposition is borne out if we consider the matter from the other end, from the standpoint of what has happened to the conception of adolescence in our own time. It begins now in pre-puberty and extends to —who knows when? Certainly its extensibility in our time has reached well beyond the age of thirty. Third, Freud is writing in this passage as an advocate of nature, sexuality, openness, and candor—and within such a context Dora cannot hope to look good. The very framing of the context in such a manner is itself slightly accusatory. In this connection we may note that Freud goes out of his way to tell us that he knew Herr K. personally and that "he was still quite young and of prepossessing appearance."[18] If we let Nabokov

[17] Freud may at this point be thinking within an even more historically anachronistic paradigm than the one that normally applied in the late-Victorian period or in the Vienna of the time. In both pre- and early-industrial Europe sexual maturity was commonly equated—especially for women—with reproductive maturity, and both were regarded as coterminous with marriageability. Ironically it was Freud more than any other single figure who was to demonstrate the inadequacy and outmodedness of this paradigm. See John H. Gagnon and William Simon, *Sexual Conduct: the Social Sources of Human Sexuality* (Chicago, 1973), p. 296.

[18] There is a fourth influencing circumstance that deserves to be mentioned. Freud appears to have worked in this case with a model in mind, but it turned out that the model either didn't fit or was the wrong one. In the case of "Katharina" in *Studies on Hysteria*, Freud had performed a kind of instant analysis with a fair degree of success. Katharina was the eighteen-year-old daughter of the landlady of an

back into the picture for a moment, we may observe that Dora is no Lolita, and go on to suggest that *Lolita* is an anti-*Dora*.

Yet we must also note that in this episode—the condensed and focusing scene of the entire case history—Freud is as much a novelist as he is an analyst. For the central moment of this central scene is a "reconstruction" that he "formed in my own mind." This pivotal construction becomes henceforth the principal "reality" of the case, and we must also observe that this reality remains Freud's more than Dora's, since he was never quite able to convince her of the plausibility of the construction; or, to regard it from the other pole of the dyad, she was never quite able to accept this version of reality, of what "really" happened. Freud was not at first unduly distressed by this resistance on her side, for part of his understanding of what he had undertaken to do in psychoanalysis was to instruct his patients—and his readers—in the nature of reality. This

---

Alpine refuge hut that Freud had climbed to one summer's day. This "rather sulky-looking girl" had served Freud his meal and then approached him for medical advice, having seen his signature in the Visitors' Book. She was suffering from various hysterical symptoms —many of which resembled those that afflicted Dora—and the story that came out had to do with attempted sexual seductions by her father, followed by her actually catching her father in the act with a young cousin—a discovery that led to the separation and divorce of the parents. The symptoms and the experiences seemed very closely connected, and as Freud elicited piecemeal these stories from her she seemed to become "like someone transformed" before his eyes. He was very pleased and said that he "owed her a debt of gratitude for having made it so much easier for me to talk to her than to the prudish ladies of my city practice, who regard whatever is natural as shameful." (*SE*, I, 125–134). The circumstances of her case and of Dora's are analogous in a number of ways, but Dora was no rustic Alpine *Jungfrau* who spoke candidly and in dialect (which Freud reproduces); she was in truth one of the prudish ladies of his city practice who was frigid then and remained so all her life.

reality was the reality that modern readers of literature have also had to be educated in. It was conceived of as a *world of meanings*. As Freud put it in one of those stop-you-dead-in-your-tracks footnotes that he was so expert in using strategically, we must at almost every moment "be prepared to be met not by one but by several causes—by *overdetermination*." (31) Thus the world of meanings is a world of multiple and compacted causations; it is a world in which everything has a meaning, which means that everything has more than one meaning. Every symptom is a concrete universal in several senses. It not only embodies a network of significances but also "serves to represent several unconscious mental processes simultaneously." (58) By the same token, since it is a world almost entirely brought into existence, maintained and mediated through a series of linguistic transactions between patient and physician, it partakes in full measure of the virtually limitless complexity of language, in particular its capacities for producing statements characterized by multiplicity, duplicity, and ambiguity of significance. Freud lays particular stress on the ambiguity, is continually on the lookout for it, and brings his own formidable skills in this direction to bear most strikingly on the analyses of Dora's dreams. The first thing he picks up in the first of her dreams is in fact an ambiguous statement, with which he at once confronts her. While he is doing so, he is also letting down a theoretical footnote for the benefit of his readers.

> I laid stress on these words because they took me aback. They seemed to have an ambiguous ring to them. . . . Now, in a line of associations ambiguous words (or as we may call them, 'switch-words') act like points at a junction. If the points are switched across from the position in which they appear to lie in the dream, then we find ourselves on another set of rails; and along this second track run the thoughts which we are in search

of but which still lie concealed behind the dream. (65)[19]

As if this were not sufficient, the actual case itself was full of such literary and novelistic devices or conventions as thematic analogies, double plots, reversals, inversions, variations, betrayals, etc.—full of what the "sharp-sighted" Dora as well as the sharp-sighted Freud thought of as "hidden connections"—though it is important to add that Dora and her physician mean different things by the same phrase. And as the case proceeds Freud continues to confront Dora with such connections and tries to enlist her assistance in their construction. For example, one of the least pleasant characteristics in Dora's nature was her habitual reproachfulness —it was directed mostly toward her father but radiated out in all directions. Freud regarded this behavior in his own characteristic manner. "A string of reproaches against other people," he comments, "leads one to suspect the existence of a string of self-reproaches with the same content." (35) Freud accordingly followed the procedure of turning back "each simple reproach on the speaker herself." When Dora reproached her father with malingering in order to keep himself in the company of Frau K., Freud felt "obliged to point out to the patient that her present ill-health was just as much actuated by motives and was just as tendentious as had been Frau K.'s illness, which she had understood so well." (42) At such moments Dora begins to mirror the other characters in the case, as they in differing degrees all mirror one another as well.

[19] Such a passage serves to locate Freud's place in a set of traditions in addition to those of literature. It is unmistakable that such a statement also belongs to a tradition that includes Hegel and Marx at one end and Max Weber and Thomas Mann somewhere near the other. It was Weber who once remarked that "the interests of society are the great rails on which humanity moves, but the ideas throw the switches." *Gesammelte Aufsätze zur Religionssoziologie* (Tübingen, 1922) I, 252. And Mann for his part regularly gave off such observations as: " 'Relationship is everything. And if you want to give it a more precise name, it is ambiguity.' " *Doctor Faustus*, Chapter VII.

Yet the unity that all these internal references and correspondences points to is not that of a harmony or of an uninflected linear series. And at one moment Freud feels obliged to remark that

> my experience in the clearing-up of hysterical symptoms has shown that it is not necessary for the various meanings of a symptom to be compatible with one another, that is, to fit together into a connected whole. It is enough that the unity should be constituted by the subject-matter which has given rise to all the various phantasies. In the present case, moreover, compatibility even of the first kind is not out of the question. . . . We have already learned that it quite regularly happens that a single symptom corresponds to several meanings *simultaneously*. We may now add that it can express several meanings *in succession*. In the course of years a symptom can change its meaning or its chief meaning, or the leading role can pass from one meaning to another. (53)

To which it may be added that what is true of the symptom can also be true of the larger entity of which it is a part. The meaning in question may be a contradictory one; it may be constituted out of a contradictory unity of opposites, or out of a shifting and unstable set of them. Whatever may be the case, the "reality" that is being both constructed and referred to is heterogeneous, multi-dimensional and open-ended—novelistic in the fullest sense of the word.

Part of that sense, we have come to understand, is that the writer is or ought to be conscious of the part that he—in whatever guise, voice, or persona he chooses—invariably and unavoidably plays in the world he represents. Oddly enough, although there is none of his writings in which Freud is more vigorously active than he is here, it is precisely this activity that he subjects to the least self-conscious scrutiny, that he almost appears to fend off. For example,

I will now take my head in my hands and suggest that his extraordinary analysis of Dora's first dream is inadequate on just this count. He is only dimly and marginally aware of his central place in it (he is clearly incorporated into the figure of Dora's father), comments on it only as an addition to Dora's own addendum to the dream, and does nothing to exploit it. (73f.) Why he should choose this course is a question to which we shall shortly return. Instead of analyzing his own part in what he has done and what he is writing, Freud continues to behave like an unreliable narrator, treating the material about which he is writing as if it were literature but excluding himself from both that treatment and that material. At one moment he refers to himself as someone "who has learnt to appreciate the delicacy of the fabric of structures such as dreams" (87), intimating what I surmise he incontestably believed, that dreams are natural works of art. And when in the analysis of the second dream, we find ourselves back at the scene at the lake again; when Dora recalls that the only plea to her of Herr K. that she could remember is "You know I get nothing out of my wife"; when these were precisely the same words used by Dora's father in describing to Freud his relation to Dora's mother; and when Freud speculates that Dora may even "have heard her father make the same complaint . . . just as I myself did from his own lips" (98,106)—when a conjunction such as this occurs, then we know we are in a novel, probably by Proust. Time has recurred, the repressed has returned, plot, double plot, and counterplot have all intersected, and "reality" turns out to be something that for all practical purposes is indistinguishable from a systematic fictional creation.

Finally, when at the very end Freud turns to deal— rudimentarily as it happens—with the decisive issue of the case, the transferences, everything is transformed into literature, into reading and writing. Transferences, he writes, "are new editions of facsimilies" or tendencies, fantasies, and relations in which "the person of the physician" replaces some earlier person. When the substitution is a simple one, the transferences may be said to be "merely new impressions or reprints": Freud is explicit about the metaphor he is using. Others "more ingeniously constructed . . . will no longer be new impressions, but revised editions." (116) And he goes on, quite carried away by these figures, to institute a comparison between dealing with the transference and other analytic procedures. "It is easy to learn how to interpret dreams," he remarks, "to extract from the patient's associations his unconscious thoughts and memories, and to practise similar explanatory arts: for these the patient himself will always provide the text." The startling group of suppositions contained in this sentence should not distract us from noting the submerged ambiguity in it. The patient does not merely provide the text; he also *is* the text, the writing to be read, the language to be interpreted. With the transference, however, we move to a different degree of difficulty and onto a different level of explanation. It is only after the transference has been resolved, Freud concludes, "that a patient arrives at a sense of conviction of the validity of the connections which have been constructed during the analysis." (117) I will refrain from entering the veritable series of Chinese boxes opened up by that last statement, and will content myself by proprosing that in this passage as a whole Freud is using literature and writing not only creatively and heuristically—as he so often does—but defensively as well.

The writer or novelist is not the only partial role taken up unconsciously or semi-consciously by Freud in the course of this work. He also figures prominently in the text in his capacity as a nineteenth-century man of science and as a representative Victorian critic—employing the seriousness, energy, and commitment of the Victorian ethos to deliver itself from its own excesses. We have already seen him affirming the positive nature of female sexuality, "the genital sensation which would certainly have been felt by a healthy girl in such circumstances" (37), but which Dora did not feel. He goes a good deal further than this. At a fairly early moment in the analysis he faces Dora with the fact that she has "an aim in view which she hoped to gain by her illness. That aim could be none other than to detach her father from Frau K." Her prayers and arguments had not worked; her suicide letter and fainting fits had done no better. Dora knew quite well how much her father loved her, and, Freud continues to address her,

> I felt quite convinced that she would recover at once if only her father were to tell her that he had sacrificed Frau K. for the sake of her health. But, I added, I hoped he would not let himself be persuaded to do this, for then she would have learned what a powerful weapon she had in her hands, and she would certainly not fail on every future occasion to make use once more of her liability to ill-health. Yet if her father refused to give way to her, I was quite sure she would not let herself be deprived of her illness so easily. (42)

This pretty strong stuff, considering both the age and her age. I think, moreover, that we are justified in reading an overdetermination out of this utterance of Freud's and in suggesting that he had motives additional to strictly therapeutic ones in saying what he did.

In a related sense Freud goes out of his way to affirm his entitlement to speak freely and openly about sex—he is, one keeps forgetting, the great liberator and therapist of speech. The passage is worth quoting at some length.

> It is possible for a man to talk to girls and women upon sexual matters of every kind without doing them harm and without bringing suspicion upon himself, so long as, in the first place, he adopts a particular way of doing

it, and, in the second place, can make them feel convinced that it is unavoidable. . . . The best way of speaking about such things is to be dry and direct; and that
is at the same time the method furthest removed from
the prurience with which the same subjects are handled
in "society," and to which girls and women alike are so
thoroughly accustomed. I call bodily organs and processes by their technical names. . . . *J'appelle un chat
un chat.* I have certainly heard of some people—doctors
and laymen—who are scandalized by a therapeutic
method in which conversations of this sort occur, and
who appear to envy either me or my patients the titilla-
tion which, according to their notions, such a method
must afford. But I am too well acquainted with the
respectability of these gentry to excite myself over them.
. . . The right attitude is: *"pour faire une omelette il faut
casser des oeufs."* (48f.)

I believe that Freud would have been the first to be amused
by the observation that in this splendid extended declaration
about plain speech (at this point he takes his place in a
tradition coming directly down from Luther), he feels it
necessary to disappear not once but twice into French. I
think he would have said that such slips—and the revelation
of their meanings—are the smallest price one has to pay for
the courage to go on. And he goes on with a vengeance,
immediately following this passage with another in which
he aggressively refuses to moralize in any condemnatory
sense about sexuality. As for the attitude that regards the
perverse nature of his patient's fantasies as horrible—

I should like to say emphatically that a medical man has
no business to indulge in such passionate condemna-
tion. . . . We are faced by a fact; and it is to be hoped
that we shall grow accustomed to it, when we have
learned to put our own tastes on one side. We must

learn to speak without indignation of what we call the sexual perversions. . . . The uncertainty in regard to the boundaries of what is to be called normal sexual life, when we take different races and different epochs into account, should in itself be enough to cool the zealot's ardor. We surely ought not to forget that the perversion which is the most repellent to us, the sensual love of a man for a man, was not only tolerated by a people so far our superiors in cultivation as were the Greeks, but was actually entrusted by them with important social functions. (49f.)

We can put this assertion into one of its appropriate contexts by recalling that the trial and imprisonment of Oscar Wilde had taken place only five years earlier. And the man who is speaking out here has to be regarded as the greatest of Victorian physicians, who in this passage is fearlessly revealing one of the inner and unacknowledged meanings of the famous "tyranny of Greece over Germany."[20] And as we shall see, he has by no means reached the limits beyond which he will not go.

How far he is willing to go begins to be visible as we observe him sliding almost imperceptibly from being the nineteenth-century man of science to being the remorseless

[20] "When the social historian of the future looks back to the first half of the twentieth century with the detachment that comes with the passage of time, it will by then be apparent that amongst the revolutionary changes to be credited to that period, two at least were of vital importance to the development of humanism: the liberation of psychology from the fetters of conscious rationalism, and the subsequent emancipation of sociology from the more primitive superstitions and moralistic conceptions of crime. It will also be apparent that this twin movement towards a new liberalism owed its impetus to the researches of a late-Victorian scientist, Sigmund Freud, who first uncovered the unconscious roots of that uniquely human reaction which goes by the name of 'guilt'. . . ." Edward Glover, *The Roots of Crime* (New York, 1960), p. ix.

"teller of truth," the character in a play by Ibsen who is not
to be deterred from his "mission." In a historical sense the
two roles are not adventitiously related, any more than it is
adventitious that the "truth" that is told often has unfore-
seen and destructive consequences and that it can rebound
upon the teller. Sometimes we can see this process at work
in the smallest details. For instance, one day when Freud's
"powers of interpretation were at a low ebb," he let Dora go
on talking until she brought forth a recollection that made
it clear why she was in such a bad mood. Freud remarks of
this recollection that it was "a fact which I did not fail to
use against her." (59) There can be no mistaking the adver-
sary tone, however slight, of this statement. It may be
replied that Freud is writing with his customary dry irony;
yet this reply must be met by observing that irony is invariably an instrument with a cutting edge. But we see him
most vividly at this implacable work in the two great dream
interpretations, which are largely "phonographic" reproductions of dramatic discourse and dialogue. Very early on in
the analysis of the first dream, Freud takes up the dream
element of the "jewel-case" and makes the unavoidable
symbolic interpretation of it. He then proceeds to say the
following to this Victorian maiden who has been in treatment with him for all of maybe six weeks:

> "So you are ready to give Herr K. what his wife with-
> holds from him. That is the thought which has had to
> be repressed with so much energy, and which has made
> it necessary for every one of its elements to be turned
> into its opposite. The dream confirms once more what
> I had already told you before you dreamt it—that you
> are summoning up your old love for your father in
> order to protect yourself against your love for Herr K.
> But what do all these efforts show? Not only that you
> are afraid of Herr K., but that you are still more afraid
> of yourself, and of the temptation you feel to yield to

him. In short, these efforts prove once more how deeply
you love him." (70)

He immediately adds that "Naturally Dora would not follow
me in this part of the interpretation," but this does not deter
him for a moment from pressing on with further interpretations of the same order; and this entire transaction is in its
character and quality prototypical for the case as a whole.
The Freud we have here is not the sage of the Berggasse, not
the master who delivered the incomparable *Introductory
Lectures* of 1916–1917, not the tragic Solomon of *Civilization
and Its Discontents*. This is an earlier Freud, the Freud of
the Fliess letters, to certain passages of which I would now
like to turn.

In May, 1895, Freud writes to Fliess to tell him why he
has not been writing to him. Although he has been over-
burdened with work, patients, etc., he is aware that such
excuses are in part pretexts.

> But the chief reason was this: a man like me cannot
> live without a hobby-horse, a consuming passion—in
> Schiller's words a tyrant. I have found my tyrant, *and
> in his service I know no limits*. My tyrant is psychology;
> it has always been my distant, beckoning goal and now,
> since I have hit on the neuroses, it has come so much
> the nearer. [italics mine]

Three weeks later he writes to Fliess to inform him that he
has started smoking again after an abstinence of fourteen
months "because I must treat that mind of mine decently,
or the fellow will not work for me. I am demanding a great
deal of him. Most of the time the burden is superhuman."
In March of the next year he tells Fliess that "I keep coming
back to psychology; it is a compulsion from which I cannot
escape." A month later he communicates the following:

> When I was young, the only thing that I longed for was

philosophical knowledge, and now that I am going over from medicine to psychology I am in the process of attaining it. I have become a therapist against my will; I am convinced that, granted certain conditions in the person and the case, I can definitely cure hysteria and obsessional neurosis.[21]

21 One might have thought that such a passage would have at least slowed the endless flow of nonsense about Freud's abstention from philosophical aspirations. To be sure, Freud is himself greatly responsible for the phenomenon. I am referring in part to the famous passage in *Inhibitions, Symptoms and Anxiety* (1926):

I must confess that I am not at all partial to the fabrication of *Weltanschauungen*. Such activities may be left to philosophers, who avowedly find it impossible to make their journey through life without a Baedeker of that kind to give them information on every subject. Let us humbly accept the contempt with which they look down on us from the vantage-ground of their superior needs. But since *we* cannot forgo our narcissistic pride either, we will draw comfort from the reflection that such 'Handbooks to Life' soon grow out of date and that it is precisely our short-sighted, narrow, and finicky work which obliges them to appear in new editions, and that even the most up-to-date of them are nothing but attempts to find a substitute for the ancient, useful and all-sufficient Church Catechism. We know well enough how little light science has so far been able to throw on the problems that surround us. But however much ado the philosophers may make, they cannot alter the situation. Only patient, persevering research, in which everything is subordinated to the one requirement of certainty, can gradually bring about a change. The benighted traveller may sing aloud in the dark to deny his own fears; but, for all that, he will not see an inch beyond his nose.

This is splendid and spirited writing; but I cannot resist suggesting that Freud is using philosophy here as a kind of stalking horse and that the earlier passage is in some senses closer to his enduring meaning. What Freud meant there by "philosophical knowledge" was knowledge or comprehension of the veritable nature of reality itself, and I do not believe he ever abandoned his belief in such knowledge. In any case, too much has been made—on both sides—of the "antagonism" between psychoanalysis and philosophy.

And in May of 1897 he writes: "No matter what I start with, I always find myself back again with the neuroses and the psychical apparatus. It is not because of indifference to personal or other matters that I never write about anything else. Inside me there is a seething ferment, and I am only waiting for the next surge forward." This is the Freud of the case of Dora as well. It is Freud the relentless investigator pushing on no matter what. The Freud that we meet with here is a demonic Freud, a Freud who is the servant of his *daimon*. That *daimon* in whose service Freud knows no limits is the spirit of science, the truth, or "reality"—it doesn't matter which; for him they are all the same. Yet it must be emphasized that the "reality" Freud insists upon is very different from the "reality" that Dora is claiming and clinging to. And it has to be admitted that not only does Freud overlook for the most part this critical difference; he also adopts no measures for dealing with it. The demon of interpretation has taken hold of him, and it is this power that presides over the case of Dora.

In fact, as the case history advances, it becomes increasingly clear to the careful reader that Freud and not Dora has become the central character in the action. Freud the narrator does in the writing what Freud the first psychoanalyst appears to have done in actuality. We begin to sense that it is his story that is being written and not hers that is being retold. Instead of letting Dora appropriate her own story, Freud became the appropriator of it. The case history belongs progressively less to her than it does to him. It may be that this was an inevitable development, that it is one of the typical outcomes of an analysis that fails, that Dora was under any circumstances unable to become the appropriator of her own history, the teller of her own story. Blame does not necessarily or automatically attach to Freud. Nevertheless, by the time he gets to the second dream he is able to write: "I shall present the material produced during the analysis of this dream in the somewhat haphazard order in which it recurs to my mind." (95) He makes such a presentation for several reasons, most of which are legitimate. But one reason almost certainly is that by this juncture it is his *own* mind that chiefly matters to him, and it is *his* associations to her dream that are of principal importance.

At the same time, as the account progresses, Freud has never been more inspired, more creative, more inventive; as the reader sees Dora gradually slipping further and further away from Freud, the power and complexity of the writing reach dizzying proportions. At times they pass over into something else. We have already noted that at certain moments Freud permits himself to say such things as: if only Dora had not left "we should no doubt have obtained the fullest possible enlightenment upon every particular of the case" (13); or that there is in his mind "no doubt that my analytic method" can achieve "complete elucidation" of a neurosis (32); or that "it is only because the analysis was prematurely broken off that we have been obliged . . . to resort to framing conjectures and filling in deficiencies." (85) Due allowance has always to be made for the absolutizing tendency of genius, especially when as in the case of Dora the genius is writing with the license of a poet and the ambiguity of a seer. But Freud goes quite beyond this. There are passages in the case of Dora which, if we were to find them, say, in a novel, would prompt us to conclude that either the narrator or the character who made such an utterance was suffering from *hubris*; in the context of psychoanalysis one supposes that the appropriate term would be *chutzpah*. For example, after elucidating the symbolism of the jewel-case and Dora's reticule, Freud goes on to write:

> There is a great deal of symbolism of this kind in life, but as a rule we pass it by without heeding it. When I set myself the task of bringing to light what human beings keep hidden within them, not by the compelling power of hypnosis, but by observing what

they say and what they show, I thought the task was a harder one than it really is. He that has eyes to see and ears to hear may convince himself that no mortal can keep a secret. If his lips are silent, he chatters with his finger-tips; betrayal oozes out of him at every pore. And thus the task of making conscious the most hidden recesses of the mind is one which it is quite possible to accomplish (77f.)

This, we are forced to recall, is from the Freud who more than anyone else in the history of Western civilization has taught us to be critically aware of fantasies of omniscience, and who on other occasions could be critical of such tendencies in himself. But not here where the demon of interpretation is riding him, riding him after Dora, whom it had ridden out. And it rides him still further, for he follows the passage I have just quoted with another that in point of mania quite surpasses it. Dora had complained for days on end of gastric pains. Freud quite plausibly connected these sensations with a series of other events and circumstances in her life that pointed to a repressed history of childhood masturbation. He then continues:

It is well known that gastric pains occur especially often in those who masturbate. According to a personal communication made to me by Wilhelm Fliess, it is precisely gastralgias of this character which can be interrupted by an application of cocaine to the "gastric spot" discovered by him in the nose, and which can be cured by the cauterization of the same spot.

At this juncture we have passed beyond interpretation and are in the positive presence of demented and delusional science. This passage was almost certainly written in 1901 as part of the first draft of the text; but it must remain a matter of puzzlement that neither in 1905, when he published the revised version, nor at any time thereafter did Freud think it necessary to amend or strike out those mythological observations.[22]

Anyone who goes on like this—and as Freud has gone on with Dora—is, as they say, asking for it. *Chutzpah's* reward is poetic justice. When Dora reports her second dream, Freud spends two hours of inspired insight in elucidating some of its meanings. "At the end of the second session," he writes, "I expressed my satisfaction at the

[22] It is pertinent to the present discussion to add that on at least one occasion in 1895 Freud directly addressed Fliess as "Demon" or "You Demon." (*Daimonie* warum schreibst Du nicht? Wie geht es Dir? Kümmerst Du Dich gar nicht mehr, was ich treibe?) Furthermore, the treatment described by Freud in the foregoing paragraph was administered by Fliess to Freud himself on several occasions during the 1890's. Throughout that decade Freud suffered at irregular intervals from migraine headaches and colds. He applied cocaine locally (one supposes that he took a healthy sniff), permitted Fliess to perform a number of nasal cauterizations, and at one point seems to have undergone minor surgery of the turbinate bone in the nasal passage at Fliess's hands.

The pertinence of the displacement of Freud's relation to Fliess into the case of Dora becomes clearer if we recall that in this friendship—certainly the most important relation of its kind in his life—Freud was undergoing something very like a transference experience, without wholly understanding what was happening to him. In this connection, the case of Dora may also be regarded as part of the process by which Freud began to move toward a resolution of his relation with Fliess—and perhaps vice versa as well.

That relation is still not adequately understood, as the documents that record it have not been fully published. As matters stand at present, one has to put that relation together from three sources: 1) *The Origins of Psychoanalysis*, ed. Ernst Kris (New York, 1950); this volume contains some of Freud's letters to Fliess, many of them in fragmentary or excerpted form, plus drafts and notes of various projects; 2) Ernest Jones, *The Life and Work of Sigmund Freud*; 3) Max Schur, *Freud: Living and Dying* (New York, 1972). The last work provides the fullest account yet available, but does not stand by itself and must be supplemented by material drawn from the other two sources.

results." (105) The satisfaction in question is in large measure self-satisfaction, for Dora responded to Freud's expression of it with the following words uttered in "a depreciatory tone: 'Why, has anything so remarkable come out?'" That satisfaction was to be of short duration, for Dora opened the third session by telling Freud that this was the last time she would be there—it was December 31, 1900. Freud's remarks that "Her breaking off so unexpectedly, just when my hopes of a successful termination of the treatment were at their highest, and her thus bringing those hopes to nothing—this was an unmistakable act of vengeance on her part" (109) are only partly warranted. There was, or should have been, nothing unexpected about Dora's decision to terminate; indeed, Freud himself on the occasion of the first dream had already detected such a decision on Dora's part and had communicated this finding to her. Moreover, his "highest" hopes for a successful outcome of the treatment seem almost entirely without foundation. The case, as he himself presents it, provides virtually no evidence on which to base such hopes—Dora stonewalled him from the beginning right up to the very end. In such a context the hopes of success almost unavoidably become a matter of self-reference and point to the immense *intellectual* triumph that Freud was aware he was achieving with the material adduced by his patient. On the matter of "vengeance," however, Freud cannot be faulted; Dora was, among many other things, certainly getting her own back on Freud by refusing to allow him to bring her story to an end in the way he saw fit. And he in turn is quite candid about the injury he felt she had caused him. "No one who, like me," he writes, "conjures up the most evil of those half-tamed demons that inhabit the human breast, and seeks to wrestle with them, can expect to come through the struggle unscathed." (109)

This admission of vulnerability, which Freud artfully manages to blend with the suggestion that he is a kind of modern combination of Jacob and Faust, is in keeping with the weirdness and wildness of the case as a whole and with this last hour. That hour recurs to the scene at the lake, two years before, and its aftermath. And Freud ends this final hour with the following final interpretation. He reminds Dora that she was in love with Herr K.; that she wanted him to divorce his wife; that even though she was quite young at the time she wanted " 'to wait for him, and you took it that he was only waiting till you were grown up enough to be his wife. I imagine that this was a perfectly serious plan for the future in your eyes.' " But Freud does not say this in order to contradict it or categorize it as a fantasy of the adolescent girl's unconscious imagination. On the contrary, he has very different ideas in view, for he goes on to tell her:

> "You have not even got the right to assert that it was out of the question for Herr K. to have had any such intention; you have told me enough about him that points directly towards his having such an intention. Nor does his behavior at L—— contradict this view. After all, you did not let him finish his speech and do not know what he meant to say to you."

He has not done with her yet, for he then goes on to bring in the other relevant parties and offers her the following conclusion:

> "Incidentally, the scheme would by no means have been so impracticable. Your father's relation with Frau K. . . . made it certain that her consent to a divorce could be obtained; and you can get anything you like out of your father. Indeed, if your temptation at L—— had had a different upshot, this would have been *the only possible solution for all the parties concerned.*" (108) [italics mine]

No one—at least no one in recent years—has accused Freud of being a swinger, but this is without question a swinging solution that is being offered. It is of course possible that he feels free to make such a proposal only because he knows that nothing in the way of action can come of it; but with him you never can tell—as I hope I have already demonstrated. One has only to imagine what in point of ego-strength, balance, and self-acceptance would have been required of Dora *alone* in this arrangement of wife-and-daughter-swapping to recognize at once its extreme irresponsibility, to say the least.[23] At the same time we must bear in mind that such a suggestion is not incongruent with the recently revealed circumstance that Freud analyzed his own daughter. Genius makes up its own rules as it goes along—and breaks them as well. This "only possible solution" was one of the endings that Freud wanted to write to Dora's story; he had others in mind besides, but none of them were to come about. Dora refused or was unable to let him do this; she refused to be a character in the story that Freud was composing for her, and wanted to finish it herself. As we now know, the ending she wrote was a very bad one indeed.[24]

[23] Fifteen years later, when Freud came to write about Ibsen, the character and situation that he chose to analyze revealed the closest pertinence to the case of Dora. In "Some Character-Types Met with in Psycho-Analytic Work" he devotes a number of pages to a discussion of Rebecca West in *Rosmersholm*. Rebecca, the new, liberated woman, is one of those character-types who are "wrecked by success." The success she is wrecked by is the fulfillment—partly real, partly symbolic—in mature life of her Oedipal fantasies, the precise fulfillment that Freud, fifteen years earlier, had been capable of regarding as the "only solution" for Dora, as well as everyone else involved in the case (See *SE*, XIV, 324–331).

[24] For what happened to Dora in later life, see Felix Deutsch, "A Footnote to Freud's 'Fragment of an Analysis of a Case of Hysteria,'" *Psychoanalytic Quarterly*, XXVI (1957), 159–167. The story is extremely gruesome. For some further useful remarks, see Erik H. Erikson, "Psychological Reality and Historical Actuality," *Insight and Responsibility* (New York, 1964), pp. 166–174.

6

Let us move rapidly to a conclusion long overdue. In this extraordinary work Freud and Dora often appear as unconscious, parodic refractions of each other. Both of them insist with implacable will upon the primacy of "reality," although the realities each has in mind differ radically. Both of them use reality, "the truth," as a weapon. Freud does so by forcing interpretations upon Dora before she is ready for them or can accept them. And this aggressive truth bounds back upon the teller, for Dora leaves him. Dora in turn uses her version of reality—it is "outer" reality that she insists upon—aggressively as well. She has used it from the outset against her father, and five months after she left Freud she had the opportunity to use it against the K.'s. In May of 1901 one of the K.'s children died. Dora took the occasion to pay them a visit of condolence—

and they received her as though nothing had happened in the last three years. She made it up with them, she took her revenge on them, and she brought her own business to a satisfactory conclusion. To the wife she said: 'I know you have an affair with my father'; and the other did not deny it. From the husband she drew an admission of the scene by the lake which he had disputed, and brought the news of her vindication home to her father. Since then she had not resumed her relations with the family. (121)

She told this to Freud fifteen months after she had departed, when she returned one last time to visit him—to ask him, without sincerity, for further help, and "to finish her story." (120). She finished her story, and as for the rest, Freud remarks, "I do not know what kind of help she wanted from me, but I promised to forgive her for having deprived me of the satisfaction of affording her a far more radical cure for her troubles." (122)

But the matter is not hopelessly obscure, as Freud himself has already confessed. What went wrong with the case, "Its great defect, which led to its being broken off prematurely," was something that had to do with the transference; and Freud writes that "I did not succeed in mastering the transference in good time." (118) He was in fact just beginning to learn about this therapeutic phenomenon, and the present passage is the first really important one about it to have been written. It is also in the nature of things heavily occluded. Instead of trying to analyze at what would be tedious length its murky reaches, let me state summarily my sense of things. On Dora's side the transference went wrong in several senses. In the first place, there was the failure on her part to establish an adequate positive transference to Freud. She was not free enough to respond to him erotically —in fantasy—or intellectually—by accepting his interpretations: both or either of these being prerequisites for the mysterious "talking cure" to begin to work. And in the second, halfway through the case a negative transference began to emerge, quite clearly in the first dream. Freud writes that he "was deaf to this first note of warning," and as a result this negative "transference took me unawares, and, because of the unknown quantity in me which reminded Dora of Herr K., she took her revenge on me as she wanted to take her revenge on him, and deserted me as she believed herself to have been deceived and deserted by him." This is, I believe, the first mention in print of the conception that is known as "acting out"—out of which, one may incidentally observe, considerable fortunes have been made.

We are, however, in a position to say something more than this. For there is a reciprocating process in the analyst known as the counter-transference, and in the case of Dora this went wrong too. Although Freud describes Dora at the beginning of the account as being "in the first bloom of youth—a girl of intelligent and engaging looks," almost nothing attractive about her comes forth in the course of the writing. (31) As it unwinds, and it becomes increasingly evident that Dora is not responding adequately to Freud, it also becomes clear that Freud is not responding favorably to this response, and that he doesn't in fact like Dora very much.[25] He doesn't like her negative sexuality, her inability to surrender to her own erotic impulses. He doesn't like "her really remarkable achievements in the direction of intolerable behavior." (91) He doesn't like her endless reproachfulness. Above all, he deosn't like her inability to surrender herself to him. For what Freud was as yet unprepared to face was not merely the transference, but the counter-transference as well—in the case of Dora it was largely a negative counter-transference—an unanalyzed part of himself.[26] I

---

[25] Dora seems indeed to have been an unlikable person. Her death, which was caused by cancer of the colon, diagnosed too late for an operation, "seemed a blessing to those who were close to her." And Dr. Deutsch's informant went on to describe her as " 'one of the most repulsive hysterics' he had ever met."

[26] That the counter-transference was not entirely negative is suggested in the very name that Freud chose to give to his patient in writing this case history. Freud's favorite novel by Dickens was *David Copperfield*. Like David, Freud was born with or in a caul—an augury of a singular destiny. On at least one occasion, Freud described his father as a Micawber-like figure. The first book he sent as a gift to Martha Bernays shortly after they had met was a copy of *David Copperfield*.

Dora, of course, was David Copperfield's first love and first wife. She is at once a duplication of David's dead mother and an incompetent and helpless creature, who asks David to call her his "child-wife." She is also doomed not to survive, and Dickens kills her off so David can proceed to realize himself in a fuller way. One could go on indefinitely with such analogies, but the point should be sufficiently clear: in the very name he chose, Freud was in a manner true to his method, theory, and mind, expressing the overdeterminations and ambivalences that are so richly characteristic of this work as a whole.

For the relevant biographical material, see Jones, I, 2, 4, 104, 174.

should like to suggest that this cluster of unanalyzed impulses and ambivalences was in part responsible for Freud's writing of this great text immediately after Dora left him. It was his way—and one way—of dealing with, mastering, expressing, and neutralizing such material. Yet the neutralization was not complete; or we can put the matter in another way and state that Freud's creative honesty was such that it compelled him to write the case of Dora as he did, and that his writing has allowed us to make out in this remarkable Fragment a still fuller picture. As I have said before, this Fragment of Freud's is more complete and coherent than the fullest case studies of anyone else. Freud's case histories are a new form of literature—they are creative narratives that include their own analysis and interpretation. Nevertheless, like the living works of literature that they are, the material they contain is always richer than the original analysis and interpretation that accompany it; and this means that future generations will recur to these works and will find in them a language they are seeking and a story they need to be told.

(1974)

COLUMBIA UNIVERSITY PRESS

562 West 113th Street, New York, N.Y. 10025

Marcus

AUTHOR

Representations

TITLE

December 31, 1990

PUBLICATION DATE

$40.00 (cl)
$16.00 (pa)

PRICE

We would appreciate receiving two copies of any review
of this book which you may publish.

Dashiell Hammett and
the Continental Op

1

Dashiell Hammett—creator of such figures in the mythology of American culture as the Continental Op, Sam Spade, and the Thin Man—was born Samuel Dashiell Hammett, in St. Mary's County, Maryland, in May 1894. The family was of Scottish and French extraction, and they were Catholic. Hammett's early years were spent in Philadelphia and Baltimore, and his formal education was brought to an end at the age of fourteen, when he left high school after less than a year of attendance. His father's relative lack of success in the world seems, at least in part, to be reflected in this decision.

For the next several years Hammett worked with indifferent success and even less interest at a number of odd jobs —on the Baltimore and Ohio Railroad, in factories, at stockbrokers', and as a casual laborer. When he was about twenty he answered an advertisement in a Baltimore newspaper, and as a result found himself employed by Pinkerton's, the most famous of American private detective agencies. The young man had found a vocation that engaged his liveliest interests. The work was challenging, exciting, adventurous, dangerous, and humorous. It took him around the country and into and out of a large variety of walks of life, classes of society, and social and dramatic situations. These experiences were formative; their influence in his education as a writer can hardly be overestimated.

In 1918 he enlisted in the Ambulance Corps of the United States Army and was stationed near Baltimore. During his year of military service he came down with influenza, which led to the activation in him of tuberculosis. It was his first encounter with the series of lung diseases from which he was eventually to die. In 1919 he returned to his work at Pinkerton and his travels and adventures in the service of the Agency. The active and arduous work of a private detective agent in the field brought on another attack of tuberculosis, and he was hospitalized in 1920 and 1921 in government hospitals on the West Coast. While he was in the hospital he became involved with one of the nurses who worked there, and they were married toward the end of 1920.

Hammett was discharged from the hospital in May, 1921, and he and his wife made their way along the West Coast to San Francisco. The town awakened Hammett's interest, and he went back to work there for the local branch of the Pinkerton Agency. He was to live in San Francisco for the next eight years, and the city provided him with the locale and material for a large part of his writing. Yet even as he was returning to work as a detective, other interests began to make themselves felt in him. He had conceived of the idea of becoming a writer, and was beginning to write bits of verse, small sketches from his experiences as a detective, and other pieces of apprentice-work. Finally, the successful solution of a case led to his leaving the Agency. Some $200,000 in gold was missing on an Australian ship that had put in to San Francisco. The Pinkerton Agency was employed by the insurance company involved to find the gold—which they believed was stashed away on the ship. Hammett and another operative were sent to search the ship, and found nothing. It was decided to send Hammett back to Australia on the ship in the belief that he might still find the missing loot. Hammett looked forward to the adventure. Just before the ship was to leave San Francisco, he made one last routine search and found the gold—it was hidden in a smokestack. He had solved the case and lost the trip to Australia. Frustrated and outdone by his own success, he handed in his resignation.

Soon after this, while working at odd jobs, Hammett began to hemorrhage again. Feeling that he had little time left to live, and that the only thing he wanted to do before he died was to write, he moved away from his family, took a cheap single room, and started to write. Sometime around here he also began to work for a local jewelry store as a writer of advertising copy. It was an odd and uncertain Bohemian existence; sometimes he lived on soup; frequently he drank too much. By the end of 1922, however, he began to break into print, with a number of small pieces in *Smart Set* and *Black Mask*. The latter, a popular pulp-fiction magazine, soon became Hammett's regular place of appearance in print, and his career and the career of the magazine traversed almost identical arcs. In October, 1923, the first story in which the Continental Op appears—in his never-to-be-varied figure as anonymous narrator—was published. From then until 1930, as Hammett's writing underwent rapid and continuous development, this was the essential (though not the exclusive) form into which his fiction was cast. It was certainly the most successful, both in itself and in its appeal to a rapidly growing audience of readers. By the middle years of the 1920's Hammett was becoming known as an original talent, an innovator in a popular form of fiction, and as the central figure in a new school of writing about crime—the "hard-boiled school," as it came quickly to be called. And it was also beginning to be recognized as being within its own context the structural equivalent of what Hemingway and the writers who clustered naturally about Hemingway were doing in their kind of writing during the same period.

By 1927 Hammett was ready to work on a larger scale. He began to publish serially, in *Black Mask*, large units of fiction that were in fact quasi-independent sections of novels. After they had been published in the magazine, he would revise them, and they would appear as volumes. *Red Harvest* was published as a volume in 1929, as was *The Dain Curse*. These two novels bring the Op's career to a climax (although three more short stories featuring the Op were later to appear), and Hammett was rapidly becoming both well known and affluent. In 1929 he invented Sam Spade and *The Maltese Falcon* and became immediately famous. This was followed at once in 1930 by *The Glass Key*. *The Thin Man*, Hammett's last published novel, and another large success, came out in 1934.

Sometime during the late 1920's Hammett's marriage—two daughters were born of it—broke up for good. His life as a writer, as he continued to prosper, remained as intense, demanding, anarchic, and casually self-destructive as it had been in the years of his apprenticeship. On the one hand, there was a great deal of heavy drinking, there was a great deal of womanizing, and an even greater deal of compulsive and wild squandering of money. On the other hand, there were rigorous bouts of self-discipline and periods of extremely intense, ascetic, and self-denying hard work. After 1930 these latter began to diminish in frequency. Hammett had left San Francisco in 1929 and moved to New York; from there in 1930, with the Great Depression setting deeply in, Hammett moved out to Hollywood. Warner Brothers had bought the film rights for *The Maltese Falcon*, and Hammett was offered high-paying work on a variety of film projects. It was here, one night in November, as he was coming out of a monumental drunk that had lasted for days, that he met a young woman named Lillian Hellman. The two were immediately attracted to one another, and there then began what was for both of them the most important relation in their lives. It was impassioned and tempestuous; it was often cruel and harsh and harmful, and there were times when neither was faithful to the other and when they went their own ways and lived apart. But in the end it endured; it lasted for thirty years, until his death.

By 1934 Hammett's career as a creative writer was finished. He did not know this, of course, and in 1932 in an interview, said that he was planning to write a play. That play never got written, but another one did. It was called *The Children's Hour*, and Hammett's work as a careful reader, stern schoolmaster, and relentlessly honest critic was instrumental in its realization. His connection with Lillian Hellman's career as a playwright was to remain close, intimate, and instrumental as the years went on.

During the 1930's Hammett continued to work at various kinds of writing and rewriting jobs in the movie industry. He also became involved, as did so many other writers and intellectuals of the period, in various left-wing and anti-fascist causes. He had become a Marxist; he had also committed himself to the cause of the Communist Party in America, and became a member of it probably sometime during 1937. Although he never surrendered his personal critical sense about the limitations and absurdities of many of his political associates and allies, both here and abroad, the commitment he had made was deep, and it was lasting, and he would pay for it in the end. It was characteristic of him—as both man and writer—that he was willing to pay the price.

Shortly after America entered World War II, Hammett —at the age of forty-eight—enlisted in the Army. Through some inexplicable sleight of hand and mouth he managed to persuade the Army doctors that the scars on his lungs that showed up on the X-rays were of no importance. He volunteered for overseas service and was sent to the Aleutians— where, among other things, he edited a daily newspaper for the troops. He apparently thoroughly enjoyed his tour of duty in the Army, and became a legendary character among his much younger fellow soldiers. When he was discharged in 1945, he was fifty-one, famous, and comparatively affluent. He had also developed emphysema. The adaptation of his novels and characters to movies and radio shows continued to bring in money, as did the steady sale of his novels. Times were changing, but his political loyalties were not. Neither were his drinking habits, which damaged and ravaged him until they brought him down in 1948 with the d.t.'s. From that time forward he never drank.

The Cold War was now on, the period identified with Senator Joseph McCarthy's name was taking shape, and many old scores were beginning to be paid off. In one of the numerous legal cases that characterized the period, Hammett was called to give evidence. He was asked to name the contributors to a fund (of which he was a trustee) that supplied bail for Communists and others who were brought to trial (in this particular case, a number of persons on trial had jumped bail and vanished). Hammett refused to testify, was found guilty of contempt of court, and was sentenced to six months in jail. He spent five months in various prisons and was then released. When he got out of prison he was an exhausted and very ill man.

His external troubles were by no means over. The money, which had once been so plentiful, was no longer there. He was blacklisted in Hollywood, and his radio shows had gone off the air. The government sued him for back taxes, won a judgment of $140,000 against him, and had his royalty, and all other, payments blocked. He took it all, as he had taken all that had come before, stoically and without complaint. He retired further into himself and lived a quiet and self-contained life until 1956, when his illness and weakness made it impossible to live alone. Thereafter he lived within the care and companionship of Lillian Hellman. In 1960 his lung condition worsened and became cancerous. He died on January 10, 1961. By his own wish, he was buried in Arlington National Cemetery. He had served the nation in two world wars. He had also served it in other ways, which were his own.

2

I was first introduced to Dashiell Hammett by Humphrey Bogart. I was twelve years old at the time, and mention the occasion because I take it to be exemplary, that I share this experience with countless others. (Earlier than this, at the very dawn of consciousness, I can recall William Powell and Myrna Loy and a small dog on a leash and an audience full of adults laughing; but that had nothing to do with Hammett or anything else, as far as I was concerned.) What was striking about the event was that it was one of the first encounters I can consciously recall with the experience of moral ambiguity. Here was this detective you were supposed to like—and did like—behaving and speaking in peculiar and unexpected ways. He acted up to the cops, partly for real, partly as a ruse. He connived with crooks, for his own ends and perhaps even for some of theirs. He slept with his partner's wife, fell in love with a lady crook, and then refused to save her from the police, even though he could have. Which side was he on? Was he on any side apart from his own? And which or what side was that? The experience was not only morally ambiguous; it was morally complex and enigmatic as well. The impression it made was a lasting one.

Years later, after having read *The Maltese Falcon* and seen the movie again and then reread the novel, I could begin to understand why the impact of the film had been so memorable, much more so than that of most other movies. The director, John Huston, had had the wit to recognize the power, sharpness, integrity, and bite of Hammett's prose—particularly the dialogue—and the film script consists almost entirely of speech taken directly and without modification from the written novel. Moreover, this unusual situation is complicated still further. In selecting with notable intelligence the relevant scenes and passages from the novel, Huston had to make certain omissions. Paradoxically, however, one of the things that he chose to omit was the most important or central moment in the entire novel. It is also one of the central moments in all of Hammett's writing. I think we can make use of this oddly "lost" passage as a means of entry into Hammett's vision or imagination of the world.

It occurs as Spade is becoming involved with Brigid O'Shaughnessy in her struggle with the other thieves, and it is his way of communicating to her his sense of how the world and life go. His way is to tell her a story from his own experience. The form this story takes is that of a parable. It is a parable about a man named Flitcraft. Flitcraft was a successful, happily married, stable, and utterly respectable real-estate dealer in Tacoma. One day he went out to lunch and never returned. No reason could be found for his disappearance, and no account of it could be made. " 'He went like that,' Spade said, 'like a fist when you open your hand.' "

Five years later Mrs. Flitcraft came to the agency at which Spade was working and told them that " 'she had seen a man in Spokane who looked a lot like her husband.' " Spade went off to investigate and found that it was indeed Flitcraft. He had been living in Spokane for a couple of years under the name of Charles Pierce. He had a successful automobile business, a wife, a baby son, a suburban home, and usually played golf after four in the afternoon, just as he had in Tacoma. Spade and he sat down to talk the matter over. Flitcraft, Spade recounts, "had no feeling of guilt. He had left his family well provided for, and what he had done seemed to him perfectly reasonable. The only thing that bothered him was a doubt that he could make that reasonableness clear" to his interlocutor. When Flitcraft went out to lunch that day five years before in Tacoma, "'he passed an office-building that was being put up. . . . A beam or something fell eight to ten stories down and smacked the sidewalk alongside him. " A chip of smashed sidewalk flew up and took a piece of skin off his cheek. He was otherwise unharmed. He stood there "'scared stiff,'" he told Spade, "'but he was more shocked than really frightened. He felt like somebody had taken the lid off life and let him look at the works.'"

Until that very moment Flitcraft had been "'a good citizen and a good husband and father, not by any outer compulsion, but simply because he was a man who was most comfortable in step with his surroundings. . . . The life he knew was a clean orderly sane responsible affair. Now a falling beam had shown him that life was fundamentally none of these things. . . . What disturbed him was the discovery that in sensibly ordering his affairs he had got out of step, and not into step, with life.'" By the time he had finished lunch, he had reached the decision "'that he would change his life at random by simply going away.'" He went off that afternoon, wandered around for a couple of years, then drifted back to the Northwest, "'settled in Spokane and got married. His second wife didn't look like the first, but they were more alike than they were different.'" And the same held true of his second life. Spade then moves on to his conclusion: "'He wasn't sorry for what he had done. It seemed reasonable enough to him. I don't think he even knew he had settled back into the same groove that he had jumped out of in Tacoma. But that's the part of it I always liked. He adjusted himself to beams falling, and then no more of them fell, and he adjusted himself to their not falling.' " End of parable. Brigid of course understands nothing of this, as Spade doubtless knew beforehand. Yet what he has been telling her has to do with the forces and beliefs and contingencies that guide his conduct and supply a structure to his apparently enigmatic behavior.

To begin with, we may note that such a sustained passage is not the kind of thing we ordinarily expect in a detective story or novel about crime. That it is there, and that comparable passages occur in all of Hammett's best work, clearly suggests the kind of transformation that Hammett was performing on this popular genre of writing. The transformation was in the direction of literature. And what the passage in question is about, among other things, is the ethical irrationality of existence, the ethical unintelligibility of the world. For Flitcraft the falling beam "had taken the lid off life and let him look at the works." The works are that life is inscrutable, opaque, irresponsible, and arbitrary —that human existence does not correspond in its actuality to the way we live it. For most of us live as if existence itself were ordered, ethical, and rational. As a direct result of his realization in experience that it is not, Flitcraft leaves his wife and children and goes off. He acts irrationally and at random, in accordance with the nature of existence. When after a couple of years of wandering aimlessly about, he decides to establish a new life, he simply reproduces the old one he had supposedly repudiated and abandoned; that is to say, he behaves again as if life were orderly, meaningful, and rational, and "adjusts" to it. And this, with fine irony, is the part of it, Spade says, that he "always liked," which means the part that he liked best. For here we come upon the unfathomable and most mysteriously irrational part of it all —how despite everything we have learned and everything we know, men will persist in behaving and trying to behave sanely, rationally, sensibly, and responsibly. And we will continue to persist even when we know that there is no logical or metaphysical, no discoverable or demonstrable reason for doing so.[1] It is this sense of sustained contradiction that is close to the center—or to one of the centers—of Hammett's work. The contradiction is not ethical alone; it is metaphysical as well. And it is not merely sustained; it is sustained with pleasure. For Hammett and Spade and the Op, the sustainment in consciousness of such contradictions is an indispensable part of their existence and of their pleasure in that existence.

That this pleasure is itself complex, ambiguous, and problematic becomes apparent as one simply describes the conditions under which it exists. And the complexity, ambiguity, and sense of the problematical are not confined to such moments of "revelation"—or set pieces—as the parable of Flitcraft. They permeate Hammett's work and act as formative elements in its structure, including its deep structure. Hammett's work went through considerable and interesting development in the course of his career of twelve years as a writer. He also wrote in a considerable variety of forms and worked out a variety of narrative devices and strategies. At the same time, his work considered as a whole reveals a remarkable kind of coherence. In order to further the understanding of that coherence, we can propose for the purposes of the present analysis to construct a kind of "ideal type" of a Hammett or Op story. Which is not to say or to imply in the least that he wrote according to a formula, but that an authentic imaginative vision lay beneath and informed the structure of his work.

Such an ideal-typical description runs as follows. The

---

[1] It can hardly be an accident that the new name that Hammett gives to Flitcraft is that of an American philosopher—with two vowels reversed—who was deeply involved in just such speculations.

Op is called in or sent out on a case. Something has been stolen, someone is missing, some dire circumstance is impending, someone has been murdered—it doesn't matter. The Op interviews the person or persons most immediately accessible. They may be innocent or guilty—it doesn't matter; it is an indifferent circumstance. Guilty or innocent, they provide the Op with an account of what they know, of what they assert really happened. The Op begins to investigate; he compares these accounts with others that he gathers; he snoops about; he does research; he shadows people, arranges confrontations between those who want to avoid one another, and so on. What he soon discovers is that the "reality" that anyone involved will swear to is in fact itself a construction, a fabrication, a fiction, a faked and alternate reality—and that it has been gotten together before he ever arrived on the scene. And the Op's work therefore is to deconstruct, decompose, deplot and defictionalize that "reality" and to construct or reconstruct out of it a true fiction, i.e., an account of what "really" happened.

It should be quite evident that there is a reflexive and coordinate relation between the activities of the Op and the activities of Hammett, the writer. Yet the depth and problematic character of this self-reflexive process begin to be revealed when we observe that the reconstruction or true fiction created and arrived at by the Op at the end of the story is often no more plausible—nor is it meant to be—than the stories that have been told to him by all parties, guilty or innocent, in the course of his work. The Op may catch the real thief or collar the actual crook—that is not entirely to the point. What is to the point is that the story, account, or chain of events that the Op winds up with as "reality" tends to be no more plausible and no less ambiguous than the stories that he meets with at the outset and later. What Hammett has done—unlike most writers of detective or crime stories before him or since—is to include as part of the contingent and dramatic consciousness of his narrative the circumstance that the work of the detective is itself a fiction-making activity, a discovery or creation by fabrication of something new in the world, or hidden, latent, potential or as yet undeveloped within it. The typical "classical" detective story —unlike Hammett's—can be described as a formal game with certain specified rules of transformation. What ordinarily happens is that the detective is faced with a situation of inadequate, false, misleading, and ambiguous information. And the story as a whole is an exercise in disambiguation— with the final scenes being a ratiocinative demonstration that the butler did it (or not); these scenes achieve a conclusive, reassuring clarity of explanation, wherein everything is set straight, and the game we have been party to is brought to its appropriate end. But this, as I have already suggested, is not what ordinarily happens in Hammett or with the Op.

What happens is that the Op almost invariably walks into a situation that has already been elaborately fabricated or framed. And his characteristic response to his sense that he is dealing with a series of deceptions or fictions is—to use the words that he uses himself repeatedly—"to stir things up." This corresponds integrally, both as metaphor and in logical structure, to what happened in the parable of Flitcraft. When the falling beam just misses Flitcraft, "he felt like somebody had taken the lid off life." The Op lives with the uninterrupted awareness that for him the lid has been taken off life. When the lid has been lifted, the logical thing to do is to "stir things up"—which is what he does.[2] He actively undertakes to deconstruct, decompose, and thus demystify the fictional—and therefore false—reality created by the characters, crooks or not, with whom he is involved.

---

[2] These homely metaphors go deep into Hammett's life. One of the few things that he could recall from his childhood past was his mother's repeated advice that a woman who wasn't good in the kitchen wasn't likely to be much good in any other room in the house.

More often than not he tries to substitute his own fictional-hypothetical representation for theirs—and this representation may be also "true" or mistaken, or both at once. In any event, his major effort is to make the fictions of others ·visible as fictions, inventions, concealments, falsehoods, and mystifications—or all, several, or any of these in a variety of permutations and combinations. When a fiction becomes visible as such, it begins to dissolve and disappear, and presumably should reveal behind it the "real" reality that was there all the time and that it was masking. Yet what happens in Hammett is that what is revealed as "reality" is a still further fiction-making activity—in the first place the Op's, and behind that yet another, the consciousness present in many of the Op stories and all the novels that Dashiell Hammett, the writer, is continually doing the same thing as the Op and all the other characters in the fiction he is creating. That is to say, he is making a fiction (in writing) in the real world; and this fiction, like the real world itself, is coherent but not necessarily rational. What one both begins and ends with, then, is a story, a narrative, a coherent yet questionable account of the world. This problematic penetrates to the bottom of Hammett's narrative imagination and shapes a number of its deeper processes—in *The Dain Curse*, for example, it is the chief topic of explicit debate that runs throughout the entire novel.

Yet Hammett's writing is still more complex and integral than this. For the unresolvable paradoxes and dilemmas that we have just been describing in terms of narrative structure and consciousness are reproduced once again in Hammett's vision and representation of society, of the social world in which the Op lives. At this point we must recall that Hammett is a writer of the 1920's and that this was the era of Prohibition. American society had in effect committed itself to a vast collective fiction. Even more, this fiction was false not merely in the sense that it was made up or did not in fact correspond to reality; it was false in the sense that it was corrupt and corrupting as well. During this period every time an American took a drink he was helping to undermine the law, and American society had covertly committed itself to what was in practice collaborative illegality.[3] There is a kind of epiphany of these circumstances in "The Golden Horseshoe." The Op is on a case that takes him to Tijuana. In a bar there, he reads a sign:

ONLY GENUINE PRE-WAR AMERICAN AND
BRITISH WHISKEYS SERVED HERE

He responds by remarking that "I was trying to count how many lies could be found in those nine words, and had reached four, with promise of more," when he is interrupted by some call to action. That sign and the Op's response to it describe part of the existential character of the social world represented by Hammett.

Another part of that representation is expressed in another kind of story or idea that Hammett returned to repeatedly. The twenties were also the great period of organized crime and organized criminal gangs in America, and one of Hammett's obsessive imaginations was the notion of organized crime or gangs taking over an entire society and running it as if it were an ordinary society doing business as usual. In other words, society itself would become a fiction, concealing and belying the actuality of what was controlling it and perverting it from within. One can thus make out quite early in this native American writer a proto-Marxist

---

[3] Matters were even murkier than this. The Eighteenth Amendment to the Constitution was in effect from January, 1920, to December, 1933, nearly fourteen years. During this period Americans were forbidden under penalty of law to manufacture, sell, or transport any intoxicating liquor. At the same time no one was forbidden to buy or drink such liquor. In other words, Americans were virtually being solicited by their own laws to support an illegal trade in liquor, even while Congress was passing the Volstead Act, which was intended to prevent such a trade.

critical representation of how a certain kind of society works. Actually the point of view is pre- rather than proto-Marxist, and the social world as it is dramatized in many of these stories is Hobbesian rather than Marxist.[4] It is a world of universal warfare, the war of each against all, and of all against all. The only thing that prevents the criminal ascendancy from turning into permanent tyranny is that the crooks who take over society cannot cooperate with one another, repeatedly fall out with each other, and return to the Hobbesian anarchy out of which they have momentarily arisen. The social world as imagined by Hammett runs on a principle that is the direct opposite of that postulated by Erik Erikson as the fundamental and enabling condition for human existence. In Hammett, society and social relations are dominated by the principle of basic mistrust. As one of his detectives remarks, speaking for himself and for virtually every other character in Hammett's writing, "I trust no one."

When Hammett turns to the respectable world, the world of respectable society, of affluence and influence, of open personal and political power, he finds only more of the same. The respectability of respectable American society is as much a fiction and a fraud as the phony respectable society fabricated by the criminals. Indeed, he unwaveringly represents the world of crime as a reproduction in both structure and detail of the modern capitalist society that it depends on, preys off, and is part of. But Hammett does something even more radical than this. He not only continually juxtaposes and connects the ambiguously fictional worlds of art and of writing with the fraudulently fictional worlds of society; he connects them, juxtaposes them, and sees them in dizzying and baffling interaction. He does this

---

[4] Again it can hardly be regarded as an accident that the name Hammett gives to the town taken over by the criminals in *Red Harvest* is "Personville"—pronounced "Poisonville." And what else is Personville except Leviathan, the "artificial man" represented by Hobbes as the image of society itself.

in many ways and on many occasions. One of them, for example, is the Maltese Falcon itself, which turns out to be and contains within itself the history of capitalism. It is originally a piece of plunder, part of what Marx called the "primitive accumulation"; when its gold encrusted with gems is painted over, it becomes a mystified object, a commodity itself; it is a piece of property that belongs to no one—whoever possesses it does not really own it. At the same time it is another fiction, a representation or work of art—which turns out itself to be a fake, since it is made of lead. It is a *rara avis* indeed. As is the fiction in which it is created and contained, the novel by Hammett.

It is into this bottomlessly equivocal, endlessly fraudulent, and brutally acquisitive world that Hammett precipitates the Op. There is nothing glamorous about him. Short, thick-set, balding, between thirty-five and forty, he has no name, no home, no personal existence apart from his work. He is, and he regards himself as, "the hired man" of official and respectable society, who is paid so much per day to clean it up and rescue it from the crooks and thieves who are perpetually threatening to take it over. Yet what he— and the reader—just as perpetually learn is that the respectable society that employs him is itself inveterately vicious, deceitful, culpable, crooked, and degraded. How, then, is the Op to be preserved, to preserve himself, from being contaminated by both the world he works against and the world he is hired to work for?

To begin with, the Op lives by a code. This code consists in the first instance of the rules laid down by the Continental Agency, and they are "rather strict." The most important of them by far is that no operative in the employ of the Agency is ever allowed to take or collect part of a reward that may be attached to the solution of a case. Since he cannot directly enrich himself through his professional skills, he is saved from at least the characteristic corruption of modern society—the corruption that is connected with its fundamental acquisitive structure. At the same time the Op is a special case of the Protestant ethic, for his entire existence is bound up in and expressed by his work, his vocation. He likes his work, and it is honest work, done as much for enjoyment and the exercise of his skills and abilities as it is for personal gain and self-sustainment. The work is something of an end in itself, and this circumstance also serves to protect him, as does his deliberate refusal to use high-class and fancy moral language about anything. The work is an end in itself and is therefore something more than work alone. As Spade says, in a passage that is the culmination of many such passages in Hammett:

> "I'm a detective and expecting me to run criminals down and then let them go free is like asking a dog to catch a rabbit and let it go. It can be done, all right, and sometimes it is done, but it's not the natural thing."

Being a detective, then, entails more than fulfilling a social function or performing a social role. Being a detective is the realization of an identity, for there are components in it which are beyond or beneath society—and cannot be touched by it—and beyond and beneath reason. There is something "natural" about it. Yet if we recall that the nature thus being expressed is that of a man-hunter, and Hammett's apt metaphor compels us to do so, and that the state of society as it is represented in Hammett's writing reminds us of the state of nature in Hobbes, we see that even here Hammett does not release his sense of the complex and the contradictory, and is making no simple-minded appeal to some benign idea of the "natural."

And indeed the Op is not finally or fully protected by his work, his job, his vocation. (We have all had to relearn with bitterness what multitudes of wickedness "doing one's job" can cover.) Max Weber has memorably remarked that "the decisive means for politics is violence." In Hammett's depiction of modern American society, violence is the decisive means indeed, along with fraud, deceit, treachery, betrayal, and general, endemic unscrupulousness. Such means are in no sense alien to Hammett's detective. As the Op says, " 'detecting is a hard business, and you use whatever tools come to hand.' " In other words, there is a paradoxical tension and unceasing interplay in Hammett's stories between means and ends; relations between the two are never secure or stable. And as Max Weber further remarked, in his great essay "Politics as a Vocation": "the world is governed by demons, and he who lets himself in for . . . power and force as means, contracts with diabolic powers, and for his action it is *not* true that good can follow only from good and evil only from evil, but that often the opposite is true. Anyone who fails to see this is, indeed, a political infant." Neither Hammett nor the Op is an infant; yet no one can be so grown up and inured to experience that he can escape the consequences that attach to the deliberate use of violent and dubious means.

These consequences are of various orders. "Good" ends themselves can be transformed and perverted by the use of vicious or indiscriminate means. (I am leaving to one side those even more perplexing instances in Hammett in which the ends pursued by the Op correspond with ends desired by a corrupted yet respectable official society.) The consequences are also visible inwardly, on the inner being of the agent of such means, the Op himself. The violence begins to get to him:

> I began to throw my right fist into him.
>
> I liked that. His belly was flabby, and it got softer every time I hit it. I hit it often.

Another side of this set of irresolvable moral predicaments is revealed when we see that the Op's toughness is not merely a carapace within which feelings of tenderness and humanity can be nourished and preserved. The toughness is toughness through and through, and as the Op continues his career, and continues to live by the means he does, he tends to become more callous and less and less able to feel. At the very end, awaiting him, he knows, is the prospect of becoming like his boss, the head of the Agency, the Old Man, "with his gentle eyes behind gold spectacles and his mild smile, hiding the fact that fifty years of sleuthing had left him without any feelings at all on any subject." This is the price exacted by the use of such means in such a world; these are the consequences of living fully in a society moved by the principle of basic mistrust. "Whoever fights monsters," writes Nietzsche, "should see to it that in the process he does not become a monster. And when you look long into an abyss, the abyss also looks into you." The abyss looks into Hammett, the Old Man, and the Op.

It is through such complex devices as I have merely sketched here that Hammett was able to raise the crime story into literature. He did it over a period of ten years. Yet the strain was finally too much to bear—that shifting, entangled, and equilibrated state of contradictions out of which his creativity arose and which it expressed could no longer be sustained. His creative career ends when he is no longer able to handle the literary, social, and moral opacities, instabilities, and contradictions that characterize all his best work. His life then splits apart and goes in the two opposite directions that were implicit in his earlier, creative phase, but that the creativity held suspended and in poised yet fluid tension. His politics go in one direction; the way he made his living went in another—he became a hack writer, and then finally no writer at all. That is another story. Yet for ten years he was able to do what almost no other writer in this genre has ever done so well—he was able to really write, to construct a vision of a world in words, to know that the writing was about the real world and referred to it and was part of it; and at the same time he was able to be self-consciously aware that the whole thing was problematical and about itself and "only" writing as well. For ten years, in other words, he was a true creator of fiction.

(1974)